Coaching Methods for Women Second Edition

Patsy Neal

Coaching Methods for Women Second Edition

▲ Addison-Wesley Publishing Company

Reading, Massachusetts
Menlo Park, California • London • Amsterdam • Don Mills, Ontario • Sydney

This book is in the
Addison-Wesley Series on Physical Education

About the Author

Patsy Neal received her B.S. degree from Wayland College (Texas) and her M.S. degree from the University of Utah. Although she is an accomplished tennis player and coach, Miss Neal is best known for her achievements in basketball. She was an All-American for three years, the 1957 National free-throw champion, a member of the American basketball team at the 1959 Pan American Games, captain of the United States team at the 1964 World Tournament in Peru, on the United States team that toured Europe and Russia in 1965, and has lectured at the Kodak Women's National Basketball Coaches Clinics. In addition, Miss Neal has been selected to *Personalities of the South, Outstanding Young Women of America, Who's Who of American Women, Outstanding Educators of America, Dictionary of International Biography,* and the *World Who's Who of Women.* The author of the books *Basketball Techniques for Women, Sport and Identity, So Run Your Race,* and co-author of *Coaching Girls and Women: Psychological Perspectives,* and numerous articles in magazines and anthologies, she has won four Freedom Foundation Awards for essays.

Preface

A tremendous amount of progress has been made in women's sports since the first edition of this book was published. Greater magazine, radio, newspaper, and television coverage has given the female athlete exposure undreamed of in the 1960s, and has opened up avenues of self-expression and physical achievement similar to those enjoyed by the male.

The expansion of girls and women's programs in the last few years has made it necessary to revise this book to reflect the present trends and concerns of coaching. Therefore, additional material on Title IX and present-day problems has been included. Since techniques and strategy have changed in some sports, many of the sections in Chapter 9 have been revised by knowledgeable coaches.

This book was designed for use in college classes on coaching techniques for women, and was the first book written specifically for the woman coach and geared exclusively to the needs of the girl and woman athlete.

This book however, was written not *only* for the woman coach, but also for the man who coaches women, for the physical education major who will be dealing with skilled athletes, for the leaders of recreational programs, for physical education instructors, and of course, for the player herself.

Because of traditional cultural and social attitudes toward women in sports, some women have been limited in their opportunities and their outlook. Many girls have not reached their full potential in sports simply because they have been defeated psychologically before they even competed. The participation of women in competitive sports has been hampered by myths and superstitions. Today, however, because we are now aware of the fact that women have a much greater capacity for physical activity and a much greater desire for sports programs than we gave them credit for in the last half century, more women are developing their talents in this field.

Woman's role in society has changed greatly in the last few decades. This change has been accompanied by a change in the public's attitude toward the woman who wishes to engage in sports. At one time, people's feelings about women athletes were so negative that a woman who considered herself a lady wouldn't think of competing in sports and risking being thought masculine, un-ladylike, or low-class. But with today's more sensible attitude toward sports for women, a girl can participate in competitive sports without losing her image of herself.

Our sports programs for women must of course be geared to women's abilities, both as performers and coaches. Nevertheless, in our efforts to open up the field for women, we must be careful not to pass over qualified men coaches in preference to less-well-qualified women coaches, just to get a woman coach. Our women should have the *best* possible coaching, whether the coach is a man or a woman.

One of our biggest problems as coaches is to enforce standards and principles that will safeguard girls who participate. However, our girls also need adequate training in the basics of human movement. If, because of poor coaching, they do not get this training, this can eventually lead to an even larger problem: failure to achieve their full potential.

If our athletic programs for women are to prosper, we must have programs that are planned by intelligent leaders who are interested in the welfare of the participants.

Naturally no one has all the answers to the problems of competition for women; so we must be willing to keep our eyes open to new possibilities in the field. And, as we seek to provide a challenging program for the highly skilled girl, we must try to motivate average players as well to reach their full potential. Therefore, we must be careful that we do not swing our programs from one extreme to another. We cannot afford to ignore the average girl and give preference to the highly skilled girl, or vice versa.

This book does not set forth a day-by-day coaching plan, but it does present the basic information a coach needs in order to work with the skilled girl.

In writing this book I have often slipped into using the feminine pronoun when referring to the coach. However, this book is intended for men as well as women; feminine connotations are only a matter of simplification in writing.

My earliest competitive experiences took place in the school system of Elberton, Georgia, and I am thankful that Georgia offered a well-rounded competitive sports program for women at a time when few states paid attention to the needs of women as well as of men.

This book is simply a written expression for the many, many opportunities that have been made available to me through the medium of sports.

Etowah, North Carolina   P.N.
December 1977

Acknowledgments

There are many people who have helped make this book possible. Dr. Katherine Ley made invaluable suggestions and comments during the writing of the original manuscript, and Wayne Tomik, physiologist at the State University of New York at Cortland, helped greatly with the research for Chapters 2 and 4.

Susan Zehrung drew the original illustrations, and George Guzzi and the art staff at Addison-Wesley created the final work.

Some individuals and publishers have been very cooperative in allowing me to use material from copyrighted sources. I am indebted to Dr. Laurence E. Morehouse and the W. B. Saunders Co. for permission to paraphrase from *Sports Medicine for Trainers*.

The excellent photographs for this book could not have been obtained without the help of Susan Hays (Indiana University News Bureau), Ellen A. Larsen (Brigham Young University Sports Information), Evelyn Lawrence (Utah State University Women's Sports Information), James Russell (University of Texas at Arlington News Service), Tommy Thompson (Madison College Sports Information), Donna Christiansen, Tommy Geddie, Paul Jackson, Dick Lowry, Carol Olson, Tom Smart, Susan Brown, Karen Kennington, Karen Morrison, *Ski Magazine*, Sundby Publications, and United States Track and Field Federation.

I am especially grateful to the outstanding coaches who have taken time to revise the sports sections in Chapter 9. These coaches, and the sports they have contributed so greatly to, are: Carol Carter, University of Utah (Skiing), Susan Fields, Western Carolina University, and Mimi Murray, Springfield College (Gymnastics), Janet Luce, Madison College (Field Hockey), Mary Ridgway, University of Texas at Arlington (Volleyball), Carol Worrell, Walters State Community College (Archery), and Kay Yow, North Carolina State University (Softball).

Others who have helped tremendously with this book are Carla Lowry, Lee Morrison, and Janet Thurgood.

Many other people have helped in different ways, and I am thankful to them even though I cannot name them all.

I am especially grateful to my mother, Mrs. Zack Thomas, to my sister, Mrs. Victor R. Bond, to my brother, Billy Neal, and to my grandmother, Mrs. Obie C. Eavenson, who have encouraged me over the years, both in my sports participation, and in my writing.

Contents

1 The Role of the Coach as Leader

We are in a very exciting and challenging period of athletics for women. Never before has the female been so free from cultural restraints and taboos as she is today. Woman's new role in our society is opening up uncountable opportunities for her to engage in play activities without the restrictions and discouragements she once had to face.

THE NEED FOR QUALIFIED COACHES

Sports programs for women in the future will depend greatly on the leadership of qualified coaches. Yet today there is a lack of experienced women coaches. One reason for this is the fact that the competitive program for girls has in the past been limited. A second reason is that the program for training women coaches at present is still limited.

Ordinarily, a person gains irreplaceable experience if he or she has been a player and has participated in competition before becoming a coach. Men can draw on many experienced players as coaches because of the expanded programs open to men, but it will be some years before developing programs for the highly skilled woman will provide enough qualified women coaches. When we take this fact into consideration, the present situation offers two possibilities: (1) Qualified men coaches can be used while at the same time women maintain control of women's programs, and (2) women coaches can be trained in classes set up for this purpose in colleges and universities.

Already, some programs are benefiting from the experience and firsthand knowledge of women athletes who have played on college teams, and who have gained added insights from coaching classes.

THE CONTRAST BETWEEN TEACHING AND COACHING

It is generally accepted that those women who are most qualified to coach are the ones who are teaching in school physical education departments; however, there is a difference between teaching and coaching, even though there is no fine line

1

separating one from the other. A good teacher does not necessarily become a good coach, or vice versa.

The person must decide whether she really wants to *coach*, or whether her real interest lies in *teaching*. The teacher tries to instruct people in fundamentals, while the coach utilizes skills that have already been learned. Teaching might involve helping the pupil build up a complete framework of movement, starting with simple movement and working up to complex ones. The coach accepts the person's framework of movement and tries to work within these limitations, making only minor changes. The teacher establishes techniques; the coach accepts established techniques, and adds to them by instilling a knowledge of strategy, desire to excel, and self-discipline.

Teaching involves performance in situations that are relaxed and comfortable; coaching involves performance under stress and in competitive situations. One should complement the other. The teacher must coach at times, and the good coach beomes a teacher when needed; one is no good without the other. A student who has been well taught is able to get the most out of good coaching because she is receptive to it. The well-coached student is more open to a learning situation in which she is being taught. When the teacher has done her job well, the good coach can carry the athlete to the height of efficiency. Although there is a difference between teaching and coaching, there is an overlapping in results and rewards.

The coach has a willing audience because the player engages in the activity voluntarily and motivation is not a problem unless the coach allows staleness to set in. The teacher may strike resistance, because the student is not always dedicated to learning, and it is the teacher's responsibility to motivate as well as to teach. But in coaching as well as in teaching, the leader's job is to bring out the best in the person, regardless of the person's motives for being in the classroom or on the playing court.

THE PHILOSOPHY OF COACHING

Some say coaching is an art; others say it is a science. Without doubt, it is both. The good coach applies scientific principles and techniques, but the great coach applies them with finesse and tact: This is the *art* of coaching. Anyone who wishes to go into coaching needs to examine his or her philosophy of coaching as it relates to teaching, and as it relates to the level of skill he or she wishes to develop.

In today's school systems, there are, basically, three levels of instruction and coaching. These levels are: (1) physical education classes, (2) intramural sports, and (3) interscholastic or varsity play.

Since work in classes is basically a teaching situation and involves little coaching, we shall not discuss it here. But those who work with intramurals and interscholastic teams need a well-thought-out philosophy of coaching if they are to span the gap between instruction of novices and coaching of the highly skilled.

This philosophy, or this differing set of values for performance at different levels of competition, can result in better sports programs. If the coach has a sound attitude toward the place of coaching, and realistic goals for her team, improvement should be the outcome.

Students who participate in varsity competition should have had the benefit of a sound intramural program beforehand, which has been organized to meet the needs of all students who want some activity beyond their physical education classes. Such an intramural program gives the person a chance to use what she has been taught in physical education classes, and thus it should emphasize utilization of skills and strategy. Instead of putting pressure on the person to excel, the intramural program should help her to improve, and to enjoy the pleasures of physical activity on a voluntary basis.

Very little individual coaching goes on during an intramural program, but clinics to aid in understanding the rules, strategy, officiating, etc., can add much to the overall program, when they are planned so that they coincide with the sports being engaged in. It is during the intramural program that people can experiment with what they know; they can try out new skills under a competitive situation that is not too intense. At the same time, they can learn to react to pressure that is limited enough to allow a player to make mistakes without losing prestige because of a lack of skill.

It is on the intramural level that coaching and teaching greatly overlap because of the difference in the level of skill: The teacher must help with basics one moment and become a coach dealing with points of stategy the next. But because of the informal atmosphere of intramurals, opportunities for coaching as such are limited, while talent in teaching and organizational work is in great demand. Since the object of intramurals is to meet the needs of all students who want activity beyond physical education classes, the person working with intramurals must be a jack-of-all-trades. This person must be patient, have a sense of humor, be able to supply words of wisdom to the uncoordinated as well as to the skilled, and must have the insight to recognize the worth of a program at this level, realizing that it is a fun-filled opportunity for exploring the potential of the self amid others of many levels of skill.

The coach of the junior varsity team steps up to a higher level of achievement, because the people who participate in this program are those who want a broader experience than that offered in the intramural program. The desire to participate in a more competitive program is usually accompanied by a greater degree of skill, and play at this level is more advanced than play at the intramural level. It is at this point that the coach becomes more of a coach, and tries to improve performance by means of organized practice sessions, drills, etc.

Junior varsity programs enable teams to compete with groups of approximately the same skill level, and people become more aware of team effort, common goals, and the importance of accomplishment. Players are further encouraged to try out different ways of performing so that they can compete most effectively. Junior varsity teams are similar to varsity teams, except that coaching is usually done over a shorter period of time and there is less stress. Potentials are still being developed, but at the same time desire and skill are channelled into a more formalized, disciplined program, with emphasis on the social aspects of competition. It is at this plateau that people become more aware of achievement due to skill and practice. The coach begins to mold individuals into a starting line-up according to ability, even though he or she usually tries to give everyone an equal opportunity to compete.

It is at the junior varsity level that demands on the individual, for both skills and social awareness, are increased. Each player must learn to cope with the demands made on her under a greater degree of pressure. Since she must respond in a group situation, her behavior becomes more important because it reflects back on the group as a whole. The individual now represents a school or an organization, and just as she is expected to exhibit more skill, she is also expected to possess more self-control, poise and social stability.

The coach has an opportunity not only to build skills, but also, at the same time, to reinforce character. If the coach is lax with respect to sportsmanship, courtesy, and common social amenities, this can result in similar laxity on the part of the athletes. At this level the coach should cultivate—in fact, demand—positive attitudes toward competition. Proper dress, a feminine appearance, and acceptable behavior are also of utmost importance, since success in athletics at this level may be the determining factor in success at the more competitive level of varsity competition.

Although individual excellence is encouraged at the junior varsity level, the primary objective should be team and individual development, good social reactions under competitive situations, and establishment of high standards in athletics.

It is on the next level—the varsity level—that coaching becomes pure coaching. The interscholastic and intercollegiate varsity coach should be selected because of merit rather than simply because she is interested and available. Competition of the interschool and varsity type is based on *achievement*, and the program must be run on this basis if the skilled girl is to gain true benefits. The right to participate is no longer granted because of a girl's desire or interest, but because of her ability to produce. Thus at this level she learns that she has to earn her privileges by hard work. Interschool and varsity competition should be reserved for the few who have excelled, and who can make the sacrifices necessary to attain excellence. Achievement is rewarded by selection to the team, trips for out-of-town games, and the chance to be a substitute or possibly even a starter.

So the philosophy of coaching includes many things. At the intramural level it means being a teacher-coach. On the junior varsity level, it means being a coach-teacher. On the interscholastic and varsity level, it means being a coach-coach. At all levels, it means setting a good example. The effective coach instills high standards in the players by demanding good performance and sportsmanlike behavior, by seeing to it that the girls are dressed well, and by teaching them to handle themselves with pride.

CHARACTERISTICS OF THE GOOD COACH

The good coach does not just happen. He or she must *want* to be a coach, and must be trained as one. A good coach should: (1) understand the workings of the human body, (2) know the best and most up-to-date methods for training and conditioning athletes, (3) have the ability to analyze and correct form, (4) have insight about how to best use personnel, (5) believe in the values of competition, (6) be aware of opportunities for personality development in sports, (7) have the qualities of dedication, enthusiasm, and initiative, (8) be capable of selflessness, (9) understand psychology, and (10) have a sense of responsibility to players and public.

Understanding of the Human Body

We know much more about the human body now than we did ten years ago, and we'll know still more ten years from now. The coach must rely on the knowledge we now have, but be aware of the research being done, and try to keep up with new developments. People used to feel that any type of strenuous exercise was harmful to the female. Yet today we know that women's physiological response to training is the same as men's [2]. We do not fully understand many aspects of competition, but we expect that research will clarify those issues that are now in doubt. A good coach, in order to prevent harm to the player and at the same time tap the woman athlete's great potential, must incorporate up-to-date medical facts into her coaching, and understand what a woman is physically capable of doing.

Knowledge of Up-to-Date Methods
of Training and Conditioning Athletes

The coach who knows the effects of exercise on the human body is able to use the best and most modern methods without unfounded fears and misconceptions. For example, there was a time when any mention of weight training for girls was met with scorn. Nowadays many coaches are improving the performance of their players by means of programs that include weight training. For many years the reason for avoiding this technique was the fear that using weights would cause a woman to become muscle-bound. However, people now realize that this fear is groundless, and that unless the program is intensive or extends over a long period—which is not usual in women's programs—weight training will not produce unsightly muscles in the female. On the contrary, it can lead to a firmness that will make the body more attractive. Thus the women's program benefits from utilization of proved methods of training and conditioning.

Ability to Analyze and Correct Form

The good coach, regardless of how much he or she knows about present-day re-search, must also be able to analyze what the athlete is doing. Then, if the athlete is not reaching her full potential, the coach can give suggestions for improve-

Happiness is having played well. (Courtesy of Indiana University News Bureau.)

ment, remembering that radical changes should not be made in the form of the skilled athlete's movements. The movements of the body are so complex that a slight correction can often make the difference between a good performance and a great one. But when an athlete thinks so much about *how* to do things that her performance suffers, the coach should be able to recognize this, and should re-emphasize the importance of her *total* movement.

The coach must be aware of the scientific principles involved in the movement of the body, but at the same time, he or she must be aware that every person will not look the same when performing these movements. The results of analysis should be an improved performance, not improved looks.

The coach's ability to *communicate* with the athlete is another vital factor in coaching. A coach who lacks tact, or who insists that only one way is correct (although other methods might be as effective), can often erase any advantages gained through a change in performance.

Ability to Use Personnel Effectively

A coach must often modify or even change systems of play according to the personnel he or she has to work with. The players, not the system, are the keys to good coaching. The plays are important only as they relate to the potential of the athletes. If the system is ineffective, it may not be the players' fault. Sometimes a system that works perfectly in practice may not succeed in a competitive situation. If so, the coach must be able to accept this fact and to make the necessary changes, even if it is in the middle of a game. The athletes, of course, must share this ability to cope with needed changes.

Belief in Values of Competition

Sports offer great opportunities for teaching good citizenship. The coach can help young athletes to learn poise, self-confidence, empathy, self-control, determination, dedication, and the difference between fairness and unfairness. Admittedly, there are occasional bad influences: There is sometimes too much pressure from fans, parents, and even coaches. Some athletes engage in sports just for the glory; some are selfish or dishonest; some display poor sportsmanship. Occasionally women athletes, under the stess of competition, give the impression of being unfeminine. At times there is too much publicity, too much emphasis on winning, too much politics. But the good to be gained from competition far outweighs the bad.

The athlete has unexcelled opportunities to live fully, give completely, make mistakes and learn quickly from them, experience winning and losing and have to take both in stride, learn to make sacrifices to achieve a goal, and feel satisfaction in achievement. In spite of fierce competition, the athlete learns how to walk off the playing field and remain friendly with the competitor. Competition forces a girl to go full-speed and yet make valid on-the-spot decisions, to depend on her own initiative, and to develop the coordination needed to carry her through situations fraught with stress.

It is the coach's responsibility to see that the players are aware of the choices between good and bad in sports, and that they do not have a victory-at-any-price attitude.

Awareness of Opportunities for Personality Development

Coleman [1] says that perhaps the most vital step a person takes in preparing to coach is acquiring a respect for the profession and an understanding of the opportunities it offers in the building of personality.

Competition does not require physical excellence only, but makes constant demands on the mental and emotional resources of the individual. The good coach knows that each of his players is continually being influenced by the many forces that are at work in competitive sports. The coach must utilize every opportunity to reinforce desirable personality traits, traits that enable the individual to be a contributing factor in our culture.

Dedication, Enthusiasm, and Initiative

Although coaching is time-consuming, and frustrating at times, work with the highly skilled is a challenge in itself, and only the dedicated coach can do justice to this challenge.

Enthusiasm is another prerequisite. Often a coach's enthusiasm can make up for a team's lack of skill, and any coach who can keep her team loving the game, and who can run a program that leaves the players wanting just a little bit more, is ahead of the coach who makes work out of play.

Keeping enthusiasm at a high level requires initiative on the part of the coach. The leader who can continually come up with a new drill or a new idea is able to keep monotony to a minimum. This usually means extra preparation before practice and a constant willingness to try something different.

Selflessness

A fine coach must be unselfish, and keep her own ambitions and need for prestige in the background. Sometimes a coach pushes a team beyond its capacity because losing is a threat to her own ego. The true coach, however, gets her reward from seeing her players develop skill and character, and cares more about the effect of the game on the athlete than the final score of the game. When a victory may hang in the balance, it's hard for a coach to do the fair thing, ignore the shouts of fans, or discipline the star player when needed. But the coach knows that team as well as individual morale depends on decisions made for the good of the team. So the good coach disregards her own prestige in favor of doing the right thing by her players.

Understanding of Psychological Reactions

In the sports world, physical skill is often overrated and mental attitude under-rated, as witness the many upsets in which unknowns meet big-time stars, and win. The psychological reactions of individuals are of crucial importance. The coach, if he or she is to get the most out of the players, must be aware of their psychological makeup, and act accordingly. Every good coach knows people cannot be all treated the same. Some people are quite coachable, while others resist coaching. Some react best to praise, while others respond only to constructive criticism; in some cases, a "chewing-out" may be necessary. As Emerson says, "Each of us needs someone to make us do what we *can*."

Thus a part of psychological coaching involves work on morale, which might be defined as an attitude of confidence, courage, and pride that renders the individual capable of meeting any situation with poise. One says that an athlete "has heart," or has "lost heart," meaning that her morale is high or low.

The psychology-oriented coach should remember that an athlete's pride can be increased by being dressed well, and by having an organized pregame warm-up that is snappy and well handled. The type of clothes or the way a warm-up is organized may not add to the skill of the players, but psychologically it can do wonders, and as a result can help the team's performance.

The coach sensitive to players' needs can also help them handle nervous tension or "butterflies." As we all know, highly motivated athletes who want to win almost always experience tension before entering competition. The problem is to keep it within bounds and to channel it so that it will improve rather than harm the person's performance. The coach should explain to the young athletes that these "butterflies" before a game can help them to perform better during the game than they did during practice sessions, provided the nervous tension is not excessive. In most cases, if the coach explains to the players that it *helps* to be nervous before the game, and that this nervous tension usually disappears right after the game starts, the athletes can better use this extra energy to good advantage. If this is not in the case of a specific athlete, the coach should try to take the player's attention away from the contest, and help her to relax before the game. Sometimes it helps to talk to the girl and try to help her understand herself and her emotions better.

The sensitive coach hesitates to change a skilled athlete's methods of performance, except to give minor suggestions that do not destroy the person's basic movement patterns. These suggestions must be presented to the athlete in a diplomatic way. And of course the coach must be careful not to destroy an athlete's confidence while trying to improve her performance, since psychological damage can take as long to heal as physical injuries.

A coach who doesn't know how to get the desired reactions from the players will find her team coming in second best, since adverse psychological reactions often lead to staleness. Therefore a coach must learn to recognize signs of emotional and psychological as well as physical stress.

One final word: For psychological effectiveness, the coach must be the boss, capable of setting requirements and making demands that the team is expected to follow. The coach must make decisions concerning the team, and make it plain that this responsibility is not going to be passed on to the players, except under certain specified circumstances.

Sense of Responsibility to Players and Public

Generally speaking, the coach has three main responsibilities: (1) to be fair to players and to help develop their fullest potential while at the same time protecting their health, (2) to create a positive public image of sports for women, and (3) to be an example of the morals, sportsmanship, health habits, and characteristics she tries to teach her players.

The coach's foremost responsibility is to her players. To fulfill this responsibility, the coach must be adaptable, imaginative, creative, and capable of being a dynamic leader, as well as a friend and a slave driver. The coach must see that sportsmanlike standards are enforced and the programs are administered in the best interests of the participants. All in all, a large order.

The coach is responsible to the public, in that the woman's sports program should make a positive contribution to society. Thus the coach must be something of a missionary and a public-relations expert, willing to take the time to inform the public of values of competitive experiences, while representing the positive aspects of sports activity herself.

Finally, the coach must learn to adjust to being continually under pressure. If the pressure—and the need to win—become so strong that the coach cannot do real justice to coaching, then the person should re-evaluate his or her goals. Perhaps this person is just not cut out to be a coach.

But if the coach can integrate her needs with those of her players, and come out with an easy and a good relationship, both with herself and with those she is coaching, then she can consider herself as having fulfilled her responsibility. Then, as the coach becomes more aware of the opportunities open to a leader in the sports field, she or he will find that coaching can be the most satisfying and challenging work there is.

BIBLIOGRAPHY

1. Coleman, Griffith, *Psychology of Coaching.* New York: Scribner's, 1932, pages 6–11.

2. Heusner, William W., "Basic Physiological Concepts as They Relate to Girls' Sports," *Proc. Second National Inst. on Girls' Sports,* Michigan State University, September 26–October 1, 1965. (Published by AAHPER, 1201 Sixteenth St., N.W., Washington, D.C.).

3. Lawther, John D., *Psychology of Coaching.* Englewood Cliffs: Prentice-Hall, 1951, pages 10–12, 126.

4. Ley, Katherine, "The Full Program at the College Level," *New York State Journal of Health, Physical Education, and Recreation,* winter issue, **18,** 2, 1965.

5. Ley, Katherine, "What Is Coaching?" *Proc. Fourth National Inst. on Girls' and Women's Sports,* Indiana University, December 3–10, 1966. (Published by AAHPER, 1201 Sixteenth St., N.W. Washington, D.C.).

2 Factors in Coaching Women

Today, most misconceptions about the effects of strenuous activity on women have been dispelled and new research findings on the subject are accessible to everyone interested in women's athletics. However, for the benefit of those who might wish some of this information in concise form, some of the research dealing with the effects of competition and exercise on women are included in this chapter.

Since women do not have the same body build that men have and thus do not have the same physical potential, the coach must carefully consider those factors that may influence a training program designed for women: (1) health / medical factors, (2) genetic/ morphological factors, (3) physiological/ metabolic factors, (4) developmental/emotional factors, and (5) environmental factors. One area that needs more research is the subject of psychological factors.

HEALTH AND MEDICAL FACTORS

It has only been in the last decade or so that we have realized that physical activities and participation in sports are not harmful to a woman. On the contrary, they can be a factor that contributes to her overall health, provided that she has no physical defects prior to engaging in strenuous exercise. Laboratory and field research point to many benefits.

Benefits of Exercise

Exercise, and the health benefits that can be gained from it, is as important to the woman as it is to the man [26]. Thus the healthy woman who participates in athletics need not fear danger to her health because there are no significant risks involved [70].

The American Medical Association has pointed out that sound sports programs can contribute a great deal to a woman's total fitness. Participation in sports activities can make her more aware of health factors, and promote in her a sense of satisfaction and achievement. The motivation provided by participation

11

in sports reinforces self-discipline in carrying out good health practices, and can lead to a more "dynamic womanhood" [2].

Observation of athletes themselves underscores the benefits of strenuous activity. Regardless of the wear and tear on their bodies, the tremendous demands on them, and the physical and emotional stress during competitive events, very few athletes miss practice or scheduled events because of illness. To use my own experience as an example, among the thousands of people I have competed with, I have known only a few who missed a competitive event because they were ill. It is true that many athletes compete while suffering from colds and other illnesses that would keep the average person in bed. This is probably due to a combination of factors: a high degree of motivation and pain tolerance, self-discipline in enduring discomfort, and an ability to bounce back quickly because of good physical fitness. Undoubtedly it is also due to the health benefits derived from strenuous exercise.

Regardless of reasons why the well-trained athlete can continue to compete when the untrained person would be unable to cope, it appears that top women athletes do not suffer any bad effects in later life from illnesses or injuries occurring during competition, either with respect to health, number of children, or ease of childbirth [1].

Exercise and the Heart

Misconceptions about the effects of sports on women have persisted not only with regard to women's health in general, but also with respect to the function of the woman's heart and its ability to withstand the strain of strenuous activity.

A study by Tuttle [78] showed that the normal heart rate of women athletes was slower than that of nonathletic women, and that they had a higher degree of physical efficiency. In a three-minute step test, Skubic and Hodgkins [72] found that trained women swimmers performed the second and third minutes of the test with slower heart rates, and that they had a slower heart rate during recovery, than women who were not conditioned.

To draw a comparison with men: Studies of men athletes by J. B. Wolffe [84] indicated that strenuous physical activity did not cause abnormal cardiac enlargement or myocardial damage so long as the person was normally healthy to begin with. As a result of his studies, Wolffe feels that the expression "athlete's heart," in its usual sense, should be redefined, since the athlete has a heart that is better developed, stronger, and that operates more economically than the heart of a person who is physically untrained.

It is now generally known that one of the three main factors in preventing coronary heart disease is regular exercise [87], and that both young and old benefit from physical activity that demands an efficient heart.

Exercise and the Menstrual Period

Ignorance of the effects of exercise on a woman's menstrual period has kept some women from participating in sports. Two studies of women athletes have helped clarify the effects of athletic competition on the menstrual cycle: Jokl [38], in a study of 543 women participants in track and field, hockey, tennis, gymnastics, and swimming, failed to find a single case of serious menstrual disability.

Erdelyi [23], in a study that involved 729 Hungarian women athletes, found that, during participation in athletics, 85.1% of the women noticed no change in the mentrual cycle, 5.6% noticed favorable changes, and 9.3% noticed unfavorable changes. (By way of comparison, consider the fact that approximately 10% of nonathletes experience unfavorable changes during the normal course of their daily lives. Thus, before blaming sports activity as the cause of unfavorable changes in the menstrual cycle, one should consider other factors as well.) Erdelyi found that the highest percentage of menstrual disorders occurred among young athletes between 15 and 17 years of age (18.0%), while only 7.4% of the adult group (18 years and older) experienced unfavorable changes during the menstrual cycle. Erdelyi concluded that women may safely continue to participate in sports activities during their menstrual periods, provided that there are no unfavorable changes in their cycles and provided that their performances don't suffer.

Other observers [3, 33, 60] also feel that women who have no menstrual disorders should be allowed to participate, during menstruation, in all types of physical activity and competition, including swimming. Pros [63] feels that if a girl is used to athletic competition, then she can continue to compete during menstruation.

Some medical people disapprove of intensive athletic competition during the first two days of menstruation [80], while others disapprove of participation in certain sports such as swimming, diving, tennis, skiing, and gymnastics at any time during menstruation because of the intense effort these sports demand and the high percentage of menstrual disorders associated with them [23].

My own belief is that participation in sports can improve a woman's general physical fitness to such a degree that participation during the menstrual period does not entail discomfort, either psychological or physical. Ordinarily, the woman athlete who has followed a sound conditioning program and has trained for competition simply forgets that it is "that time of the month." I have never known a topnotch woman athlete who missed a competitive event because she was menstruating, or one who blamed poor performance on this factor alone. If a woman does experience discomfort or poor performance, it may be due to social and psychological conditioning over a period of years rather than an inability to perform well during menstruation.

Some studies [23, 47] have indicated that if a woman's performance does sag during the menstrual cycle, the sag occurs during the premenstrual period or the first two days of menstruation, with the best performance coming during the postmenstrual phase. However, there is usually no letdown in performance, and most women athletes are capable of performing at their average level during menstruation [1, 23, 62, 66].

Far from having an adverse effect on a woman's menstrual habits, participation in sports, by strengthening her abdominal muscles, can eliminate many symptoms of dysmenorrhea [18, 29, 30] and thus one by-product of a sports program is often an improved menstrual cycle.

The sport that is most controversial with respect to competition during menstruation is swimming. Studies [3, 5] indicate that swimming is not generally a causative factor in menstrual disturbances, and that women who have been ardent swimmers usually go through life relatively free of obstetrical and gynecological difficulties. If a girl does complain of pain, a change in the menstrual cycle, or a lag in performance while she is participating in swimming (or in any other sport), she should be given a thorough physical examination to rule out other possibilities before one assumes that these bad effects are a result of swimming or strenuous activity. If the results of these tests indicate that the girl has trained too hard, then she should not practice or compete during her menstrual period.

Top-flight women athletes compete every day, many of them while they are menstruating. No one watching them compete could point out which ones are menstruating, because their performances and their psychological attitudes toward competition do not vary with the time of the month. In fact, women can not only compete while they are menstruating, but can excel in their performances. In the 1956 Olympics in Melbourne, six gold medals were won by women who were menstruating at the time they competed [16].

Exercise and Childbirth

Another common worry connected with women engaging in competitive sports is that it may adversely affect a woman's child-bearing function. The few studies that have been done in this area indicate that women athletes have fewer complications during pregnancy and childbirth than nonathletes [23], possibly because of women athletes' strong muscles (especially in the abdominal and pelvic region), overall physical fitness, and ability to relax in the face of pain and discomfort.

Generally, women athletes have no more trouble than non-athletes in adjusting to marriage and motherhood, although they may marry at an older age [23]. A study by Astrand [5] supports findings that women athletes have normal desire for marriage and children, and that sports training has no adverse effect on fertility.

During the early months of pregnancy, a woman can usually continue to participate in sports, except those that involve body contact or bumps [16]. However, she should not participate in those sports that involve unnecessary risks, although spontaneous abortion as a result of strenuous exercise is rare [47]. (Another interesting fact about the 1956 Melbourne Olympics is that three women participants were pregnant [16].)

After a woman athlete has had a baby, she should allow some time to elapse before continuing her training and competition on a serious basis. Charles [16] suggests a 3-month interval, while Pros [63] advocates a wait of 4 months.

GENETIC AND MORPHOLOGICAL FACTORS

Evolution and heredity have resulted in a woman's having certain physical traits and structure that make her ability to perform different from a man's. In planning sports programs for women, we should consider these differences.

Differences Between Men and Women

The differences in body type and body composition of men and women are probably not as great as some would believe. However, let us list some of them, based, of course, on men and women of average size.

1. The woman has a narrower shoulder than the man [43, 50, 80].
2. The male is taller than the female [80].
3. The female's center of gravity is lower than the male's [50, 51, 80].
4. The woman's arms and legs are proportionately shorter than the man's [51].
5. The woman has a smaller lung capacity than the man [50, 80].
6. The woman's pelvis is wider and shallower than the man's [43, 50, 51, 80, 83].
7. The female's heart is smaller than the male's [80].
8. Some skeletal differences begin at birth, with some bones in the female ossifying before those in the male [50, 80].
9. The angle of the female's arm is slightly different from the male's [43, 51, 80].
10. The male has a longer growth period than the female; the female matures earlier [50, 71, 80].
11. Women have more fat or adipose tissue than men [51].
12. The woman's thumbs are proportionately shorter than the man's, while the index fingers are longer [77].
13. The femur is more oblique in the female than in the male [83].
14. The female has approximately 36% muscle [51, 77], the male 43% [51].

These differences do have some implications for athletic programs for women. Since the woman does have narrower shoulders, broader hips, and an inward inclination of the arms, most women find it hard to engage in activities in which the body must be supported for any length of time by the arms. The angling of the arms may also make throwing more difficult for the woman than for the man.

Having broader and heavier hips may also mean that the woman may not be able to run as well as the man. The obliquity of the femur may also lead to a mechanical disadvantage for the woman in running when compared to the male.

Since the woman is generally not as tall as the man, she is at a disadvantage in jumping and in running events, in which speed depends on length of stride. However, this shortness gives her an advantage in events that rely heavily on stability, since her center of gravity is lower than a man's.

The fact that the woman's hands have thumbs that are shorter and index fingers that are longer than a man's gives her an advantage in activities that demand dexterity. One often reads about women's ability to play better golf than men around the greens, where touch is more important than power.

The woman's earlier maturation makes her less susceptible than the man to bone and joint injury during adolescence, while the extra fat adds protection against bruises and helps keep her warm in a cold environment. However, a woman's adipose tissue forces her to expend more energy to gain the same results a man does, since she must move a greater amount of dead weight because of tissue that consists of fat rather than muscle.

Differences Among Women

Women vary greatly among themselves in their traits and structure. Therefore, in guiding a program of women's athletics, one must also consider each woman's overall body type. The bounds within which any athlete has to work are set to some degree by heredity. Some physical characteristics may limit a person severely in one specific sport, while other characteristics may greatly help the person perform well in another sport. Height is an advantage to the basketball player, but a disadvantage to the gymnast and the tumbler. The woman who is overweight or proportionately fatter than average may be at an advantage in swimming great distances or in throwing events that demand power, but at a disadvantage in activities in which the body weight must be supported or which involve jumping and running.

One of the better-known classifications of men's bodies was formulated by W. H. Sheldon, whose classifications may also be applied to women. According to Sheldon, there are three basic body types: (1) *endomorphs*, characterized by roundness and softness of body, (2) *mesomorphs*, who are muscular, with large bones, and (3) *ectomorphs*, who are slender and relatively thin and small-framed. It should be remembered that these body types can overlap.

Generally, endomorphs excel in the one sport in which weight is an advantage rather than a disadvantage: long-distance swimming. Most swimmers who can cover great distances, such as the English channel, are obese or of stocky build, with fat concealing the muscles. The insulating property of adipose tissue enables the fat person to maintain body temperature in cold water over a long period of time. In addition, the specific gravity of adipose tissue is less than that of muscle, so that the buoyancy of the swimmer is increased [51]. Mesomorphs can usually excel in events that demand speed, strength, and endurance. People who are a combination of endomorph and mesomorph are usually good at sports that require strength and a certain amount of speed and endurance, such as the shot put and discus throw, as well as middle-distance runs. The ectomorph, though at a disadvantage in events demanding strength and stability, may do well in endurance events and jumping events, since there is a limited amount of body mass to move, and in running events in which length of stride is important.

The tall person can successfully compete in basketball, badminton, tennis, golf, softball, swimming, most track and field events, and volleyball, if she can control her body well and if she has adequate strength to move her long limbs. Long legs and arms not only help the person in activities in which reach is important, but allow a greater range of motion and a greater coverage of a specific area. Long arms can also improve one's performance in sports that require throwing (for example, the discus and the javelin) or batting and hitting (for example, tennis and softball), since the longer the arm used as a lever, the greater the speed and velocity of the object thrown or hit. The tall volleyball player not only gets more power from the hitting action on a spike, but she also has an angle advantage as a result of her longer reach. A fencer has a definite advantage if her arms are longer than the opponent's, and a high jumper has an easier time clearing the bar if her legs are longer and her center of gravity higher than average.

The short girl can compete well in tumbling, diving, hockey, skiing, and ice skating. The fact that her short limbs enable her to tuck her body in tight helps the tumbler and diver to execute movements, somersaults, and spins with speed and overall body control. A low center of gravity and greater stability helps the short hockey player by enabling her to maintain balance and to start, stop, and change direction quickly, and also aids her hand-eye coordination, since her body is low and close to the ball. The low center of gravity is a definite advantage in skiing, in which speed and sharp turns as well as body balance are imperative. The short ice skater has the same advantage.

This is not to say that a short girl cannot excel in a specific sport such as basketball or tennis, or that a tall one will never be any good in a sport such as tumbling or skiing. Some of our greatest athletes do not fit the expected mold: Billie Jean King has been one of the world's best tennis players, yet she is relatively short. She counteracts her height disadvantage with skill, quickness of reactions, hustle, and determination. In golf—in which height gives extra leverage and consequently more power and distance—Sandra Haynie has competed exceptionally well and yet weighs about 107 pounds and is petite.

One can't say that selection of an athlete for an activity is more important than training, or vice versa. Ideally, a coach could select an athlete who had all the qualifications for a specific sport and then train her to be a top competitor. But desire and interest can be such great motivating factors that an athlete with lesser physical attributes can compete on even terms with one having all the physical characteristics, but less motivation.

The woman who *does* choose a sport in which her height, weight, or overall body type put her at a disadvantage must accept the facts and be willing to face up to the options open to her. First, both the coach and the athlete must realize that there are limitations to what the girl can accomplish when she is competing with someone else who is equally motivated and who in addition has physical characteristics that are an advantage in the given sport. Second, the girl must be willing to work harder to counteract the disadvantages of body type. For instance, the heavy basketball player may have to work very hard on endurance and speed in order to keep up with the slender girl, while the thin girl may have to utilize speed and try to develop additional strength in order to compete with the muscular, stocky girl in the shot put or some other event that depends on strength and body weight. Third, the person must have extraordinary determination and hustle. Motivation and mental attitudes play a tremendous part in athletics, and often psychological factors outweigh physical ones.

Some studies, in fact, have even shown that body type is not a large determining factor in some performances. Patterson [57], for example, found no significant correlation between women's success in swimming and their height and weight. Watson [81] found that the relationship between college women's body measurements and their ability to throw a baseball was low, with respect ot both accuracy and distance. Perbix [58] indicated that there was no relationship between women's somatotype ratings and their trunk extensions, although the same study found that there seem to be significant relationships between mesomorphy and strength and power, and that women physical education majors have more dominant mesomorphic traits than woman in other fields. In a study of men, Pierson [61] found that there seems to be little relationship between speed of reaction and height, weight, body fat, or lean body mass.

Do Sports Masculinize Women?

Another subject of contention is whether women lose their femininity if they are athletes. The natural desires of women in the past for play activities and athletic competition have been inhibited because of this misconception, and even today there are evidences that the myth persists that girls who participate in a sports program acquire masculine characteristics.

Participation in sports does not masculinize women [43]; the belief that it does has no foundation, since the great majority of women who participate in athletics show no signs of masculinization even after competing for years [23].

True, there are always a few women to be found engaging in sports who have masculine characteristics; these characteristics may give them some advantages because of the structure of their bodies. However, Carpenter [11] measured the factors that influenced the athletic performance of college women and found that the two most important ones were power and muscular strength, while the third factor measured—masculine type of build—had less influence. This study indicated that there is no significant correlation between a woman's athletic performance and femininity of body type.

However, Cress and Thorsen [19], in a study of college women, found a higher correlation between androgyny ratings and motor performance than between androgyny ratings and somatotype ratings. They also found that masculinity of physique showed a significant positive correlation with pure speed, the 50-yard dash, the Sargent jump, arm strength, and the Humiston test.

For some time there have been rumors that certain countries entered men, disguised as women, on some of their women's Olympic teams. In the 1968 Olympics, to ensure that women would be competing against women, female participants had to pass not only a visual checkup, but they also had to pass the buccal smear and karyotype (chromosome patterns) tests. These tests are based on the theory that masculinity and femininity are determined by the characteristics of chromosomes. However, as pointed out in an article in *Sports Illustrated* [88], the reliability of these tests has been questioned, on the basis that more than one criterion must be involved in determining the sex of an individual.

Today, athletes do not have to undergo visual inspection, but cells from inside the mouth or hair follicles are examined microscopically for the female chromosome pattern.

When women athletes do show evidences of masculinity, there is no proof that participation in sports is the cause of it. It is more likely that the athletes already had these characteristics before they began to take part in athletics. After all, there are exceptions to the norm in any field of endeavor. The feminine women participating in sports—and they are in the majority—should not be judged on the basis of the few exceptions who are masculine. One has only to look at some of the women who have won medals in the Olympic Games to see that a woman can be feminine and talented in sports at the same time. Wilma Rudolph, Peggy Fleming, and Dorothy Hamill are examples (to name but a few).

Participation in sports, therefore, does not seem to masculinize women. It is just that our culture has imposed its own code of conduct on both women and men, and when anyone exhibits behavior that varies from this code, a false label is attached to that person. In most cases, this code of conduct is based on scant knowledge of the physiological, morphological, or psychological workings of the male or female. The code has assigned cultural roles on the basis of sex, and reinforced them over the years until people have generally accepted certain traits as being masculine and certain others as being feminine. Yet confusion is arising because, although society at large accepts one role as feminine and another as masculine, science has led many people to question the cut-and-dried division between these roles. And women themselves are reaching out and seeking a more vital role that will allow them greater development professionally, socially and physically. The age-old limitations on women, aptly defined by the Germans as *Kinder, Küche, Kirche,* are beginning to fade. And there are many questions that need to be answered as to the real meaning of masculinity and femininity.

Are strength and endurance purely masculine traits, or can women engage in activities that require these two factors and still remain feminine? Does aggressiveness belong only to a man, grace only to a woman? Are courage and the ability to endure pain strictly masculine traits, or can women be courageous and train themselves to continue physical exercise in spite of discomfort? Is it feminine to bear pain with fortitude only during an involuntary experience like childbirth, but masculine to do so under voluntary, competitive athletic conditions? Steinhaus [76], for one, feels that women should be allowed to compete, within their own limits, without being labeled masculine or unladylike, and raises the important question of whether our "forced, false, male-made standard of femininity" isn't preventing women from developing their personalities fully.

Men and women *both* are capable of kindness, aggression, physical and mental self-discipline, strength, and endurance. Men and women *both* can be strong, can endure, can run, jump, laugh and cry. These capabilities are not sex-dependent, although the degree of accomplishment may be limited by sex. But, to women as well as men, the development of one's physical potential is as necessary to well-being as the development of the mind or spirit. Thankfully, society is beginning to banish the pejoratives "tomboy" and "sissy."

*Women also enjoy sports activities. (Courtesy of Indiana
University News Bureau.)*

Women should be encouraged to be athletes—not to emulate men athletes—but so that women too may enjoy the benefits of health and the psychological satisfaction of competition as part of a full and a satisfying life.

PHYSIOLOGICAL AND METABOLIC FACTORS

There are some physiological and metabolic differences between men and
women: At every age the woman's metabolic rate is lower than the man's [33,
50]. Her heart is smaller, and thus the rate of her heartbeat is faster than a man's,
both at rest and during exercise, with a slower return to normal during the recovery period following strenuous activity [51].

Women have lower systolic and diastolic blood pressures than men [33, 80]
and their smaller thoracic cavity and lungs seem to make women's respiratory
movements faster than men's [80]. The average woman has 25-30% less lung capacity than the average man, although physically trained men and women appear
to utilize the anaerobic processes to the same extent [9]. The male has more red
blood corpuscles and a greater supply of hemoglobin than the female [33, 50, 51,
80].

Strength

The female has only about 78% as much muscular strength as the male [52].
Furthermore, she has less muscle in relation to her size than the male. Yet there
does not seem to be any impairment in the workings of her muscles because of her
sex [80]. These differences simply mean that women do not have as much total

strength as men. But women's muscles function with the same efficiency, the difference being not in the ability to perform but in the proportion of muscle to body mass.

Speed and Endurance

Klafs and Arnheim [43] believe that before puberty girls can equal—and in some cases surpass—the performances of boys in the same age group, in athletic feats that involve speed, strength, and endurance. Shaffer [71] contends that girls and boys respond about the same until approximately 14 years of age, and then the girls tend to drop off in both endurance and caliber of performance. Whether this decline in girls' performances after puberty is due to cultural restrictions and the role expected of the female or to morphological or physiological limitations is an unsolved question. A study by Jones [41] indicates that this drop in performance is not due to physical limitations, since, according to his findings, post-menarcheal girls have more strength than premenarcheal girls of the same age.

Jokl [39] believes that for most girls the peak of endurance comes at age 14, and that, to develop their potential to the utmost, girls should start training for endurance events *before puberty.* He feels that training during this period, when physiological development is a a maximum, would give better results, and that the effect of this conditioning would be to improve performances over a period of years.

Skubic and Hodgkins [73] feel that younger girls do better than older ones in situations that involve endurance. In their study, junior high school girls did significantly better on a cardiovascular test than high school or college women.

Shaffer [71] points out that since endurances, strength, and coordination seem to be related to maturation, the age of girls excelling in sports will become even lower because of the fact that girls are maturing at a younger and younger age.

Because of their physiological and metabolic makeup, girls seem better equipped to compete in activities that involve endurance than in ones that rely greatly on strength and power [33]. A fundamental principle of the physiology of exercise is that training produces similar physiological responses in men and in women [33], although there is a difference between them in the degree of potential which can be developed through training [9]. The training program for women should not be noticeably different from that for men except for the degree of intensity and level of achievement sought.

People over the years have been concerned that too much strain and stress might be placed on the female during training and competition. I believe that the makeup of the human body, especially the woman's, is more capable of adjusting to intense demands on it during conditioning and competitive situations than many realize. This view was also taken by Dr. Allan J. Ryan when he was questioned about the matter [66]; he replied that we shouldn't worry because he didn't feel we were even close to the point of too-great strain yet.

Performance and Age

As the athlete ages, some physiological changes may affect his or her ability to perform. After 30, maximum oxygen intake declines progressively as the athlete gets older [9, 51, 56], making it more difficult to engage in strenuous activity for long periods. There also appears to be an increase in lung ventilation while the athlete is participating in submaximal work [56]. Strength and the ability to keep up performance demanding a high degree of coordination seems to decline with age [51, 56]. However, as pointed out by Brouha [9], the ability to perform well and to reach maximum performance is dependent more on the physical fitness of the athlete than on a set chronological age.

This view is supported by Morehouse and Rasch [51] who believe that if training is continued, there may be very little decline in physical fitness in later years. They also point out that the ability to do light work stays at a high level beyond 60 years of age, although an athlete past 30 can maintain a high level of athletic performance only if he or she progressively increases the amount of training and conditioning. This means that older athletes can successfully compete with younger ones provided they are willing to spend more time and effort to achieve the same results.

An example of what conditioning means has been Dr. Thomas K. Cureton, Jr., of the University of Illinois, who in his middle sixties often gave demonstrations involving two hours of running, swimming, etc., that wear down younger participants [87].

Men athletes taking part in the Olympics seem to turn in their best performances when they are between 17 and 30 [42]; athletes engaging in events that demand speed and agility are younger than those taking part in events that demand endurance [37, 42].

Of course, there are exceptions to these generalizations about age and performance. Some athletes with great motivation and self-discipline can maintain a high caliber of performance in events that involve both strength and endurance well beyond 30. Others lose interest and drive before 30, and therefore do not reach their maximum potential. Some of the young champion swimmers retire before the age of 20.

DEVELOPMENTAL AND EMOTIONAL FACTORS

Girls today mature at an earlier age than ever before. The average age for menarche has dropped almost a year and a half over the past hundred years [79], while the average adolescent has gained approximatedly 1/2 inch in height and 3 pounds in weight per decade [71]. Better living conditions and improved nutrition and health are thought to be contributing factors, but perhaps increased protein in the diet and changes in endocrine functioning brought about by added psychological stress may also be causes of earlier maturation [79].

Going for the tip. (Courtesy of USU Women's Sports Information.)

Maturation

The girl's pattern of growth is much faster than the boy's, with the girl's prepubertal growth starting 2 to 3 years before the boy's. The male has the greatest acceleration in his growth pattern in his fourteenth or fifteenth year and the girl in her twelfth [50], or before menarche [71].

Menarche marks a change in the physical growth and development of the girl. Her strength improves, but her motor ability begins to taper off [25, 41, 71]. Espenschade [25] maintains that girls' development in motor performances changes little after puberty, although boys' continues to improve, but stresses the fact that adolescent sex differences have other causes besides capacity, such as training, previous experience, and motivational factors. Jones [41] found that the increase in strength brought about by growth acceleration starts approximately a year before menarche in girls and reaches a peak about the time of menarche, with all girls eventually attaining similar levels of strength at a late age, even though their growth patterns differed.

Motor Ability

Motor ability in activities that require strength and power seems to be closely related to body size and build at all ages, while motor ability in activities that involve balance and coordination seems to have little relationship to a person's physique or body strength at a particular age, although the ability to perform them does improve with age [25].

A study by Phillips et al. [59], which used the Kraus-Weber test to determine the muscular fitness of elementary school children, showed that girls scored higher than boys at all age levels, partly because of the flexibility items. They also found that flexibility for both sexes decreased as age increased, and the the flexibility of girls decreased to a greater extent than that of boys; thus the older children were closer to the same flexibility level.

Hanson [86], in testing students in grades 1 through 6, found that boys scored higher than girls in motor performance except in two categories: rope-skipping and balance. Generally, girls and boys in one grade level were superior in performance to girls and boys in the grade below them.

Although boys continue to increase their performance scores in running, jumping, and throwing from childhood to the last year of high school, girls' improvement continues only until they are about 13; at the same time, even though girls generally exhibit no further improvement in motor ability, there is an increase in their physical size and strength beyond the age of 13. This lack of motor improvement may possibly be due to changes in the body build brought about by adolescence, but it is more likely due to a lack of interest and motivation on the part of the girl, due to cultural pressures [24,25].

Social and Cultural Influences

It is possible that as cultural influences, psychological attitudes, and the expected roles of the male and the female become less constricting, we may discover that girls exhibit a greater variation in range of motor skills than one finds in a comparison between boys and girls.

Women can reach a higher degree of achievement in sports than previously thought, as shown by the accomplishments of the Russian women athletes. Some of the greatest gains in the Soviet Union's international competitive standing have resulted from the performance of its women athletes. Recently, because of the interest in the U.S. in our standing in international competition, the United States has also improved its records in some areas. This interest has given women more motivation to engage in athletics and to strive for their maximum potential.

The main reason that American women have had scant interest in sports in the past is that cultural taboos have choked out any natural motivation they might have had to engage in competitive activities, and have forced them to assume the protective coloration society demands: marrying, raising a family, and being a good homemaker. Although for centuries men have been urged to show their courage, endurance, strength, skill, and aggressiveness in sports activities, girls who showed an interest in running and jumping, or in strenuous physical exercise, have been labeled tomboys. This area was thus off limits to any feminine girl. Over the years, the conflict between girls' natural capacity and desire for physical activity and the socially acceptable role for women was so great that many people believed that competitive activities endangered a woman's health and femininity.

In 1957, the Sixth National Conference on Physicians and Schools [64] made public a statement that the physical makeup of girls was such that they could take part in sports just as readily as boys, if it weren't for the social mores that had imposed limitations on girls.

Cassidy [13] observed that the girl has been deprived of the chance to reach her highest potential because of the belief that girls should be protected from the "evils and stresses in competitive athletics."

Jokl [38], in a survey of Olympic athletes, pointed out certain social implications that are beyond the limits of the sports world. He remarked that those countries which did not enter women in the Olympic games also had high child mortality and higher overall rates of morbidity and mortality. Countries such as the United States, Russia, and the British Commonwealth nations had a high participation and success ratio, which paralleled the social advancement and industrialization of these countries.

Several studies involving male athletes have indicated that high school athletes are better adjusted and exhibit more leadership ability than nonathletes [8, 12, 20, 68], while at least one study [28] indicates that high school girls who participate in athletics are personally and socially better adjusted than those who do not.

In a 1954 study of college extramural and varsity programs for women, White [82] found that in 61% of extramural programs and in 39% of varsity competitions, women experienced no undesirable results from the sports program. When the programs proved to unsatisfactory, the problem most often mentioned was demand on faculty and/or student time.

A society's sociological, philosophical, and psychological concepts determine the direction of the sports programs for its women at a given time and place. Since these concepts have changed greatly in Western society in the past few years, a truer concept of the male's and female's roles in the sports world has been evolving, although the evolution will continue for generations.

Once the social mores have been examined and scientific evidence replaces superstition and myth, sports and competition for girls may prove to be a powerful tool for educating them. It is not hard to identify the biological and psychological differences between men and women, but the sociological, philosophical, and psychological limitations imposed by society invoke more subtle reactions, and conceivably play a greater part in the public apathy toward women's sports than the biological differences between the sexes.

ENVIRONMENTAL FACTORS

Any athlete's performance can be greatly affected by changes in the environment. Going from one climate to another or from one altitude to another forces the body to adjust to the different external stresses on it.

In order for the body to maintain a state of homeostasis, it must keep a balance between the heat being produced internally and the heat being lost externally. Metabolic processes, such as the working of muscles during exercise, cause an increase in internally produced heat. The body can also gain heat from contact with the environment, such as playing on a warm day or swimming in a pool that is overheated. The body can regulate this accumulation of heat in several ways; for the athlete, most of the heat is lost through the evaporation of perspiration during strenuous activity. Therefore humidity plays a role in the performance of the athlete, because when humidity is high, perspiration does not evaporate as quickly, and the body is not able to regulate its temperature as easily, as when the humidity is low.

Adjustment to Climate

It is easier for an athlete to adjust from a hot to a cold climate than from a cold to a hot. In a cold climate, the heat dissipated from the working muscles is partly counterbalanced by the cool environment. At the same time, the athlete competing in a cold environment can regulate body temperature by increasing or decreasing the amount of clothes worn, while in a hot environment a certain minimum of clothing must be maintained. If an athlete wears too much clothing during competition under cold conditions, such as skiing, the body must get rid of excess heat just as it does in a warm climate.

The real problem arises when an athlete must compete in hot weather. When the external temperature is above 80°, the body undergoes certain physiological changes in order to cope with the added stress caused by heat. The body metabolism rises, there is a water loss through perspiration (some marathon runners lose as much as 4 to 5 liters of water through sweating), there is a salt loss, the pulse rate becomes higher, and the heart's output of blood per beat is lower [42]. There is an increased load placed on the cardiovascular system, as it must keep the blood supply going to three different areas simultaneously; (1) surface blood vessels, which are dilated to aid in cooling the body, (2) muscles that are being used during the exercise, and (3) the brain [10]. The athlete has problems during competition when, either because of a lack of conditioning or a lack of acclimatization, her heart is unable to supply these three areas adequately.

When the body is unable to cope with the heat load placed upon it, the athlete may suffer from cramps, exhaustion, or even have a heat stroke. Ordinarily, an athlete suffering from heat cramps can help the body in its effort to maintain a balance between heat production and heat loss by replenishing the fluids and salt that have been lost through competition and by resting and cooling off when the heat load is too great. If the athlete continues to play, exhaustion may follow; the athlete may suffer dizziness and, in extreme cases, unconsciousness. Fainting is the body's way of preventing extensive harm to itself, since the body becomes inert and has a chance to regain a homeostatic condition. However, if an athlete is highly motivated and has an intense drive to compete, the preliminary signs of cramps, dizziness, and even momentary fainting spells may be ignored, and a heat stroke may result which can be fatal.

Women seemingly cannot handle heat stress as well as men [21,27,32] because physiologically it takes more effort for them to maintain a heat balance in a hot environment [32]. However, since heat acclimatization helps keep the body temperature lower, allows the heart to work more efficiently, and keeps the blood pressure more stabilized [10], women as well as men can benefit from acclimatization to heat.

Buskirk and Bass [10] believe that acclimatization to heat can be accomplished by working out in a heated room 2–4 hours every day for a period of 7–10 days before a competitive event in a hot climate. They state that once this acclimatization to heat is reached, the body is able to maintain this state of acclimatization for one to two weeks, even though there is no further exposure to heat.

The coach and the athlete should remember that if conditioning has been done in a cool environment, the athlete is not conditioned for competition in a hot environment, since the body is under more stress to balance the heat load.

If the athlete will take adequate fluids and salt before and during competition, wear light clothes that allow maximum evaporation of perspiration, work out under similar heat conditions 7–10 days before the meet or game, and pace herself to allow cooling periods when possible, she should be able to perform well even in unaccustomed heat. The coach can help the athlete by scheduling events early in the morning or in the evenings to avoid the worst part of the heat during the day.

Adjustment to Altitude

Another environmental problem is performance at high altitudes. Although much more research needs to be done in this area, it now seems that while athletes in events such as sprints (which can be done anaerobically) and other events that require effort of less than a minute are not affected by altitude, athletes performing distance runs and events that demand endurance or effort for more than a minute *are* affected [6,15].

Changing from a lower to a higher altitude presents problems to the athlete because of the decrease in total barometric pressure as one goes to higher altitudes. As a result of the lower pressure, there is not as much oxygen in the blood, and consequently, the working muscles and other active tissues do not get an adequate supply of oxygen. This makes it impossible for the athlete to carry on intensive effort over a long period of time. Short periods of effort can be accomplished anaerobically, so that performance at the time does not suffer from the low oxygen content in the blood, but the recovery period takes longer. During recovery, the oxygen debt is not repaid at the same rate as it is at lower altitudes, and the lower barometric pressure thus results in a slower recovery period. When work is done over a long period of time aerobically, an oxygen debt builds up, even at sea level. This results in a less efficient performance because of the inadequate oxygen supply.

An athlete's body *can* become acclimatized to altitude [6,7,15,42], resulting in more oxygen being carried in the blood and greater efficiency of the lungs and cardiovascular system, which leads to a greater working capacity and therefore a better performance.

The best results come when physical training is combined with acclimatization [6,42]. Although there is a difference in opinion as to exactly how long it takes an athlete to become acclimatized, it has been shown that changes in the blood which can limit endurance are brought about shortly after the athlete goes to a higher altitude [6]. Thus if an athlete (or team) doesn't have time to become acclimatized before competing at a higher altitude, the trip should be so planned that the athlete can compete as soon as possible after arrival.

Balke [6] advocates a minimum of one week for acclimatizing purposes for an increase of 3000 feet in altitude, while Cervantes and Karpovich [15] believe that an altitude such as Mexico City has should require 9–13 days of acclimatization, for sprinting events and approximately 3 weeks for endurance events, such as swimming 400 meters.

Some things do seem to be evident. Competition at high altitude does have its dangers, as shown by the high number of athletes who have collapsed during and after exertion. One of the most frightening cases of exhaustion was that of Ron Clarke of Australia, who in the 1968 Olympics at Mexico City, collapsed at the end of the 10,000-meter race and had to be given oxygen for 10 minutes before he regained consciousness [89].

A second fact that seemed to be brought out by the 1968 Olympics was that, if a competition is to be held at some place that has a high altitude, anyone who lives at high altitude the year round has a definite advantage over a person from a sea-level environment, even though the sea-level athlete may train at high altitude for months before he competes. The Kenyan runners, who came from an altitude comparable to that of Mexico City, surprised the sports world with their domination of the distance events [90,91].

Roger Bannister feels strongly that a sea-level athlete can never become completely acclimatized for competition at high altitude, and feels that it is unfair to the majority of athletes to hold the Olympics or similar competitions at high altitude, such as that of Mexico City [92].

Adjustment to Water

Another environmental problem arises in swimming. Swimming presents a different adjustment to heat regulation, since the athlete cannot lose heat as easily through perspiration evaporation. The problem is intensified because water temperature varies greatly from pool to pool. When the water is too warm during

Sheeler–Winton Invitational Swim Meet. (Courtesy of Dick Lowy, Hialeah, Florida.)

endurance events, the inability of the body to balance heat production and heat loss can affect performance just as in any other environment in which over-heating occurs. If the water is too cold, the body has to expend energy to main-tain normal body heat, thus depleting the energy that could be used for optimum performance. Standarized pool temperatures, based on research dealing with the best temperature for optimum performance in speed and endurance events, certainly helps swimmers' performances.

Swimming poses another problem for the girl who is menstruating and who does not ordinarily use tampons. According to Anderson [3], most girls can use tampons without difficulty and without impairment to their virginity. Therefore swimming during the menstrual period should not hamper the girl.

SUMMARY

1. Most physiological research indicates that sports competition for women is not detrimental to their health, normal function, or well-being. When a sane conditioning program precedes a sane competitive program, the normal woman may participate in vigorous athletic competition. The average woman can be happier and healthier as a result of sports activities.

2. There are differences between men and women morphologically, physiologi-cally, metabolically, and psychologically. However, these differences are not as great as they were once thought to be. It is possible that there are greater differences between the performances of different girls than there are between the performances of girls and boys.

3. There have been, and still are, cultural and social influences that greatly handicap the performance of the woman athlete. The strength of these influences changes with the times, but we seem to be emerging into an era in which women's participation in athletic events does not carry negative connotation as in the past, although women still are not now—and may never be—encouraged to the extent that men are.

4. Because of the biological differences between the male and the female, most women are incapable of equalling the performances of most men in strength, power, and endurance events. Therefore women's achievements in sports should not be compared with men's, although there are some activities in which women can hold their own against men. Competition should not pit men against women, and when coed competition involves pitting a man and a woman against another team consisting of a man and a woman, care should be taken to equalize the teams.

5. Educators should be careful that they do not set up inflexible programs on the basis of the "average." As a result of regional, educational, social, philosophical, psychological, and cultural influences, as well as biological differences, the difference between the performances of one woman and another can be tremendous. Coaching the woman athlete should thus be done on an individual basis, taking into consideration the ability and potential of each person. At the same time, coaches should be selected on the basis of their qualifications, not on the basis of their sex.

6. Physiologically, women react to training in the same way that men do. The differences are basically those of capacity, with the woman having a lower level of performance. Training programs for men and women, therefore, may differ in degree and intensity, but not necessarily in technique.

7. Participation in sports does not have a harmful effect on the normal function of the reproductive system. Although opinion is not unanimous, the medical profession generally maintains that women can take part in physical activity during menstruation without harm. Some authorities feel that a woman who is menstruating should avoid events in which maximum effort is demanded of her, and avoid swimming, for which training involves long exposure to water. Others feel that there need be no restriction placed on the woman during menstruation. So long as the woman does not experience any abnormal change in her cycle, however, she should feel free to train and to compete during menstruation. There is no evidence that participation in stressful competition has a detrimental effect on the normal processes of pregnancy and childbirth; on the contrary, there is evidence that they are aided by participation in sports.

8. The belief that participation in sports tends to masculinize women is a myth. A person's body size and structure is regulated by the endocrine glands, and although muscles may increase in size because of a program that requires much high-resistance exercise, women seldom engage in this type of training program. Some people mentally associate all women athletes with the image

of the huge Russian shot putter or discus thrower. However, the Russian woman is a product of her heredity and genetic background rather than the sport. The large body frame and potential for power were there long before she started training for the event; otherwise she would never have chosen an activity demanding strength. Or, even if she had, she would never have attained Olympic caliber without this large body build. For every Tamara Press, there are hundreds with the grace and beauty (though not necessarily the skill) of Dorothy Hamill and Nadia Comaneci.

9. We still don't know everything there is to know about women and competition, or for that matter about men and competition. The area of sociological and psychological factors is a relatively unexplored one, in which we definitely need more research.

BIBLIOGRAPHY

1. AAU, *Study of the Effect of Athletic Competition of Girls and Women.* New York: AAU, n.d.

2. AMA, "Sports Opportunities for Girls and Women," *Journal of Health, Physical Education, and Recreation,* **35**, 46, November-December, 1964.

3. Anderson, Theresa W., "Swimming and Exercise During Menstruation," *Journal of Health, Physical Education, and Recreation,* **36**, 66–68, October 1965.

4. Astrand, I., "Aerobic Work Capacity in Men and Women, with Special Reference to Age," *Acta Phisiologica Scandinavica* **49**, Supplement 169, 1960.

5. Astrand, P.O., *et al.,* "Girl Swimmers, with Special Reference to Respiratory and Circulatory Adaptation and Gynaecological and Psychiatric Aspects," *Acta Paediatrica Supplement,* 147, 1963.

6. Balke, Bruno, "Work Capacity and Altitude," in *Science and Medicine of Exercise and Sports,* edited by Warren R. Johnson. New York: Harper, 1960, Chapter 18.

7. Balke,B., and J.G. Wells, "Ceiling Altitude Tolerance Following Physical Training and Acclimatization," *Journal of Aviation Medicine,* **29**, 40, 1958.

8. Biddulph, Lowell G., "Athletic Achievement and the Personal and Social Adjustment of High School Boys," *Research Quarterly,* **25**, 1–7, 1954.

9. Brouha,L., "Physiology of Training, Including Age and Sex Differences," *Journal of Sports Medicine and Physical Fitness,* **2**, 3–11, March 1962.

10. Buskirk, Elsworth R., and David E. Bass, "Climate and Exercise," in *Science and Medicine of Exercise and Sports,* edited by Warren R. Johnson, New York: Harper, 1960, Chapter 17.

11. Carpenter, Aileen, "Strength, Power, and 'Femininity' as Factors Influencing the Athletic Performance of College Women," *Research Quarterly,* **9**, 120–125, May 1938.

12. Carter, Gerald C., and J.R. Shannon, "Adjustment and Personality Traits of Athletes and Non-Athletes," *School Review,* **46**, 127–130, February 1940.

13. Cassidy, Rosalind, "Critical Issues in Physical Education and Athletics," *Journal of Health, Physical Education, and Recreation,* **35**, 16–17, June 1964.

14. Cearley, Jess, "Linearity of Contributions of Ages, Heights, and Weights to Prediction of Track and Field Performances," *Research Quarterly*, **28**, 218, October 1957.

15. Cervantes, Jose, and Peter V. Karpovich, "Effect of Altitude on Athletic Performance," *Research Quarterly*, **35**, 446–448, October 1964.

16. Charles, A.H., "Women in Sport," in *Injury in Sport*, edited by J.R.Armstrong and W.E. Tucker. London: Staples Press, 1964.

17. Coffey, Margaret A., "The Sportswoman—Then and Now," *Journal of Health, Physical Education, and Recreation*, **36**, 38, February 1965.

18. Connolly, Olga, "Let Them Participate," *DGWS Track and Field Guide, 1964–1966*, Washington D.C.: AAHPER, 1964.

19. Cress, Carolyn L., and Margaret A. Thorsen, "Morphological Bisexuality as a Factor in the Motor Performance of College Women," *Research Quarterly*, **35**, 408–417, October 1964.

20. Derian, Albert Steven, "Some Personality Characteristics of Athletes Studied by the Projective Method," unpublished master's thesis, University of California, Berkeley, 1947.

21. de Vries, H.A., *Physiology of Exercise for Physical Education and Athletics.* Dubuque, Iowa: Wm.C. Brown Company, 1966. Chapter 26, "The Female in Athletics."

22. Edwards, H.T., "Lactic Acid in Rest and Work at High Altitude," *American Journal of Physiology*, **116**, 367, 1936.

23. Erdelyi, G.J., "Gynecological Survey of Female Athletes," *Journal of Sports Medicine and Physical Fitness*, **2**, 174–179, September 1962. (Also called "Women in Athletics" and distributed at the First National Institute for Girls' and Women's Sports, Norman, Oklahoma, November 1963.)

24. Espenschade, Anna, "Development of Motor Coordination in Boys and Girls," *Research Quarterly*, **18**, 30–44, March 1947.

25. Espenschade, Anna, "Motor Development," in *Science and Medicine of Exercise and Sports*, edited by Warren R. Johnson. New York: Harper, 1960, Chapter 22.

26. *Exercise and Fitness*, special report of the Joint Committee of the American Medical Association and the American Association for Health, Physical Education, and Recreation. *Journal of Health, Physical Education, and Recreation*, May 1964.

27. Folk, G.E., *Introduction to Environmental Physiology*. Philadelphia: Lea and Febiger, 1966.

28. Hale, Creighton J., "Athletics for Pre-High School Age Children," *Journal of Health, Physical Education, and Recreation*, **30**, 19, December 1959.

29. Hamer, M.C., "Dysmenorrhea and Its Relation to Abdominal Strength," *Research Quarterly*, **4**, 229–237, March 1933.

30. Harris, Ruth, and C. Etta Walters, "Effect of Prescribed Abdominal Exercises on Dysmenorrhea in College Women," *Research Quarterly*, **26**, 140–146, May 1955.

31. Henry, F.M., and W.E. Berg, "Physical and Performance Changes in Athletic Conditioning," *Journal of Applied Physiology*, **3**, 103, 1950.

32. Hertig, B.A., *et al.*, "Artificial Acclimatization of Women to Heat," *Journal of Applied Physiology*, **18**, 383–386, March 1963.

33. Heusner, William W., "Basic Physiological Concepts as They Relate to Girls's Sports," Proceedings of Second National Institute on Girls' and Women's Sports, Michigan State University, September 26–October 1, 1965. (Published by AAHPER, 1201 Sixteenth St., N.W., Washington, D.C.)

34. Houston, C.S., and R.L. Riley, "Changes During Acclimatization to High Altitude," American Journal of Physiology, 149, 565, 1947.

35. Johnson, P.B., et al., Physical Education: A Problem-Solving Approach to Health and Physical Fitness. New York: Holt, Rinehart, and Winston, 1966.

36. Jokl, Ernst, Nutrition, Exercise, and Body Composition. Springfield, Ill.: Charles C Thomas, 1964.

37. Jokl, Ernst, et al., Sports in the Cultural Pattern of the World, A Study of the Olympic Games of 1952. Helsinki, Finland: Institute of Occupational Health, 1956.

38. Jokl, Ernst, "The Athletic Status of Women," Amateur Athlete, 33, 14, May 1962.

39. Jokl, Ernst, "The Athletic Success of Young Girls," Amateur Athlete, 34, 20-21, January 1963.

40. Jokl, Ernst, "Youth and Swimming Records," Amateur Athlete, 34, 24-25, October 1963.

41. Jones, Harold E., "The Sexual Maturity of Girls as Related to Growth in Strength," Research Quarterly, 18, 135–143, May 1947.

42. Karpovich, P. V., Physiology of Muscular Activity, sixth edition. Philadelphia: W. B. Saunders, 1965.

43. Klafs, Carl E., and Daniel Arnheim, Modern Principles of Athletic Training. St. Louis: C. V. Mosby, 1963.

44. Koenig, Fran Becker, "Conditioning and Competition Related to Postpubescent Women," unpublished paper, Michigan State University, 1965.

45. Ladell, W. S. S., "The Effects of Water and Salt Intake Upon the Performance of Men Working in Hot and Humid Environments," Journal of Physiology, 127, 11-46, 1955.

46. McCurdy, J. H. and Leonard A. Larson, The Physiology of Exercise. Philadelphia: Lea and Febiger, 1939.

47. "Menstruation and Sport," British Medical Journal, December 21, 1963, 1548.

48. Metheny, E. L., et al., "Some Physiologic Responses of Women and Men to Moderate and Strenuous Exercise," American Journal of Physiology, 137, 318, 1942.

49. Meyer, Margaret H., and Germaine Pella, "The Effect of Hard Laboratory Exercise on the Total and Differential Leucocyte Count of Young Women," Research Quarterly, 18, 271, December 1947.

50. Moore, Roy B., "An Analytical Study of Sex Differences as They Affect the Program of Physical Education," Research Quarterly, 12, 587–608, October 1941.

51. Morehouse, Laurence E., and Philip J. Rasch, Sports Medicine for Trainers. Philadelphia: W. B. Saunders, 1963.

52. Morris, Carrie Belle, "Measurement of the Strength of Muscle Relative to the Cross Section," Research Quarterly, 19, 295–303, December 1948.

53. Morton, Henry W., Soviet Sport. New York: Collier Books, 1963.

54. Neal, Patsy, "Personality Traits of 1959 Pan-American Athletes as Measured by the Edwards Personal Preference Schedule," unpublished master's thesis, University of Utah, 1963.

55. Neilson, N. P., and F. W. Cozens, *Achievement Scale in Physical Education Activities.* Sacramento: California State Department of Education, 1934.

56. Norris, Arthur, and Nathan W. Shock, "Exercise in the Adult Years, With Special Reference to the Advanced Years," in *Science and Medicine of Exercise and Sports,* edited by Warren R. Johnson. New York: Harper, 1960, Chapter 24.

57. Patterson, Jane K., "The Effects of Competitive Swimming Training on Girls in Relation to Selected Anthropometric and Strength Measurements, " *Swimming Techniques,* **2,** 14, April 1965.

58. Perbix, Joyce, "Relationship Between Somatotype and Motor Fitness in Women," *Research Quarterly,* **25,** 84–90, March 1954.

59. Phillips, Marjorie, *et al.,* "Analysis of Results from Kraus-Weber Test of Minimum Muscular Fitness in Children," *Research Quarterly,* **26,** 314–323, October 1955.

60. Phillips, Marjorie, Katherine Fox, and Olive Young, "Sports Activity for Girls," *Journal of Health, Physical Education, and Recreation,* **30,** 23, December 1959.

61. Pierson, William P., "Body Size and Speed," *Research Quarterly,* **32,** 197–200, May 1961.

62. Pierson, William R., and Aileen Lockhart, "Effect of Menstruation on Simple Reaction and Movement Time," *British Medical Journal,* 796–797, March 23, 1963.

63. Pros, J. R., "Current Literature: Some Errors in Engaging Women in the Physical Education," *Journal of Sports Medicine and Physical Fitness,* **4,** 192, September 1964.

64. *Report of the Sixth National Conference on Physicians and Schools.* Bureau of Health Education, Chicago: American Medical Association, 1957.

65. Research Committee, DGWS, "Recommendations from Women Doctors and Gynecologists About Sports Activities for Girls," *Journal of Health, Physical Education, and Recreation,* **30,** 23, December 1959.

66. Ryan, Allan J., "Consultants Answer Questions," *Values in Sports.* Washington, D.C.: AAHPER, 1962.

67. Ryde, D., "Effect of Athletic Competition on Girls and Women," *Practitioner,* **177,** 73, 1956.

68. Schendel, Jack, "Psychological Differences Between Athletes and Non-Participants in Athletics at Three Educational Levels," *Research Quarterly,* **36,** 52–67, March 1965.

69. Scott, Gladys, and W. W. Tuttle, "The Periodic Fluctuation in Physical Efficiency During the Menstrual Cycle," *Research Quarterly,* **3,** 137, March 1932.

70. Shaffer, Thomas E., "Misconceptions in Athletics and Physical Education," *Journal of School Health,* **33,** 349, October 1963.

71. Shaffer, Thomas E., "Principles of Growth and Development as Related to Girls Participating in Track and Field Gymnastics," Proceedings of First National Institute on Girls' and Women's Sports, Norman, Oklahoma, November 1963. (Published by AAHPER, 1201 Sixteenth St., N.W., Washington, D.C.).

72. Skubic, Vera and Jean Hodgkins, "Cardiovascular Efficiency Test Scores for Junior and Senior High School Girls in the United States," *Research Quarterly*, **34**, 191–198, May 1963.

73. Skubic, Vera, and Jean Hodgkins. "Cardiovascular Efficiency Test Scores for Girls and Women," *Research Quarterly*, **35**, 184–192, May 1964.

74. Smith, Lafayette, "The Girls in the Olympics," *Today's Health*, **42**, 28, October 1964.

75. Steinhaus, Arthur, "Exercise and the Female Reproductive Organs," *Toward an Understanding of Health and Physical Education*. Dubuque, Iowa: Wm. C. Brown,1963.

76. Steinhaus, Arthur H., "What Are We Doing to Our Girls?" (letter to the editor), *Journal of Health, Physical Education, and Recreation*, **35**, 6, November-December, 1964.

77. Tuttle, W. Gerald, "Women *Are* Different from Men," *Science Digest*, **14**, 69–72 September 1943.

78. Tuttle, W.W., and H. Frey, "A Study of the Physical Efficiency of College Women as Shown by the Pulse-Ratio Test," *Research Quarterly*, **1**, 17–25, December, 1930.

79. Ulrich, Celeste, "The Tomorrow Mind," *Journal of Health, Physical Education, and Recreation*, **35**, 17, October, 1964.

80. Ulrich, Celeste, "Women and Sport," *Science and Medicine of Exercise and Sports*, edited by Warren R. Johnson. New York: Harper, 1960, Chapter 26

81. Watson, Katharine G., "A Study of the Relation of Certain Measurements of College Women to Throwing Ability," *Research Quarterly*, **8**, 131, October 1937.

82. White, Christine, "Extramural Competition and Physical Education Activities for College Women," *Research Quarterly*, **25**, 344–363, October 1954.

83. Williams, Jesse F., *The Principles of Physical Education*. Philadelphia: Wm. B. Saunders, 1932.

84. Wolffe, J.B., "Heart of the Athlete," *Journal of Sports Medicine and Physical Fitness*, **2**, 20–22, March 1962.

85. Youngen, Lois, "A Comparison of Reaction and Movement Times of Women Athletes and Non-Athletes," *Research Quarterly*, **30**, 349, October 59.

86. Hanson, Margie, "Motor Performance Testing of Elementary School Age Children," Ph.D. dissertation at University of Washington, Seattle, 1965.

87. *The Healthy Life*, a Time-Life special report. New York: Time Incorporated, 1966.

88. Underwood, John, "Games in Trouble," *Sports Illustrated*, **29**, 45, September 30, 1968.

89. Bannister, Roger, "A Debt Was Paid Off in Tears," *Sports Illustrated*, **29**, 22, November 11, 1968.

90. "The Olympics' Extra Heat," *Newsweek*, October 28, 1968, pages 74–80.

91. Underwood, John, "A High Time for Sprinters—and Kenyans," *Sports Illustrated*, **29**, 19, October 28, 1968.

92. Bannister, Roger, "A Debt Was Paid Off in Tears," *Sports Illustrated*, **29**, 22, November 11, 1968.

93. Brown, C. H., J. R. Harrower, and M. F. Deeter, "The Effects of Cross-Country Running on Pre-Adolescent Girls," *Medicine and Science in Sports,* **4:**1-5, 1972.

94. Chapman, E. A., "Cardiovascular Adaptation of the Female Intercollegiate Athlete," *Women and Sports Conference Proceedings* (Western Illinois University), 1973, pp. 170-184.

95. Kane, John E., "Psychology of Sport with Special Reference to the Female Athlete," *Women and Sport: A National Research Conference,* (D. V. Harris, Ed.), Penn State HPER Series No. 2, 1973.

96. Larned, Deborah, "The Feminity Test, A Woman's First Olympic Hurdle," *Women Sports,* July, 1976, pp. 9-11.

97. Sinning, W. E., and Lindberg, G. D., "Physical Characteristics of College Age Women Gymnasts," *Research Quarterly,* **43:**226-234, 1972.

98. Zaharieva, E., "Olympic Participation by Women: Effects on Pregnancy and Child-birth," *JAMA,* **221:** 992-995, 1972.

3 Organizing and Selecting the Team

One of the most important duties of a coach is to choose the personnel he or she is to work with. Selection of players is no easy job. Some people, when they report to practice early in the season, are out of condition. Because of fatigue and lack of timing, they don't look good in the first sessions. Others look great early, but improve only slightly as the season wears on. Still others are intent on personal goals and do not work well toward team objectives. Thus a determining factor in any season's record is the coach's ability to choose players wisely and mould them into a working unit. If there are personality problems—either between the coach and certain players or between team memers—they should be resolved at the beginning of the season. If these problems persist, they can multiply and destroy what would otherwise be a good team.

Unless the coach knows the players well, psychological factors may show up only late in the season. A coach has to seek just the right tone of voice or the right words to bring out the best in some people. Some players can't perform in a relaxed and confident way until a certain amount of rapport has been established between themselves and the coach.

In selecting players, the coach must look to the future as well as the present, remembering to work not only for the season at hand but for the following season as well, and must bear in mind the following factors: (1) organization of the team, (2) practice sessions, (3) determining players' potentials, and (4) cutting the squad.

ORGANIZATION OF THE TEAM

The coach who wants the best opportunity to select players must organize workouts so that all interested persons will know what is expected. Publicity should include the details of practice time, place, who is eligible to try out for the team, etc. For the best results, one should utilize all the usual media: boards, assemblies, school papers, and posters. The first notice should be given several weeks in advance, followed up by other publicity, right up to the day of beginning workouts.

The first meeting should give the girls a chance to become familiar with each other and with the coach. It is important that each girl know right from the start what the coach will expect of the team during the season. Things that should be stressed are:

1. Importance of attending practice
2. Training rules
3. Conduct and attitude
4. Teamwork, individual and team pride, and individual effort
5. Eligibility requirements: grade point average must be maintained, players must carry so many hours, etc.
6. Tentative season schedule

One should allow time for questions and answers about anything that is not clear to the participants.

PRACTICE SESSIONS

A definite time should be set up for practice each day. Since time and facilities are usually limited, each team member should be ready for practice on time. Any tardies or absences should be cleared through the coach.

Although there is disagreement as to the effects of warm-ups, most coaches feel that they are worth while, and include them both in practice sessions and before games. Drills and exercises should be chosen to develop the timing, coordination, endurance, and strength needed for the specific sport being engaged in. One should aim at a *gradual* increase of endurance and strength, so that the peak of development is reached at the end of the season.

The players' mental attitude in these first practice sessions can set the pace for the rest of the year. If the coach is enthusiastic, has a positive attitude, and instills confidence and desire in the players from the start, there will be no problem of having to "get the team up" for each game or meet. Unless players are overworked or become stale during the season, the morale established at the beginning will rise with each new accomplishment.

Although the coach must be aware of each player and her abilities, and must be approachable by each player, at the same time she must be in control. A team has to be committed to the authority of the coach. However, this dedication must be earned. The coach who is prepared each day, who is professionally qualified, and who has had experience in the coaching field (or at least understands skills and strategy) is one who has earned the right to speak with authority and who can guide her team well. This doesn't mean that the coach should not listen to suggestions from the players. Open discussion should be invited, but the final decision is the coach's responsibility.

Practice sessions should be used wisely. During rest periods, the coach or a skilled player should give oral instructions and demonstrations. Chalkboard talks and walk-through drills often clarify questions and eliminate confusion later, when players have to execute a maneuver at full speed. If players must sit on the bench during scrimmage or games, they should always be taking part in the action mentally, preparing themselves for the moment when they will go in as substitutes.

Loafing should not be permitted. A player who "goofs off" in practice also tends to slack off in actual competition, or else will not be able to play the entire game at full speed. If a player becomes too tired to continue hustling during practice sessions, she should be encouraged to ask for a substitute rather than loafing through the rest of the practice.

Where applicable, isometric exercises, weights, and other devices should be used to increase the strength of the players. For sports that require endurance, practice should include running, jumping rope, and drills to increase the efficiency of the cardiovascular system.

Fine skills that demand precision, timing, and quick reflexes should be practiced at the beginning rather than at the end of the workout because of the fatigue factor, although in most cases these skills also need to be used when fatigue has set in. If a player attains perfection in these skills when she is fresh and rested, she will be able to execute them better when she is tired.

The amount of time allotted to workouts should depend on the skill level and the age of the group being coached.

Most skills should be practiced under actual competitive situations. To a hockey player trying to perfect her dribble in a congested area, practice against one or two opponents is much more effective than dribbling for hours by herself. Practice makes perfect only if skills are performed correctly and under the right circumstances.

Drills and practice techniques should be varied in order to prevent monotony and eventual staleness. Preseason practice sessions should provide motivation that will keep players on their toes until the actual competition begins. When staleness does set in, a few days of rest or a change in scenery is often enough to snap a team back into top form. For instance, if a track team becomes tired from running laps around the stadium, the coach can renew motivation by holding practice sessions on a beach or in another area.

Preseason workouts should allow all participants an equal chance to show what they are capable of doing, as well as giving the coach an idea of each girl's potential. After the coach has cut the squad, she should use practice sessions to perfect systems of play, improve individual and team skills, and develop mental and physical fitness.

DETERMINING PLAYERS' POTENTIALS

It is always hard to gauge a person's potential accurately. Some girls are late starters; others look great at the beginning but fail to improve later on.

When deciding whether a girl has the skills or the potential to make the team, the coach must consider several aspects of the girl.

1. Mental attitude
2. Dedication and willingness to sacrifice
3. Physical development
4. Health
5. Capability for teamwork
6. Love of the game
7. Skill

In most cases, mental attitude makes or breaks the athlete. Many who start out without much skill become champions purely because of desire and positive attitudes. Others must overcome tremendous physical handicaps: Ben Hogan and Glenn Cunningham are just two who have proved the power of having "heart," or the desire to compete.

A person who will not quit, even against big odds, and who will scramble and scrap down to the wire is often preferable to a person with more skill but less desire to compete. The girl whose attitude is "I can" has the potential of being a better player than the girl whose attitude is "I will if I feel like it."

A person's dedication and willingness to sacrifice in order to perfect her skills is usually what makes the difference between a good athlete and a great one. Training for a sport is hard, time-consuming work, and the great athlete must be willing to forgo many pleasures in order to excel. The girl who prefers late parties, smoking, and drinking to achieving her top potential as an athlete will find it hard to excel. The self-discipline necessary for constant conditioning is impossible to anyone who is not dedicated to the game; if she is, then the goal outweighs the work.

In junior high and high school, the physical development of the girl must be taken into consideration. Because the growth of each individual varies, some junior high school girls may already have reached the peak of their growth spurt, while others may not even have started. A girl who is gaining rapidly in height and weight needs time to learn to control her new size. Many girls who are experiencing a spurt in growth may appear awkward, uncoordinated, and unskilled, but these same girls may turn out to be the best athletes after their growth has leveled off and they have learned to control their bodies.

The overall health of a girl is of course a vital factor. Many great players and teams have been weakened by recurring injuries or illnesses. And any girl who is a hypochondriac naturally has a demoralizing effect on the team. Therefore all girls should have medical exams before the training period, and the coach should keep an eye on their health as the season advances.

In team sports, the importance of teamwork is immeasurable. A girl who is a "ball hog," or who risks making the big play herself rather than giving the opportunity to someone who has a better chance will hinder a team. The best shooters and spikers are not always the best players; for every shooter and spiker, there must be someone who can get the ball *to* them. A team composed of girls who work together well, and who are intent on winning and looking good as a team, is much more effective than a team composed of girls working as separate units and striving for outstanding individual performances rather than an outstanding team performance.

Love of the game involves many things: the thrill of being able to control the body and mind while competing in tense situations; the joy of running, of jumping and throwing, of using strength and coordination; the satisfaction of knowing oneself in many different situations and moods. To take part in a sport after one has stopped loving it is no longer rewarding. Love, dedication, and sacrifice must be a sigificant part of competition.

Skill, though often overemphasized, is nevertheless necessary. Regardless of how much a player wants to excel, unless she has perfected the fundamentals of her sport, she can't go beyond a specific point in her development. The champion has usually perfected both her skill and her mental attitude; and one without the other is a handicap. The coach should encourage both aspects of her athletes.

CUTTING THE SQUAD

Once a coach has had a chance to see what each girl can do, and has tried to assess the potential of each, she must cut the squad. This can be one of the hardest job she encounters, because often her judgments about a person's potential will turn out to be wrong. Even so, the coach must have enough faith in herself to act in accord with her judgments until they are proved wrong.

The squad should be cut down to a number that can be worked with easily. In most cases, this means two complete teams plus a couple of substitutes to ensure that enough players will be available for game situations. When travel is necessary, the coach may have to cut the squad down even further. The traveling squad should be subject to change, dependent on the improvement of individual players as the season progresses.

In cutting the squad, the coach must evaluate not only individual performances, but team performance as well. Play combinations should complement each other, and girls selected for the squad should fit the play of others on the team. The effectiveness of having several good players on a squad is decreased if they are like so many mismatched parts of a whole. ·

Telling a girl that she has not made the team requires tact and sympathy. A coach must decide whether to make the announcement in front of all the girls, or to take each girl aside individually. Sometimes a written announcement posted on the bulletin board is the easiest for the coach (but not always for the girl who has been cut from the team).

It should be stressed that any girl who is cut from the team for one particular season should be encouraged to try again next year. The coach should also try to tell each girl what skills she needs to work on in order to improve her chances of making the squad next time. In this way the coach, even while cutting the team, helps the potential athlete rather than dampening her love for the sport.

4 Training, Conditioning, and Reduction of Injuries

Training and conditioning are the only ways to build up the stamina, endurance, strength, speed, and flexibility that the body of the athlete requires. Training demands not only the sweat and pain of physical exertion, but the mental trait of self-discipline. For most athletes, exercise is performed under a controlled program in which the discipline is imposed by the coach; but the finer points of conditioning, such as getting enough sleep, eating the right foods, and abstaining from drugs, smoking, and drinking rest with the individual's self-discipline and motivation.

First, before any type of training program, each girl must have a thorough medical examination and must be pronounced fit for strenuous activity. Second, every coach should understand the principles of athletic training and conditioning and their results, and be familiar with up-to-date methods. Especially should the coach realize the importance of gradual conditioning over a period of time rather than a crash program of a few days or weeks.

PRINCIPLES OF TRAINING AND CONDITIONING

Training produces physiological changes in the athlete which enable her to perform more efficiently. Brouha [5, 6] and Morehouse and Rasch [34] have pointed out these changes:

1. An athlete's muscles become larger, stronger, and more efficient than the nonathlete's.
2. The athlete's heart beats more slowly, and there is a greater volume of blood circulated with each stroke.
3. There is a retarded progressive fall of systolic blood pressure.
4. The athlete needs less oxygen for moderate loads of work, but consumes a greater amount of oxygen during exhaustive work.
5. The athlete has lower pulse rate and blood pressure during submaximal exercise.

6. The exchange of oxygen and carbon dioxide between lungs and the blood is more efficient in the athlete.

7. Pulse rate and respiration of an athlete return to normal more quickly after exertion.

8. There is less lactic acid formed in the muscles of an athlete for a given amount of exercise, which enables athletes to perform longer before exhaustion.

9. The dissipation of body heat during submaximal work is more efficient in an athlete.

10. For an athlete, there is less pulmonary ventilation for a given load, resulting in slower breathing rate and deeper breathing.

All these physical advantages enable the athlete to exert less effort than the nonathlete to produce the same amount of force; the athlete also displays better neuromuscular coordination and has more efficient cardiovascular function and increased pulmonary ventilation. As a result, the athlete's body uses energy and handles waste materials more efficiently than the nonathlete's. Her muscles have more oxygen and her blood circulates better (this aids in heat control). The coach's duty is to so train the athlete that these physical changes do take place.

The fundamental aspects of training and conditioning which the coach must bear in mind are: (1) demand, (2) sequence, (3) regularity, (4) maintenance, (5) specificity, (6) retrogression, (7) staleness, (8) rest and sleep, and (9) individual differences.

Demand

A person in good physical condition adapts to the demands placed on his or her body either adequately or poorly, depending on the training stimulus. The more the athlete does, the more she will be capable of doing, and vice versa, although some factors such as heredity, previous training, nutrition, and so forth do set a limit to her ability to perform. Once she reaches this limit, there will be no improvement in her performance regardless of how much training she undertakes. Someone who is in excellent condition may maintain her level of fitness with less effort than it took her to attain it. However, if training stops, she drops back to a lower level of ability.

After a few weeks of training, the athlete reaches a plateau where there is no longer an improvement in performance. Regardless of the time spent in practice, improvement will result only if there is an increase in the work rate [5]. There is also a fine line in training beyond which continued stress can either improve performance or lead to the state known as staleness.

Many coaches use the principle of overload in order to increase the demands on the players, and therefore to improve their performances. That is, the coach makes the athletes adapt to additional stress in order to develop strength and endurance by demanding that their bodies do more than they have previously.

Getting ready for competition. (Courtesy of UTA News Service, James Russell.)

If the athlete wants to build up strength, she must work with a heavier load (one that offers greater resistance) and fewer repetitions. If she wants to build up muscular endurance, she should use a light load (little resistance) and many repetitions[39].

Sequence

Some athletes try to do a whole season's work in one day. But to eliminate injuries and get the best results, the athlete should start on a level that is within her capabilities, and then increase the work load slightly each day until she attains the fitness she feels is necessary to perform at maximum efficiency.

Many athletes become discouraged when they reach a plateau and seem to level off. Yet if the athlete just sticks to her planned program and continues to increase her exercises gradually, she will find that self-discipline and perseverance pay off, and that she will attain a new level of skill. Training should not be done haphazardly, but should follow an orderly progression so that the body has time to adapt to the demands on it.

Regularity

If an athlete wants to do well in competition, she must train continuously. A person who trains faithfully one week and takes the next week off can rarely reach a peak performance. The frequency of workouts depends on the person's goals. An Olympic competitor may find that two or three practice sessions a day are required, while the college athlete may find that daily workouts suffice. For the person who just wishes to be generally fit for daily living, three workouts a week may be adequate.

Whatever the conditioning program is, the athlete must perform her exercises regularly to get the desired results, for irregular practice periods result in erratic performance.

Maintenance

The effects of exercise are reversible if the conditioning program is stopped. However, when the athlete has achieved the desired level of conditioning, she does not have to expend as much effort or time in order to maintain this level, provided that she engages in her conditioning program regularly and does not decrease the intensity or decrease the work load.

Specificity

When an athlete is conditioned for one sport, this does not necessarily mean that she is in condition for another, even though both sports may require endurance or strength. Timing, efficiency of movement, and physiological adjustments geared to badminton, for example, may not enable one to play tennis with the same effectiveness. To operate with a minimum of wasted motion and a maximum of coordination, the athlete must train specifically for a particular sport.

Retrogression

Shortly after her training has started, an athlete may feel that she is losing ground rather than improving. However, this is a normal reaction, because the body may be unable to adapt itself immediately to the demands placed on it. And if the body has to cope with other handicaps such as inadequate sleep or poor eating habits, the athlete may experience other periods of retrogression. These slumps should not be confused with a normal difference in performance from day to day, nor should they be confused with staleness. Environmental stimuli and internal changes, as well as psychological factors, can cause variability of performance. The coach and the athlete must expect that some days will be better than others; but good athletes keep variability in performance to a minimum.

Staleness

Staleness is a steady decrease in performance. Some symptoms of it are continuous fatigue, irritability, sleeplessness, possible loss of appetite and weight (though some may overeat and gain), increased tendency to worry, indigestion, and in some cases, headaches and nausea. Physiological changes occurring during staleness include a higher heart rate and a higher lactic acid concentration than that normally resulting from a given amount of exercise [6], though only rarely does a coach have the time or the means to measure this. If the coach finds that the conditioning program is resulting in staleness, she should decrease the work load for a few days. If this does not help, she may need to stop training completely for a couple of days. Participation in an entirely different activity during this time can give players the fresh mental outlook and physical rest needed to eliminate staleness.

Rest and Sleep

If the athlete is to cope with the added stress on her body resulting from an intensive training program, adequate sleep and rest are very important. Schoolwork, practice, and social life together take up a great deal of time; usually the thing that gets short-changed is the time set aside for rest and sleep. People vary as to the amount of sleep they need. One girl may get along fine on six hours, another may need ten. If a person can go to bed and get up each morning without any trouble, and with a rested feeling, then she is probably getting an adequate amount of sleep. Irritability, a need for afternoon naps, excessive fatigue, etc., should be taken as signs that the person may not be getting enough sleep. Most athletes should allow 8 to 10 hours for sleep, to allow their bodies a chance to recover from the tremendous demands placed on them. Loud noises, excessive light, extreme room temperatures, and uncomfortable beds are impediments to sleep, and should be avoided. Regular hours for going to bed and getting up help one to sleep well. If the athlete is tense or overtired, she should try to put aside all worries before going to sleep.

Individual Differences.

Each person differs in capacity to engage in strenuous activity at the beginning of a conditioning program. Therefore, programs should be flexible enough to meet the needs of the individual. If the coach cannot arrange for highly individualized programs, the beginning point of the conditioning program should be such that even the most out-of-condition girl can handle the overload without harmful effects; or the coach should match each girl with others of similar ability for workouts.

TRAINING THE ATHLETE

In training and conditioning athletes, the coach must think about four main elements: (1) strength, (2) endurance, (3) flexibility, and (4) speed

Strength

The coach can use three types of exercises to improve athlete's strength [38]: (1) the lifting of body weight, with several repetitions, (2) adding external weights to specific parts of the body being moved, with fewer repetitions, or (3) isometric contractions. All these methods utilize tension in the specific muscle group to be developed.

*Isometric contraction** is contraction that produces partial or maximum tension in a muscle *without* movement in a joint, and takes place when antagonistic muscles work against each other with equal force, or when a muscle group works against a stationary external object. In most isometric exercises, muscles contract for a maximum of six seconds, then relax. The contractions and rest periods are continued for a specific number of times. Isometric exercises can be used to increase strength in specific muscles of the body and to maintain muscle tone, but their value in increasing total physical fitness is probably not as great as some coaches believe.

Isotonic contraction is contraction that produces partial or maximum tension in a muscle *with* movement in a joint. For instance, pushing against an immovable weight causes isometric contraction, while pushing against a movable one causes isotonic contraction.

Isotonic exercises are better utilized in circuit training because of the range of motion possible when there is movement of the joint. Neither isometric nor isotonic exercises are sufficient in themselves for general conditioning purposes, but they have their place when combined with other methods.

Muscles become stronger only when they must do more than they have done before. Repetition, without overloading, has little effect on strength. The best results seem to come from using about 75% of maximal force in isotonic exercises, and about two-thirds maximal force in some exercises.

People used to think that girls would become musclebound if they used resistance and overload exercises to build up their strength. Women especially were apprehensive about this method of training because they did not wish to lose their femininity while competing, or look like Amazons because of their muscle development. Nowadays, people realize that this fear has no basis if the exercises allow a complete range of motion, or if extensive weight-training is not used over a long period of time. Many women athletes are now improving their performances by weight training.

If the athlete is to develop strength rapidly, the muscles must work against a heavier resistance to overload than usual. To do an exercise many times with a light resistance will result in increased endurance but not increased strength. As strength increases and the athlete finds the work easier to handle, the work load should be progressively increased [3].

Endurance

Endurance is the ability to engage in activity for a long time without undue fatigue. If a girl's endurance is low because she is not conditioned for the activity, her performance may suffer, since fatigue impairs one's ability to maintain a high level of work. If she continues to play after fatigue has set in, she may eventually get to the point we call exhaustion. When that happens, she can no longer keep going.

---

*Research on isometric contraction was first published by Dr. Theodor Hettinger and Dr. Erich Müller in 1953.

Exhaustion, or neuromuscular fatigue, results from an accumulation of acid waste materials, lack of adequate oxygen in the working muscles, or failure or efficiency in the neuromuscular (nerve-muscle) junction [3]. It seldom occurs during competition unless the girl has failed to follow a sound conditioning program, or else is so "up" for the event that she continues to compete even though she is highly fatigued. Intense motivation or psychological factors can force her to overcome physical fatigue through mental determination. Exhaustion, or the body's inability to meet the demands placed on it, is a safety valve that prevents the athlete from going beyond a point that would result in harmful effects if the exertion were to be continued.

There are two kinds of endurance: muscular and circulatory-respiratory (better known as *wind*). Several factors can affect endurance. A strong girl can naturally perform work for a longer period than a girl who lacks tonus or strength in her muscles. When the athlete competes in an event that requires the lifting of heavy loads—such as tumbling, free exercise, or routines on uneven parallel bars—her endurance depends greatly on her strength. When a muscle is strong, its fibers may not all have to contract to perform a movement: this enables some of the fibers to rest. When certain muscle fibers can relax while others are contracting, the resting fibers get a richer blood supply and more oxygen, allowing the athlete to continue movement over a long period of time. Thus the athlete with strong muscles can work longer than the athlete with weaker ones. So when an event demands endurance and allows the athletes no chance to rest, strength is a definite advantage.

Another factor in endurance is the skill of the performer. Good athletes use less energy in a given activity than less-skilled ones because the skilled athlete's movements are more efficient and relaxed. Established patterns of movement that have been used over and over are easier to execute and are done with a minimum of waste motion. This means that, when endurance is a factor, the skilled athlete has an advantage over the less-skilled one.

A third influence on endurance is the efficiency of the athlete's circulatory and respiratory systems, since an increase in waste products in the blood can result in fatigue. The amount of oxygen debt (see page 28) the athlete can tolerate limits her endurance, because the oxygen debt is related to the amount of lactic acid built up in the muscles. Therefore an athlete's muscular endurance depends on her ability to adjust to the buildup of waste products in her body, and her ability to dispose of these waste products. Of equal importance is the ability of her heart, blood vessels, and lungs to take in and use oxygen.

The reason that records are being broken today is that athletes are conditioning themselves to go full speed for a longer period of time than they used to. However, because of the limitations of the body, no one can go full speed forever. The less effort the athlete has to use in a certain sport, or the slower she has to move during competition, the longer she can participate in that activity.

Work that requires brief but maximum effort, such as lifting a heavy weight, can be repeated only three or four times before fatigue sets in. If the exertion is less intense, a reduction in performance does not occur so quickly. For sports such as running, swimming, bicycling, and skiing, maximum effort can be exerted for only approximately 30 seconds. Most runners can give their maximum effort and maintain their top speed for about 300 yards, but then the speed must be reduced or the runner may become exhausted [34].

In order to develop endurance, the athlete must be willing to sustain effort even when she is tired. However, for psychological and sometimes physiological reasons, there must be a balance between work and rest. The more time the athlete has to recover, the more blood is pumped to the muscles to supply oxygen and other needed materials and to remove waste products; this enables the athlete to continue work without as much fatigue as she would have had if there had been no rest. Müller [35] pointed out that it is what the body does during rest periods that is important because as long as the body is able to recover at a rate that keeps pace with the fatigue, then the athlete is able to continue. Now if a girl increases the work load and goes beyond the point of comfort while she is training, she improves her endurance, because physiological changes take place to meet the stress on the body. These changes speed up the rate of recovery, so that the highly conditioned athlete needs less rest or recovery time than the poorly conditioned one. Therefore, when a person is striving for a higher level of endurance, rest is important, but so is the acceptance of pain or discomfort.

An athlete can build up endurance by repeatedly taking part in a specific event. However, if the event does not always demand a great deal of the athlete, her physiological systems are not all forced to perform at maximum efficiency, and thus she may not be able to build her endurance to its peak by this method. In order to improve her endurance (and also her performance), she should not only participate in her chosen sport, but she should include special overload exercises in her practice sessions.

Regardless of pace, endurance depends primarily on the intake of oxygen and the ability of the circulatory system to carry oxygen to the muscles. When an athlete is using up energy faster than she can take in oxygen to meet her body's demand, she builds up an *oxygen debt*. If she is unable to rest or slow down long enough to replenish this oxygen, she will eventually become exhausted and unable to perform. When the body has an inadequate oxygen supply during intense effort, it uses *anaerobic* energy sources. If, on the other hand, the athlete slows down and has enough oxygen coming in to supply the muscle tissues and to get rid of waste products (lactic acid), she is said to be working *aerobically* and within her steady-state capacity. An athlete who has an adequate oxygen intake can continue to participate in the sport for a long time without undue fatigue.

Pace.   In endurance events, the athlete must conserve energy in order to finish the event; therefore, a basic objective of the coach in training the athlete is to develop the best pace for her. Good athletes have a steady pace, worked out to provide a rhythm that will conserve energy and avoid fatigue too early in the competition. In a running event, for example, the athlete should distribute the

Out of the blocks. (Photograph by Audiovisual Center, Indiana State University, courtesy of United States Track and Field Federation.)

work output evenly except for the closing moments, when she should give the final "kick" and go all out in the finish. She uses the greatest amount of energy at the beginning of the race when she must overcome the inertia of starting from a standstill to build up to the maximum speed she wants to hold throughout the race. This acceleration from a standing start to a maximum speed takes approximately 6 seconds, or 30–40 yards, and once the girl hits the desired speed, she expends energy to maintain momentum and to carry out the physiological changes going on in her body. It is more economical to maintain a steady pace than to decelerate and then accelerate, for any energy saved by slowing down is quickly used up when the athlete speeds up again [34].

The beginning athlete often starts out at a fast pace in hopes that she can get a big lead before she tires, but her rapid expenditure of energy leads to a high oxygen debt early in the race, forcing her to run the last part in a fatigued state. The same thing happens when the athlete suffering from butterflies expends her excess energy by engaging in the warm-up session too strenuously, or by unnecessary movements at the beginning of the contest. It pays to budget one's energy and channel it constructively throughout the competition.

Flexibility

Flexibility concerns the range of motion in the joints. The good athlete needs not only strength and endurance, but average or above-average joint movement.

A person's flexibility is limited by the bony structure of his or her body, but the range of motion is also influenced by the elasticity of muscles, tendons, and ligaments. This elasticity can be improved by means of stretching exercises.

The range of motion in a given joint depends on: (1) the length of ligaments and other tissues around the joint, (2) the length and elasticity of muscles and tendons concerned with flexion of the joint, (3) muscle and fat that may limit movement in the joint, and (4) the bony structure of the joint. To improve flexibility, the athlete should use progressive exercises in which force is gradually increased and the duration of the held position is lengthened [3].

To maintain a desired level of flexibility, a girl should perform each exercise through a full range of motion. To increase flexibility, she must continue to perform the exercise until she can actually feel the muscle or muscles being pulled. During warm-up periods most athletes do stretching exercises, because they know that having a full range of motion leads to greater ease of movement during competition.

When a person stops activity, either by choice or because of injury, the muscles and tendons tend to lose their elasticity and ligaments no longer have their normal extensibility. The athlete who gains weight may also lose some flexibility due to the added body fat, because fat can restrict flexibility if it reduces internal elasticity of the muscle or if it limits movement at the joint. The same thing can happen when muscles are overdeveloped.

McCue [28] found that a girl can improve her flexibility to a significant extent within 3 weeks by engaging in mild exercise. She also found that people who could jump better had a higher mean score in flexibility of the hip and trunk during flexion, and that the underweight person had a greater mean hip flexion than the overweight one, although the overweight person had a greater mean for lumbar extension.

Speed

Is there such a thing as building up speed? Naturally, there is a limit to the speed any given person can attain, but a girl certainly should be able to build up her speed to her maximum potential, just as she builds up strength, endurance, and flexibility.

Youngen [49] found that women athletes were significantly faster than women nonathletes in speed of arm movement and reaction time, and that—although tennis players, fencers, and field hockey players differed significantly in speed of movement—there was not a significant difference in their reaction times.

One might assume that the speed of performing specific movements can be improved through training, but that the initial reaction or reflex time does not differ significantly among trained, skilled players.

One could describe speed in running as being due to a combination of reflex time (reaction to starting gun or signal), strength (especially in the legs), endurance, and flexibility. All these factors together give a person a specific response within a given time. Since running speed depends on the length of the stride and the number of strides in a given amount of time, the person must work on flexibility of the legs and ankles, and must also increase strength in order to make the thrusts against the ground more forceful.

CONDITIONING METHODS

There are many methods for training the athlete, but *fartlek,* interval training, circuit training, and weight training seem to be the methods most widely used at present.

Fartlek*

This type of training is used widely to build endurance in the athlete. *Fartlek* is a Swedish word, which is usually translated "speed play." It allows the individual a certain amount of freedom, since it consists of the athlete running at a pace that she decides on, the pace being adjusted according to her feeling that she should speed up or slow down.

   Fartlek is simply a pace that becomes slow or fast depending on the athlete, and consists of jogging, sprinting, jogging, walking, sprinting, etc., as the athlete varies her running to develop endurance. Usually the athlete trains while running cross-country, partly because it does not get so monotonous, and partly because of the space needed for running. However, any area with adequate space—such as a golf course, football or soccer field, or a standard track—may be used.

   The disadvantage of this method lies in the very fact that the pace, distance, etc., are controlled by the athlete. If this method is to be effective in building up endurance, the athlete must force herself to run while she is tired. Therefore some people don't gain as much from using this system as they should. It is very hard to exert oneself to the point of pain; it takes great motivation and self-discipline.

Interval Training

Unlike *fartlek,* which is regulated by the athlete, *interval training* is controlled by the coach. In this type of training program, the athlete takes a fast lap for a preset distance, then a slower lap to allow time for recovery, then another fast lap.

   To increase endurance, the athlete can: (1) run the first lap at a greater speed or go a longer distance, (2) run a shorter distance for the interval or recovery lap, and (3) run a greater number of fast and slow laps. Some people hold to the theory that, since the athlete trains at higher speeds during interval training than during competition, there is an increase in speed as well as endurance. Interval training is used extensively throughout the world, especially by runners and swimmers.

   When the athlete is first beginning her training program and effort is intense, most coaches prefer that the recovery lap be 2 or 3 times longer than the fast lap. Then, as the conditioning program progresses, the recovery lap is shortened. The athlete has to learn to adjust to this shorter recovery period while maintaining her speed on the next fast lap. The coach must keep the length of the rest interval adequate to meet the demands of the effort phase. For hard, maximal work, the recovery phase (slow jogging, walking, etc.) should be 2 to 3 times as long as the ef-

---

*Originated by Gosta Holmer of Sweden.

fort phase, while light work might have a time ratio of one to one. To determine whether the rest interval is adequate, the coach can measure the athlete's pulse.

When the coach has planned the program well, the athlete is able to develop her endurance gradually, until she can run a race at full speed. To allow sufficient time for progressive conditioning, the coach must start interval training well in advance of the competitive program. The importance of this training during the off-season and pre-season is stressed in Chapter 5.

To prevent staleness during endurance work, the coach can use *fartlek* training for 3 or 4 weeks and follow it up by interval training. Many track coaches, when they use interval training to prepare athletes for middle-distance runs, follow one of two theories: (1) *Over-distance,* in which the athlete runs farther than she is going to run during competition (for instance, running 550 yards in practice to prepare to run 440 in competition), or (2) *under-distance,* in which the athlete runs a shorter distance at full speed during practice (for instance, running 330 yards in practice, as fast as possible, to prepare to run 440 in competition).

For an athlete who is training for an event that requires running endurance, here are some suggestions for workouts (although of course all workouts depend on the condition of the player).

Monday	*Tuesday*
1. Warm up using stretching exercises.	1. Warm up using stretching exercises.
2. Jog around track once, then alternate jogging and sprinting while going around track again.	2. Jog around track once, then alternate jogging and sprinting while going around track again.
3. Run four 220's at full speed; try to increase time each week.	3. Run 550 yards, using pace for first 440 yards.
4. Rest four minutes between each 220 (by jogging or walking).	4. Rest 4 minutes (jogging or walking).
5. Jog and walk 2 to 3 laps	5. Run 660 yards, using pace for first 440 yards.
6. Go in for shower.	6. Rest 4 minutes (jogging or walking).
	7. Jog and walk 2 to 3 laps.
	8. Go in for shower.

Circuit Training*

Circuit training increases muscular strength and endurance. In circuit training an athlete goes from one exercise station to another in a planned sequence and in the shortest possible time.

In planning a circuit training program, one chooses exercises to fit the needs of the individual. Each of these exercises is then numbered and assigned to a cer-

---

*Program developed by R.E. Morgan and G.T. Adamson.

tain area (called a station). The athlete progresses from one station to another, performing a specific number of repetitions at each station. The circuit is usually repeated three times, although the number of times the athlete does the exercise depends on the individual and the training program. When the athlete has completed the circuit, her time should be recorded.

In circuit training, the athlete can increase her strength and endurance by (1) doing a greater number of exercises at each station, (2) doing the exercises in a shorter length of time, or (3) combining (1) and (2).

If the work load (number of exercises to be performed) is to be kept consistent, the athlete can develop strength and endurance by gradually decreasing the time it takes her to go around the circuit.

This method of training emphasizes time rather than resistance, and is based on the theory that the athlete can increase her strength and endurance by working harder in a given length of time or by exerting the same amount of energy in less time. The circuit usually consists of 9 to 12 exercises, each requiring about half the athlete's maximum ability. At the beginning of the training program, the girl, while being timed, completes three rounds of the circuit without a rest period. To improve her level of conditioning, she tries to complete the circuit in one-third less time than her previous recorded time; when she reaches *this* level, the work load is increased, she is retested to see how long it takes her to complete this circuit three times, and then a new goal is set up, with a shorter time [34].

Circuit training is usually used to develop general all-round physical fitness, rather than specialized performance in a specific activity. However, if the specialist makes a wise choice of exercises, circuit training can hold many benefits for her if she combines it with practicing the fine points of the given sport.

Circuit training can be set up for one person or for groups, can be planned for any time period, does not require a lot of equipment, and gives motivation to the individual to compete against her own record. An additional benefit is that the athlete can follow her progress as she tries to beat her own time. Having the athlete pair up with another person of approximately the same skill level can also increase motivation.

Here are two examples of circuit programs.

Station 1.   Jog in place slowly for 2 minutes.

Station 2.   Do 15 modified push-ups.

Station 3.   Do 25 sit-ups.

Station 4.   Jump rope for 1 minute.

Station 5.   Work with weights: 8 overhead presses; 8 two-arm curls; 8 half-squats with weight on shoulder; 8 heel raises; 8 supine pullovers.

Station 6.   Basketball chest pass against wall from 5 feet away, 15 times.

Station 7.   Stretching and flexibility exercises: Touch toes 20 times from standing position; 20 bear hugs; from sitting position bob three times and touch toes, repeating 8 times.

Station 8.   Do 25 jumping jacks.

Station 9.   Isometric exercises: Push one fist against the other; grasp fingers and pull in opposite directions; put hands behind head and pull forward; put hands on forehead and push backward (five times each for a count of 6 seconds).

Station 10. Run 4 laps around the gym.

Station 1.   Jog 1 lap, then sprint one lap around gym.

Station 2.   Jump into air as high as possible 8 times.

Station 3.   Throw medicine ball for distance 3 times.

Station 4.   Do 30 modified pull-ups.

Station 5.   Flexibility and stretching exercises: Do the "inchworm" three times; kick right leg up and touch left hand 10 times; kick left leg up and touch right hand 10 times; do 30 big arm circles.

Station 6.   Broad jump for distance 3 times.

Station 7.   Make 10 free throws.

Station 8.   Do 25 sit-ups.

Station 9.   Walk on hands and feet for 15 yards.

Station 10. Run 440 yards.

Weight Training

Weight training is the use of weight in exercising to develop muscle power and strength by the overload principle. Weight training should not be confused with weight lifting, which is the lifting of heavy weights with the goal of lifting more pounds than the opponent can. The confusion between weight lifting and weight training is probably the reason for the negative feelings about the use of weights in a woman's training program, since weight lifting is usually associated with powerful, muscled men, and has a masculine connotation. However, one can use weight training to improve a girl's general fitness and to raise her level of performance in a particular sport while at the same time adding to her femininity by improving her figure and muscle tone, since her muscles are strengthened by carefully selected weight training exercises.

In many events, strength is a prerequisite to success: the discus and javelin throw, gymnastics, swimming, and so forth. By increasing her strength with weight training, the girl also increases her chance to compete well.

A weight-training program usually involves repeating exercises a certain number of times, with workouts 2 or 3 times a week. The number of repetitions is gradually increased until a maximum number is reached. Then the work load is increased by adding additional weight, after which the girl goes back to the number of repetitions she started with. Increasing the work load increases strength. Girls who are able to handle only a small weight at the beginning of a weight-training program may need a preliminary program of calisthenics before training with weights. Specific exercises with weights are given on pages 62–63.

In order to start a girl off with the right amount of weight, the coach must test her at the beginning of the program to determine how much strength she has. The girl should start with a weight load that she can handle for 8 repetitions (of a specific exercise) without overstraining. (The number of repetitions in a set varies, but it has been suggested that the woman's program should use a set of 8 at the beginning [31].) The movements should be continuous; the weights should be lifted and lowered slowly. Unless the eighth repetition is fairly hard, then the load is too light for that person and there will not be an adequate gain in strength. When the athlete has increased her strength to the point at which she can do 12 repetitions of a given exercise, she should increase the weight load (usually an increase of 5 pounds is enough for girls) and then go back to 8 repetitions with the added weight load.

Other [45] have suggested that a girl start with a weight she can lift 4 to 5 times, and that she continue to exercise with this weight until she can perform the exercise 10 times. Then 2½ to 10 pounds are added and the girl goes back to 5 repetitions. Some coaches prefer that exercises start with 8 to 10 repetitions with an increase of 2 until 20 repetitions are reached, at which time more weight is added and the girl goes back to 8 to 10 repetitions. This builds muscular endurance as well as strength.

Isometric, Isotonic, and Isokinetic Exercises

The use of isometric and isotonic exercises in training was discussed on page 46. Basically, isotonic exercises involve movement through a range of motion in the presence of resistance, or a load. Isometric exercises involve work against an object that does not move.

Isokinetic exercise is a principle of exercising that involves work against a resistance or a load while movement occurs at a mechanically regulated rate of speed. The mechanical device sets up a resistance that helps develop dynamic tension in a muscle or a muscle group during the shortening range and at a specific and optimal shortening speed [50].

EXERCISES TO INCREASE STRENGTH, ENDURANCE, FLEXIBILITY, AND SPEED

In setting up an exercise program or a training schedule, the coach should keep several principles in mind:

1. Regular practice sessions should be held; the length of the sessions should be consistent with the level of skill and fitness of the girl or girls involved.

2. The program should be set up to meet the needs of each individual. Since individual needs vary, the coach may have to modify or adapt parts of the program to fit the needs of certain girls.

3. So that the girls will perform specific exercises properly and thereby obtain the best results, the coach should explain the exercises and conditioning program clearly.

4. The coach should vary exercises in order to prevent the girls from getting bored and to eliminate staleness.

5. The training program should be progressive, the work load being gradually increased to allow the body to make the needed adjustments.

6. In order to prevent pulled muscles, strains, etc., the coach should see to it that an adequate warm-up period precedes any strenuous exercise.

7. For best results, exercises to increase strength, endurance, flexibility, and speed must be combined with practice of the specific skills the performer will be using.

The coach must carefully select the exercises for each individual engaging in a specific sport. Some girls need development in certain areas, while others need general overall fitness. Here are a few exercises that help athletes develop their overall physical fitness by increasing strength, endurance, flexibility, and speed.

Exercises for Increasing Strength

A. *Abdomen*

1. Back-lying position, hands grasped behind the head, knees bent with heels on the floor. Curl up to a sitting position and touch right knee with opposite elbow. Go back down, come up again and touch left knee with right elbow. Repeat.

2. Back-lying position, arms extended at sides and legs stretched out on floor. Bend knees and slide heels up close to hips, then pull knees to chest. Lower feet to floor close to hips and extend legs out on floor again.

3. Back-lying position, arms extended out at shoulder level. Bring heels along floor to hips. Pull knees to chest, lifting pelvis off floor. Lower knees slowly to the left while rotating pelvis in that direction. Bring knees back over chest. Lower hips and go back to the starting position. Go to right side and continue alternately.

B. *Legs and Hips*

1. In a standing position, with arms extended in front of body, bend knees and go down to a half-squat position. Keep most of weight on toes and balls of feet. Go back to standing position and continue. Hold 5-pound weight on shoulders and do the same.

2. Begin in a standing position with feet spaced comfortably. Bend knees and go down to a half-squat, keeping weight on toes and balls of feet, then jump upward, extending arms in the air while jumping as high as possible. May be varied by holding weights on shoulders.

3. Side-lying position. Lift leg straight upward slowly as far as possible and then return leg slowly to starting position. Repeat several times. Turn onto other side and repeat with other leg.

4. From a standing position, start with left foot forward, knees slightly bent, then change positions of feet with an easy jump. The knees should bend and relax on the jump to absorb the shock of the lunge. Continue exercise while alternating feet.

C. *Calves, Ankles, and Feet*

1. Place balls of feet on an object that is about 2 inches thick. Lift heels off floor by rising up onto toes and balls of feet as high as possible. Extend arms in front of body for balance. Hold this position for 6 seconds, return to starting position, and repeat.

2. Draw a small circle on the floor within reaching distance of a bench. Then, sitting on the bench, pick up marbles with the toes and place them in the circle.

3. Sitting on bench, curl up a towel with the toes.

4. Remain in a sitting position on a chair or bench and lift one leg, moving foot in a circle. Change direction of circle. Repeat with other foot.

5. Stand on board or mat, with toes over edge. Grip board or mat with toes, curling them and grasping tight with them. Relax and repeat.

D. *Shoulders, Neck, and Chest*

1. Face-lying position, head turned to left or right, hands grasped behind back. Pull shoulder blades together, using a smooth and even motion. Hold position for a count of 6, then slowly relax shoulder muscles. Repeat.

2. Lie in same position with arms at shoulder level, elbows bent at an approximately 90-degree angle. Bring shoulder blades together, then lift arms from mat. Hold position from 3 to 5 seconds. Return to starting position. Repeat.

3. Modified push-up position. Let chest down halfway to floor and then hold for a count of 3 seconds. Return to starting position. Repeat.

4. Face-lying position, arms stretched out over head. Raise arms off floor as far as possible, while keeping elbows straight. Hold for count of 6, then return to starting position. Repeat.

5. Same position as above. Lift up one arm at a time.

6. Stand about arm's length from a wall. With arms extended, place hands against wall. Then, bending elbows only, allow body to move toward wall. Push body away from wall and return to starting position. Repeat.

7. Hang from a bar with palms toward face. Pull up until chin is above bar, hold a few seconds, then lower body slowly to extended position.

E. *Arms, Wrist, and Fingers*

1. Use a two-arm support on parallel bars, keeping body in a vertical position. Bend elbows and lower body slowly. Return to starting position.

2. Use a modified pull-up position (on chinning bar, parallel bars, etc.) with palms toward face. Bend elbows, pulling chest to bar, or until elbows form a 90-degree angle. Return to starting position and repeat.

3. Use modified push-ups, putting most of weight on fingers rather than on palms of hand.

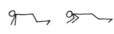

4. Sitting on floor, push hips and body up by pressing fingers against floor.

F. *Upper Back*

1. Face-lying position. Clasp hands at small of back, extend arms toward feet while bringing shoulder blades together. Then raise head and shoulders

off the floor. Hold about 6 seconds. Relax and return to starting position.

2. Face-lying position. Grasp fingers behind head, raise elbows off floor, pull shoulder blades together, and raise head and chest off floor. Hold 3 to 5 seconds. Return to starting position.

3. Kneel, sitting on heels with hands clasped in small of back. Bend forward from hips, placing forehead on mat. Extend arms backward and upward, holding position for about 6 seconds. Lift head as arms are extended backward.

Exercises for Increasing Endurance

1. Jump rope, using any movement with feet. Jump continuously for 3 to 5 minutes. Increase time each practice session.

2. In a standing position, interchange feet with a hopping motion. Movement may be sideward, backward, etc.

3. Run in place, lifting knees high. Alternate with sprints and distance runs if space is available. Spot run in bursts if space is limited.

4. Jump upward repeatedly, as high as possible, at a fast pace.

5. Step up onto a bench approximately 18 inches high, then step down. Continue for 2 to 3 minutes, then change legs for the step up onto the bench. Increase time as endurance improves.

6. Engage in vigorous activity in the chosen sport, such as making fast break in basketball, swimming lengths of pool as fast as possible, etc.

Exercises for Increasing Flexibility

A. *Trunk, Hips, and Pelvic Region*

1. In standing position, swing one leg forward and backward as far as possible. After several repetitions, exercise the other leg in the same way.

2. Standing with feet 3 or 4 inches apart and parallel to each other, bend forward from waist while

keeping knees straight. Touch hands to floor
until you can feel the stretch and tension. Hold
for count of 6 and return to starting position.

3. Sit on floor with legs extended in front of body.
Reach with hands and bend forward from waist
while trying to reach beyond toes. Hold for count
of 6. Return to starting position.

4. Lie on back. Bring one knee to chest and grasp
leg just below knee while pulling knee toward
chest until you feel a definite stretch in the muscles. Hold for a count of 6. Return to starting
position.

5. Following above directions, bring both knees to
the chest.

B. *Heel Cords*

1. Stand about arm's length from a wall, keeping
feet 3 to 4 inches apart and flat on the floor.
Lean forward, keeping head, shoulders, hips,
chest, and ankles in alignment. Keep bending the
elbows until you feel stretch behind the knees and
in the calves of the legs. Hold for approximately
6 seconds. Return to starting position.

C. *Shoulders and Back*

1. Sit with knees crossed and arms folded across
chest. Move chin down to chest and curl forward
in an attempt to touch the forehead to the knees.
Hold for count of 6. Return to starting position.

2. Hang from stall bar or other fixed bar. Turn
palms outward and hang with back to wall and
stall bars. Hang as long as possible. Repeat after
rest.

D. *Arms, Neck, and Shoulders*

1. Sit with legs crossed. Hold arms at shoulder
level, with elbows bent and hands in front of
chest. Pull elbows back, hold 6 counts, and return to starting position.

2. Stand with feet approximately shoulder width
apart. Extend arms out to the side at shoulder
level. Have arms make circles, starting with small

circles, and gradually going into larger ones. Reverse direction.

3. Move head around in a circle by dropping head forward, moving it to the side, backward, to opposite side and then forward again. Reverse direction.

4. Standing, grasp hands behind back. Extend arms and pull shoulder blades together. Relax and repeat.

Exercises for Increasing Speed

1. Run in place, lifting knees high. Speed up tempo and then slow it down, etc.

2. Get into sprinter's position and push off hard by extending ankles and knees.

3. Get in sprinter's position and interchange feet, reaching out and backward as far as possible with the legs. (This is also excellent for developing endurance.)

4. Sprint and jog, increasing sprinting distance or decreasing jogging distance each day.

5. Run up inclines or along the beach or on any surface that requires more effort than normal running.

6. Practice starts and stops, keeping body weight low. Start up as quickly as possible and then stop in one step. Vary by having someone blow whistle to indicate stops and starts.

7. Use arms in running, exaggerating pumping motion until using the arms becomes natural.

Exercises with Use of Weights

1. Hold weights at chest. Push weights upward over head until arms are extended. Lower to chest again.

2. Hold weight below waist with arms extended. Lift up to shoulder level, then lower to extended arm position again.

3. With weight on shoulder behind head, do half-squats.

4. With weight on shoulder behind head, raise body onto toes.

5. Back-lying position, knees bent and weight behind head. Curl forward and do a modified sit-up.

6. Back-lying position, legs extended. Hold weight directly above chest, keeping arms extended. Move weight toward legs, then back up above chest, then move toward head. Repeat.

7. Lie on bench or table face down, with arms hanging down on each side. Lift weights up and then lower.

8. Lie on back with weight resting on chest. Push weight straight up away from chest until arms are extended. Lower weight back to chest.

9. Sit with weight resting on shoulder behind head. Lift weight straight upward until arms are extended. Lower weight back to shoulders.

10. Sit on table with legs hanging over the side. Place weight on foot. Extend leg upward and then lower. Alternate weight to other leg.

11. Tie a 2–3 pound weight to a stick or a bar with a rope. With arms extended forward at shoulder level, wind weight to bar slowly. Reverse hand motions to lower weight to floor.

12. Holding weights in each hand, go into half-squat, them jump forcefully upward.

13. Stand with feet comfortably spread, a dumbbell in each hand, palms facing body. Raise arms sideways until weights are level with shoulders. Lower hands to side and repeat.

Isometric Exercises*

1. Sitting or standing, hold arms at shoulder height with elbows bent. Press palm of one hand against fist of other hand, exerting equal tension to keep arms from moving.

2. Sitting or standing, hold arms at shoulder height with elbows bent. Hook fingers together. Pull

---

*Maximum tension should be exerted for 4–6 seconds.

outward as hard as possible while keeping same arm position.

3. Sitting or standing, grasp hands behind back. Pull outward with both arms. Have someone push arms outward while you try to resist and maintain your arm position.

4. Sitting, place hands under thighs and pull upward with arms resisting pull with legs. Push down against floor in reverse arm action.

5. Stand in an open door with arms against wall. Push outward. Then, catching door jamb, pull inward.

6. Sit on floor. Place fingers on floor next to hips and push down. Lift hips up and hold, exerting pressure with fingers.

7. Go into modified push-up position. Lower body halfway to floor. Hold for 6 seconds.

8. Place legs inside legs of a partner so that ankles touch. Push outward with legs while other girl pulls inward with equal tension. Exchange positions.

DIET AND NUTRITION

Since athletic competition requires great exertion, an athlete's muscles and other tissues must have an adequate supply of the right food components. The foods she eats must provide the carbohydrates, fats, proteins, minerals, water, and vitamins her body needs for normal development. At the same time these foods must enable her body to function at its best under competition, should contain variety, but not be of such quantity or kind that she becomes overweight.

Carbohydrates are the sugars and starches found in foods such as breads and cereals, fruits, potatoes, candy and other sweets, etc. Carbohydrates are broken down into *glycogen* and stored in the liver and muscles. When energy is needed, glucose is supplied quickly from these two reservoirs. However, the greater part of the excess is converted in the liver and stored as fat in the body.

Fats are compounds of *glycerol* and *fatty acids*. Glycerol, when it is oxidized, can be utilized as energy for muscular work; fatty acid is oxidized to form a coenzyme. Fats form a reserve for the production of heat and energy, and are used as body fuel just as carbohydrates are. However, fat that has been stored is used only when the intake of carbohydrates is not adequate to meet the body's demands.

In order for the body to grow, repair tissues, manufacture gland secretions and digestive juices, and fight disease, it needs adequate protein. Protein differs from fats and carbohydrates in that it is almost never stored as fat or used for energy unless excessive amounts are present. Meat, eggs, or milk should provide approximately a third of the protein consumed daily. Protein molecules are broken down during the digestive process into simple units called *amino acids,* and it is in this form that protein is absorbed from the intestinal tract and used by the tissues.

Vitamins are organic compounds that are essential to good health. They do not furnish energy or build tissue, but act as catalysts which are necessary in the utilization of energy and the regulation of metabolism. A diet that is well-balanced and varied usually supplies all the vitamins that are necessary.

Minerals help develop strong bones and teeth, and help regulate many essential body processes. Again, a well-balanced diet supplies all the minerals needed. In the case of some minerals, excessive amounts may do as much harm as insufficient amounts. Foods such as milk and milk products, green vegetables, and lean meat provide the minerals the body needs.

Water is necessary to life as it serves as a solvent and diluting factor, helps transport body fuels and waste products, regulates body temperature, and serves as a lubricant. If balance is not maintained between water loss and water intake, the person becomes dehydrated and body functions suffer.

Diet and the Performance of the Athlete

The human body, as it tries to maintain good working order, acts as a homeostatic mechanism. Due to the strenuous demands of competition, an athlete's body may demand more food than a nonathlete's in order to supply the materials necessary for the working body. The nonathlete may be able to maintain homeostatic balance with less intake of calories. The girl who is in training and under competitive conditions must have the foods needed for growth, development, repair, and function, but at the same time must keep herself at the weight desired for competition. An oversupply of calories leads to unnecessary pounds, which will handicap the athlete in competition. Adequate nutrition must not be confused with overeating. The quality of food eaten is more important than the quantity.

Some interesting facts about nutrition and the athlete have been found. In an early study of marathon runners, it was found that at the end of a race there was a definite fall in the runners' blood-sugar level. The runner's fatigue and his blood-sugar level, at the end of the race, seemed to be closely related. The athlete's exhaustion was similar to that found in progressive insulin shock. The investigators of these early studies suggested giving sweets to the athletes during the race, but later studies indicate that sugar during competition does not effect aerobic work capacity, although it may have some value in helping the athlete to recover from fatigue, and to get prepared for later work [34].

Another factor research has uncovered is that sugar, as it is being digested and absorbed, depletes the body of fluid, and therefore tends to lead to a state of dehydration. It has been suggested that heavily sweetened tea with lemon may provide the sugar needed, while keeping the body adequately supplied with needed fluids [34].

Other studies have indicated that the intake of fat tends to be high in people engaged in hard work under severe environmental conditions. Fatty tissue not only serves as a protection against bruises and as an insulation against cold, but as a reservoir of energy, since fat is stored as reserve fuel. The meal high in fat is digested more slowly, and because of this slow passage of the meal from the stomach, the athlete does not feel hunger as quickly. However, in the athlete's diet, fat elements should not be more than double the carbohydrates. One disadvantage of a high-fat diet is that this slow movement of the food through the digestive tract allows decomposition, and—since some athletes have sensitive membranes lining the stomach and intestines which can be irritated by some of the products of food decomposition—the result can be diarrhea [34].

Mathews *et al.* [26] suggest that the athlete should taper off activity 48 hours before competing to allow the liver to replete the glycogen stores. Mayer [27] feels that if the activity is especially demanding, the athlete might be better off eating 4 or 5 lighter meals each day rather than the usual 3.

Where once coaches and athletes felt that they had to have a high intake of protein the day of competition to keep up their strength, scientists now feel that protein is not the best food for events requiring endurance.

Many athletes are now using a process called "carbohydrate loading" to increase their energy during the day of a meet or a game. The object of "carbohydrate loading" is to store up more glycogen in the muscles than the body would under normal circumstances. This is done by: (1) exhausting the glycogen stored in the muscles and liver by working out very hard about a week before the competitive event, (2) keeping the glycogen content of the muscles low by eating mostly proteins and fats for three days (2-4 days before the meet), (3) building up the glycogen in the liver and muscles again by eating mainly carbohydrates for three days before the competition, and (4) eating light and easily digested foods on the day of competition.

Using this process, the athlete might follow this schedule: (1) Seven days before the game, run several miles. (2) Four to six days before the game, eat mostly protein such as meat, fish, eggs, cheese, and fats (butter, oil). (3) One to three days before the competition, fill up on carbohydrate foods such as bread, potatoes, spaghetti, fruits. (4) The day of the game, eat light foods such as soup and gelatin desserts.

Some of the advantages of carbohydrate loading are that stamina is increased, more fluid is retained in the body (more easily replaces water lost while sweating), and the athlete can eat large amounts of many things he or she enjoys 2-4 days before competing. Some of the disadvantages of carbohydrate overloading are that it can cause the athlete to gain weight; it creates an unbalanced diet and restriction of some of the essential nutrients found in other foods; it is uncomfortable training when the body is deprived of glycogen for three days, and carbohydrate loading is not effective when it is used often (also cannot be used effectively for successive events because it takes the body 48 hours to refill its glycogen stores) [57, p. 64].

Some medical people do not feel that carbohydrate loading is good and could create health problems when used over a long period of time.

There are some who feel the low-carbohydrate phase of the diet is not necessary, and who have received extra stamina benefits simply by taking a long run to deplete the glycogen supplies 3–4 days before the race or meet, and then by eating mainly carbohydrates several days before the competition [55, p. 76].

The use of liquid food, before practice or games, has helped many athletes to compete better. Woods [48] reports that the 1961 University of Arizona football team had a liquid food supplement 30 to 40 minutes before each practice. The coaches of this team felt that endurance and stamina of the players increased 5 to 15% as a result. The team that year had the best record in the history of the school.

The University of Nebraska football team [23] used a liquid meal called Sustagen in place of the pregame meal with the following results:

1. There was no significant weight change.
2. Players had some feelings of hunger, but this was solved by giving them toast, honey and peaches with syrup along with the liquid food.
3. Nausea and vomiting were eliminated.
4. Stamina seemed to improve.
5. Diarrhea as result of emotional tension continued.
6. No cramps resulted.
7. There was greater gastrointestinal motility.

There have been some studies of wheat germ [7,8] and its effect on the performance of the athlete. However, it seems that at present athlete's performances cannot, by such dietary additives, be improved to a point that is better than the performances they turn in when they eat a regular balanced diet [10]. Other fads, such as vitamin supplements, have also been used in an effort to obtain better than the performances but, again, these help only if the athlete is not getting the right foods in an all-round good diet.

The athlete's daily diet should include meat, cheese, fish, eggs, milk, vegetables, fruits, and whole-grain cereals, unless an allergy to one of these foods exists. A well-balanced diet from the "fundamental four" [15] food groups (milk and milk products, meat and meat substitutes, vegetables and fruits, and bread and cereals) gives the athlete's body enough nutrition to meet the demands of competition.

A high-carbohydrate diet on the day of competition might consist of:

BREAKFAST

½ grapefruit with sugar, or orange juice
Cereal with milk and sugar (corn flakes, oatmeal, etc.)
1 or 2 eggs (poached or boiled)
Ham or bacon
Toast with jelly
Glass of milk

LUNCH

Soup (vegetable, cream of mushroom, chicken noodle, etc.)
Meat (roast beef, fish, chicken, etc., baked or broiled)
Salad (tossed, potato, etc.)
Vegetable (creamed potatoes, creamed corn, green beans, etc.)
Bread
Milk or tea

DINNER or PREGAME MEAL*

Broiled steak
Baked potato
Bouillon
Toast and honey
Cake
Tea

Water is especially important to the athlete. If the body is to operate efficiently, water must be replenished when the athlete has perspired greatly. The athlete often sweats out large amounts of water during a workout. The loss of water is no problem as long as she takes in enough fluids before, during, and after intensive activity. However, when there is excessive perspiration there is also a loss of body salt. This lessens the body's ability to retain water, which may lead to dehydration. Dehydration keeps the athlete from performing up to standard, and may lead to weakness and muscle cramps. Thus an athlete who perspires heavily or must compete in a hot gymnasium or warm climate should replace the lost water and salt. Some athletes prefer to add more salt to their food at the table; others take salt tablets. When drinking during and after competition, the athlete should avoid very hot or very cold fluids, or stomach cramps may result.

The Pregame Meal

The person who plans the pregame meal must consider how digestion influences the athlete's performance, and what nutrients the food will supply to aid that performance.

---

* If competition is at night; otherwise this meal would take the place of lunch.

No athlete should eat a meal just before competing; preferably she should eat 3 to 4 hours before competition. What is in her stomach may effect her performance, especially with respect to its speed of absorption. A high-fat diet takes longer to digest. The longer it stays in her stomach, the longer it requires oxygen for metabolism. On the other hand, a high-protein meal requires the presence of water, which might otherwise be utilized in perspiration and temperature regulation, and also demands oxygen for its metabolism. Again, this oxygen could otherwise be used by the muscles. A high-carbohydrate meal, however, gives fuel for quick energy, which is needed by the athlete.

Any foods that might irritate the stomach, such as salads, spices, beans, etc., should not be eaten before a game. The athlete who knows which foods are hard for her to digest should forgo these on the day of the game.

The pregame meal should be free from tension and noise, and should please the athlete, for she will probably already be thinking about the game to come and will be a little nervous. Many coaches have their own ideas about pregame meals for their athletes. Because of individual differences and food preferences, it is impossible to say that one specific diet should be followed by the athlete. Supplements over and above a sound diet will not affect an athlete's performance physically, but it's possible that they will affect her psychologically. Therefore, if an athlete feels she must have a particular food at the training table or the pregame meal, her morale might benefit from having it even though there is no physical gain.

There are no miracle supplements that can help the athlete perform better. Neither does one meal make a big difference in the body's efficiency. Diet must be dealt with wisely the year around, especially every day the athlete is in training. Nutrition is the same for athletes as for other people. The difference lies only in the quantity of food.

Here are some suggestions for pregame meals.

Pregame Meal A	*Pregame Meal B*	*Pregame Meal C*
Bouillon	Consomme	Cream of chicken soup
Broiled beefsteak	Baked fish	Roast beef
Baked potato with butter	Creamed potatoes	Macaroni and cheese
Peas	Cooked carrots	Green beans
Toast and honey	Rolls with jelly	Rolls and honey
Peach in heavy syrup	Pudding or gelatin dessert	Custard or ice cream
Milk, water, or tea	Milk, water, or tea	Milk, water, or tea

Substitutions can be made when finances are limited, so long as the diet remains a balanced one (for instance, fish can be substituted for steak, gelatin dessert for ice cream, etc.).

DRUGS

Stimulants

Stimulating drugs are sometimes used in an effort to improve athletic competition. The use of drugs, regardless of the amount or frequency, is a question that every coach must answer in the light of ethical and medical aspects. The use of drugs by athletes cannot be justified on ethical grounds because fair play and good sportsmanship is the essence of athletics. Nor can one justify the use of drugs as an artificial means of bettering performance when the whole objective of sports is to teach the person to meet stress well and to depend on her own resources in competitive situations. When drugs are used without medical supervision, they can be harmful both physiologically and psychologically. When used indiscriminately, they may lead to addiction.

One of the participants in the 1960 Olympic Games, the Danish cyclist Knud Jensen, collapsed during the 100-kilometer race and died later. An investigation showed that he had taken a drug called Ronicol, which stimulates circulation by dilating the blood vessels. His death resulted from the combination of exertion, high temperature, and the effects of the drug [46].

Some of the drugs most commonly used in athletics, and their effects, are the following [34].

1. *Ephedrine.* Elevates blood pressure, speeds up heart rate, constricts peripheral blood vessels, causes greater cardiac output, dilates the bronchioles, and stimulates the respiratory center. Has little effect on persons not suffering from asthma or emphysema.

2. *Amphetamine* (benzedrine, dexedrine). Greatly stimulates the central nervous system. Speeds up the respiratory center and increases cardiac work and output. Used to cover fatigue symptoms caused by physical exertion.

3. *Desoxyephedrine.* Stimulates heart and central nervous system. Hides effects of fatigue, but does not make recovery from fatigue faster. May become addictive.

4. *Nikethamide.* Has been taken by European athletes to compensate for the vasomotor circulatory disturbances resulting from violent physical exertion. When too much is taken, convulsions and death may occur because of respiratory paralysis.

5. *Pentylenetetrazol.* Stimulates central nervous system and cardiovascular system; has been widely used by European athletes.

6. *Digitalis.* Increases the strength of cardiac contraction. Has been used in treatment of congestive heart failure, but should not be used by normal people.

7. *Nitroglycerin.* Relaxes smooth muscles. May have unpleasant side effects. When used in excessive doses, it converts hemoglobin to methemoglobin and anemia results.

Another drug that has come on the scene in athletics is the *anabolic steriod* which is a male hormone. It is used to aid in muscle-building. Consequently, some women athletes use this drug in an effort to increase their strength.

The use of drugs has become such a problem in men's athletics that the International Amateur Athletic Federation has taken a strong stand on it. The IAAF has the power to prevent any athlete from participating in amateur athletics if he is found to be using drugs to improve his athletic performance [46]. A stronger stand was also taken in the 1968 Olympics to prevent athletes from using drugs to improve their performance [51].

More modern techniques being experimented with by some countries to improve the athlete's performance while bypassing drug tests include "muscle booster" machines and transfusion of the athlete's own blood. The machine has electrodes that send painless current into specific muscles, forcing the muscle to contract under the electronic impulses, resulting in an increase of muscle strength by 50% (this machine has been used widely in the Soviet Union). Although athletes deny using the blood transfusion process, experiments in this area have been used in Sweden and in Finland. The process involves taking about two pints of blood from an athlete, refrigerating it, and reinjecting the athletes' red blood cells four weeks later (at which time the athlete has rebuilt the normal supply of blood and has additional red cells as a result of the transfusion, allowing the athlete to utilize oxygen more effectively) [54].

When we consider all the facts, the use of any type of drug or machine—either as a stimulant or depressant—in athletics cannot be justified on any grounds. The coach must strictly prohibit the use of drugs. The chance that the athlete might experience harmful effects from using drugs is enough of a deterrent to outweigh any benefit that might accrue if she used them.

Smoking and Drinking

Because of the widespread use of tobacco and alcohol by both athletes and non-athletes, the facts about them should be mentioned here. Even though the Surgeon General and many other authorities have recently published evidence as to the harmful effects of smoking, many people still smoke. Yet there is a significant relationship between lung cancer and smoking; heavy cigarette smokers run 20 times as great a risk of lung cancer as nonsmokers. Other health hazards that seem to be connected with smoking are cancer of the mouth, larynx, esophagus and bladder. Heart and circulatory diseases are found much more often among male smokers than nonsmokers, and respiratory diseases such as asthma and emphysema are greatly worsened by smoking [52].

Tuttle and Frey [42] found that smokers are at a disadvantage in physical efficiency in comparison with nonsmokers. Questionnaires tabulated by Cureton [7] showed that 93% of track and field athletes at the 1956 Olympics at Melbourne did not smoke while in training, and 83% had never smoked in their lives.

The athlete undoubtedly has more to lose by smoking than the average person because it is necessary for her body to operate at optimum conditions.

The American Medical Association has indicated that there is acute impairment of pulmonary fuction in young smokers, and that smoking brings about significant decreases in breathing capacity. Smoking also greatly hampers the ability of the body to utilize oxygen efficiently. Since the above functions are so important in the athlete's ability to perform well, the American Medical Association has stated that there is no doubt that athletes should not smoke [15].

The effects of alcohol depend on the intake and the individual's reaction to it. However, even small amounts can effect judgment, perception, reflexes, and inhibitions. Alcohol reduces the athlete's endurance because it slows down the removal of lactic acid, which results in fatigue. Alcohol is a depressant, both mentally and physically; this puts the athlete at a disadvantage, since she must operate at full speed.

Some European athletes do drink light wines or beer (sometimes even at the training table). Coaches in the U.S. vary in their training rules on alcoholic beverages: Some coaches permit them any time except the day of the game or meet, and some don't allow them at all.

Some argue that athletes who are mature should make their own decisions on this question. Others argue that drinking and training do not mix. I feel that anything detrimental to an athletes's training should be eliminated. Present knowledge seems to indicate that smoking or drinking hurts the athlete's performance. Therefore the coach should stand as firm on this issue as she or he does on proper sleep, diet, and so forth.

REDUCTION OF INJURIES

Chances for a great team often vanish when good players are injured. Once a player has received an injury, it is too late to think about what could have been done to prevent it. Thus the coach must try to eliminate in advance any factors that might lead to injury.

First, the coach should try to prevent injuries. Second, after an athlete has been hurt, the coach must try to prevent further injury. Third, the coach must try to get the athlete back into playing condition as soon as possible.

Prevention of Injuries

Adequate warm-up periods, good techniques in performing, and gradual conditioning can prevent many injuries. An athlete should never start strenuous activity without a warm-up period, which should be long enough to limber her up but not so long that she becomes tired before the game or practice session even begins. Warm-ups are especially needed when it is cool, or when the girl is sore or stiff from previous workouts or contests. The same thing works in reverse: Heavy practice sessions should taper off and end with light activity, to give the girl's system a chance to adjust to the letdown in demands on it.

Another aid to safety: The coach should be careful not to demand too much of the players. Forcing them to keep going when they are tired is asking for trouble, since tired muscles invite injuries.

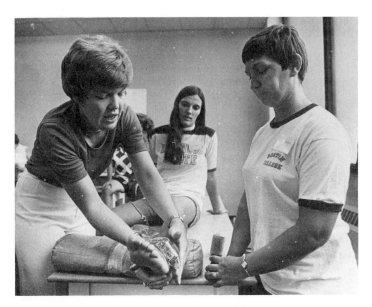

Treatment by trained personnel. (Courtesy of Indiana University News Bureau.)

Treatment of Injuries

Immediate treatment of such injuries as sprains, scrapes, and pulled muscles can reduce not only the pain but also the length of time the athlete will be out of action. However, the coach must never treat an injury if she is not sure of the extent of it; she should refer the girl to a doctor at once. A doctor or nurse should be on the scene during all competitive contests. If a trainer is not on hand during practice sessions, the coach should know where to get professional help quickly.

The pain and swelling of sprains can be reduced by immediate application of ice packs; later on, alternating hot and cold packs can keep swelling and soreness to a minimum. Scrapes should be washed, treated with a mild antiseptic, and covered with a clean dressing. Blisters should also receive immediate care, lest they coninue to be irritated.

Pulled muscles require rest. At the first sign of a strained or pulled muscle, the coach should take the girl out of the game and wrap a supporting bandage or tape around the weakened area. Here again ice is good for reducing the pain and swelling.

Always remember that *only* a qualified person should make a diagnosis or undertake treatment.

Preventing Reinjury

It is important to get the player back into playing condition as soon as possible. When a girl is injured and out of action for a while, she is bound to have some weakness in the muscle or joint affected. The coach should have her do specific exercises to help strengthen that area before allowing her to participate in the regular training program. If the coach fails to do this, a reinjury may occur. Since a player naturally tends to favor an injured area, the coach must watch for a change in the girl's technique in performance. If the change in movement is extreme, another joint or muscle may be put under too much stress and the athlete may end up with an even worse injury.

Reentering Competition

The longer the athlete is out of action, the less range of movement she will have in the joint that was injured. Because of this, the coach must start rehabilitation as soon as possible, with exercises that will rebuild the weak muscles, such as progressive resistance exercises. A well-planned exercise program, with stretching, bending and other flexibility exercises, improves the range of movement in stiff joints.

One of the big problems of an athlete who has been injured is the psychological factor. The pain resulting from the injury can cause the athlete to favor the hurt area out of fear of reinjury, even though the injury may have healed. If the athlete is pushed too hard before the injury has completely healed, and a reinjury does occur, this fear may become so deeply instilled that it will take the girl a long time to get over it. The coach can help her by making sure that she has regained the use of the injured joint or muscle and is in top condition before allowing her to compete again, and by trying to reinforce her confidence in her ability to play the game at her usual pace.

In summary: To reduce injuries, the coach must see that her girls are conditioned and trained well, have proper warm-up periods, use their muscles correctly to prevent strains from incorrect techniques, are treated immediately after injury, and have a sound and a wise reconditioning program.

It goes without saying that every athlete should be covered by an insurance policy and that parents of the athletes recognize the fact that the school or organization bears no financial responsibility for athletes' injuries.

BIBLIOGRAPHY

1. Armbruster, David A., Robert H. Allen, and Bruce Harlan, "Conditioning," in *Swimming and Diving*. St. Louis: C. V. Mosby, 1958, Chapter 13.

2. Bannister, R. G., "Muscular Effort," *British Medical Bulletin*, **12**, 3222, 1956.

3. Barney, Vernon, Cynthia Hirst, and Clayne Jensen, *Conditioning Exercises*. St. Louis: C. V. Mosby, 1965.

4. Broer, Marion, *Efficiency of Human Movement*. Philadelphia: W. B. Saunders, 1960.

5. Brouha, Lucien, "Physiology of Training, Including Age and Sex Differences," *Journal of Sports Medicine and Physical Fitness*, **2**, 3–11, March 1962.

6. Brouha, Lucien, "Training," in *Science and Medicine of Exercise and Sports*, edited by Warren R. Johnson. New York: Harper, 1960, Chapter 21.

7. Cureton, Thomas K., "New Training Methods and Dietary Supplements Are Responsible for Many of the New Records." *Athletic Journal,* **45,** 12–14, January 1962.

8. Cureton, Thomas K., "What About Wheat Germ?" *Scholastic Coach,* **29,** 24, November 1959.

9. DeLorme, T. L., and A. L. Watkins, *Progressive Resistance Exercise.* New York: Appleton-Century-Crofts, 1951.

10. DeVries, H. A., *Physiology of Exercise for Physical Education and Athletics.* Dubuque, Iowa: Wm. C. Brown, 1966.

11. Durnin, J. V. G. A., "The Influence of Nutrition," in Proceedings of the International Symposium on Physical Activity and Cardiovascular Health, *Canadian Medical Association Journal,* **96,** 12, March 25, 1967.

12. Epskamp, R., "Rx for Distance Runners," *Athletic Journal,* **43,** 16, March 1963.

13. Fait, Hollis, *et al., A Manual of Physical Education Activities.* Philadelphia: W. B. Saunders, 1961.

14. Guild, W., "Pre-Event Nutrition," in *Exercise and Fitness.* New York: Athletic Institute, 1960.

15. Hein, Fred V., and Dana L. Farnsworth, *Living.* Chicago: Scott, Foresman, 1965.

16. Hemmingway, A., "Physiological Bases of Training," *Ergonomics,* **2,** 133, February 1959.

17. Henry, F. M., and W. E. Berg, "Physical and Performance Changes in Athletic Conditioning," *Journal of Applied Physiology,* **3,** 103, 1950.

18. Hettinger, T., *The Physiology of Strength.* Springfield Ill.: Charles C Thomas, 1961. 1961.

19. Humphrey, James H., *et al., Reading in Health Education.* Dubuque, Iowa: Wm. C. Brown, 1964.

20. Jensen, Clayne R., "The Controversy of Warm-Up." *Athletic Jornal,* **47,** 24, December 1966.

21. Jokl, E., *Sports in the Cultural Pattern of the World.* Helsinki: Institute of Occupational Health, 1956.

22. Kiputh, R. J. H., *Swimming.* New York: A. S. Barnes, 1942.

23. "Liquid Pre-Game Meal," *Scholastic Coach,* **31,** 56–58, January 1962.

24. Logan, G., and Egstrom, G. H., "The Effects of Slow and Fast Stretching on the Sacrofemoral Angle," *Journal of the Association for Physical and Mental Rehabilitation,* **15,** 85, 1961.

25. Luke, G. Brother, *Coaching High School Track and Field.* Englewood Cliffs, N. J.: Prentice-Hall, 1958.

26. Mathews, D. K., R. W. Stacy, and G. N. Hoover, *Physiology of Muscular Activity.* New York: The Ronald Press, 1964.

27. Mayer, J., "Nutrition and Athletic Performance," *Physiological Reviews,* **40,** 369, 1960.

28. McCue, Betty F., "Flexibility Measurement of College Women," *Research Quarterely,* **24,** 316, 1953.

29. Metheny, E. L., *et al.*, "Some Physiologic Responses of Women and Men to Moderate and Strenuous Exercise," *American Journal of Physiology,* **137,** 318, 1942.

30. Meyer, Margaret H., and Germain Pella, "The Effect of Hard Laboratory Exercise on the Total and Differential Leucocyte Count of Young Women," *Research Quarterly,* **18,** 271, December 1947.

31. Miller, Kenneth D., *Track and Field for Girls.* New York: The Ronald Press, 1964.

32. Morehouse, L. E., "Physiological Bases of Strength Development," *Exercise and Fitness.* New York: Athletic Institute, 1960.

33. Morehouse, L. E., *Physiology of Exercise,* fifth edition. St. Louis: C. V. Mosby, 1967.

34. Morehouse, L. E., and Philip Rasch, *Sports Medicine for Trainers.* Philadelphia: W. B. Saunders, 1963.

35. Müller, E. A., "The Physiological Bases of Rest Pauses in Heavy Work," *Quarterly Journal of Experimental Physiology,* **38,** 205, 1953.

36. Osius, Theodore G., "Food for the Training Table," *Scholastic Coach,* **30,** 64–67, October 1960.

37. Rasch, Philip, and Roger Burke, *Kinesiology and Applied Anatomy.* Philadelphia: Lea and Febiger, 1963.

38. Scott, Phebe, and Virginia Crafts, *Track and Field for Girls and Women.* New York: Appleton-Century-Crofts, 1964.

39. Sorani, Robert, *Circuit Training.* Dubuque, Iowa: Wm. C. Brown, 1966.

40. Steinhaus, A. H., *Toward an Understanding of Health and Physical Education.* Dubuque, Iowa: Wm. C. Brown, 1963.

41. Taylor, Henry Longstreet, "Exercise and Metabolism," in *Science and Medicine of Exercise and Sports,* edited by Warren R. Johnson. New York: Harper, 1960, Chapter 8.

42. Tuttle, W. W., and H. Frey, "A Study of the Physical Efficiency of College Women as Shown by the Pulse-Ratio Test," *Research Quarterly,* **1,** 17–25, December 1930.

43. Van Itallie, Theodore, Leonardo Sinisterra, and Fredrick J. Stare, "Nutrition and Athletic Performance," in *Science and Medicine of Exercise and Sports,* edited by Warren R. Johnson. New York: Harper, 1960, Chapter 15.

44. Vannier, Maryhelen, and Hally Beth Poindexter, *Physical Activities for College Women.* Philadelphia: W. B. Saunders, 1964.

45. *Weight Training in Sports and Physical Education.* Editorial committee: Frank D. Sills, Laurence E. Morehouse, and Thomas DeLorme. Washington, D. C.: AAHPER, 1962.

46. Wilt, Fred, "From the Desk of Fred Wilt," *Track Technique,* **25,** 770, September 1966.

47. Wilt, Fred, "Training Trends in Distance Running," *Scholastic Coach,* **6,** 10, February 1964.

48. Woods, Richard R., "Liquid Food—An Aid to Athletes," *Athletic Journal,* **43,** 50, September 1962.

49. Youngen, Lois, "A Comparison of Reaction and Movement Times of Women Athletes and Non-Athletes," *Research Quarterly*, **30**, 349, October 1959.

50. Perrine, James J., "Isokinetic Exercise," *Journal of Health, Physical Education, and Recreation*, **39**, 40, May 1968.

51. Underwood, John, "Games in Trouble," *Sports Illustrated*, **29**, 45, September 30, 1968.

52. *Smoking and Health*, Report of the Advisory Committee to the Surgeon General of the Public Health Service. Princeton, New Jersey: D. Van Nosstrand, 1964.

53. Mortensen, Jesse P., and John M. Cooper, *Track and Field for Coach and Athlete*. Englewood Cliffs, N. J.: Prentice-Hall, 1959.

54. "Enter the Muscle Booster," *Asheville Citizen*, Fri., July 16, 1976, p. 32.

55. *Food for Fitness*, Mt. View, California: World Publications, 1975, pp. 75–79.

56. Moore, Bobbie, "Do or Diet for the Old Home Team," *Sports Ill.*, April 1, 1974, pp. 62–64.

57. Sands, Susan, "The Search for the Ultimate Spinach," *WomenSports*, October, 1974, pp. 36, 64–68.

5 Planning the Season

Planning the season can be fun and exciting. A coach must start with a basic idea and mould her team in a desired direction. If she does a good job of coaching, by the season's end she will reach the goal she set out to reach.

OBJECTIVES FOR THE SEASON

One often thinks of "the season" as the time during which competitive meets are held. However, taking into account the specialization and year-round training programs of highly skilled athletes, the coach should include the off season, the preseason, and the season itself in her planning. If the coach is working with a person who is of Olympic caliber, or is an outstanding competitor on a national level, she will probably want to work out a program of year-round practice of the skill involved, tapering off during the off season just enough to prevent staleness. However, most athletes prefer to devote the off months to an activity that has no connection with their chosen competitive field. This change in activity eliminates staleness and boredom and brings the athlete back to her sport with a refreshed mental attitude.

Whether the coach considers the season as being year-round, several months, or only a month or so, there are some objectives she should keep in mind as she plans the program: (1) conditioning the athlete, (2) helping her perfect her skills, and (3) seeing to it that the athlete is mentally prepared.

Conditioning should be a gradual process, beginning at a level that will not produce excessive fatigue and working progressively until the athlete is at peak condition for competition. The coach and the player must be aware that development of the cardiovascular, muscular, and respiratory systems can be accomplished only by taking the athlete beyond what she normally does. This means simply that discomfort is going to be necessary. An athlete who is unaware of the fact that conditioning means keeping on when the lungs burn and the muscles ache and the heart feels as though it is pounding a hundred times a minute will probably feel it is the end of the world for her. But this pain is necessary if the athlete is to reach a new level of conditioning.

The coach's second objective is to help the athlete improve her skills and perfect her coordination so that during the competitive event she can move naturally and without conscious thought. The adage "Practice makes perfect" is misleading, for practice makes perfect only if the person has practiced correctly, with the right techniques.

During practice sessions the coach should try to polish the rough spots and smooth out errors of performance. Once the athlete gets into competition, she must feel confident that she can perform her task without worrying about *how* she should do it.

The good coach should be aware of current material in her field and should pass this information on to her players. She should not be afraid of changing her coaching methods if someone proves that a new method is better, and she should seek up-to-date aids in getting the most out of the athlete. Many coaches use film to catch the athlete in motion in order to study her movements at a pace that can be regulated by the projector. Others plot the movements of their athletes. Some analyze each movement step by step to determine whether the athlete is getting the most out of her talents. Regardless of the method the coach uses to help the athlete perfect her skills, the coach must be tactful and remember that there is more to the individual than physical skills. Suggestions made at the right moment and in the right tone of voice are an important factor in coaching the skilled athlete.

The coach's third objective in planning the season is to see that her players are mentally prepared. With the stress on perfection in the sports world, and with the tendency of the top athlete to put in four to six hours a day practicing, an athlete's ability to enter competition mentally refreshed is one of the biggest factors in efficient performance. The stale athlete feels no joy in competition, and consequently does not have that extra spark of energy that is so important. Athletes who train the year around, or train steadily for months on end, generally do experience staleness. It is a natural reaction to stress, and simply means that the athlete needs a different outlook on her competition. In most cases, she only needs to get away from her sport for a few days and relax completely by engaging in an activity that is altogether different. A coach can help ward off staleness by varying the means for practicing: A change in drills, a change in environment for workout sessions, even a change in equipment might bring about the desired result. The coach should use her imagination to make practice a challenge and fun, and should be aware of the player's temperament and emotions, which usually give warning of approaching staleness.

Another factor in mental preparedness is understanding the strategy of the competitive event. Thinking while playing is an important part of competition. The athlete's ability to adjust plays a large role here, for strategy often involves a change to counteract the plans of the opponent. Strategy is connected with the ability to analyze, and after analysis, to come up with a plan of action that is effective. Naturally, because of the limit on time-outs, the coach can't stop game action and give suggestions at any point where new strategy should be employed.

Therefore the coach should help her players to react in an intelligent, thinking way under game conditions.

Taking into account these three objectives—conditioning, perfection of skills, and mental alertness—the coach can usually break the season down into three parts: (1) off-season, (2) preseason, and (3) competitive season.

The off-season. Unless an athlete is in training for international competition, there are usually several months during which she is not involved in her sport. These months should be used to maintain a high plateau of physical conditioning and to regain a fresh mental attitude.

During the off-season, the athlete should participate in activities that demand a lot of her physically, especially in endurance and strength. If she has been competing in track and field during the season, then gymnastics, hockey, speedball, tennis, swimming, basketball, etc., would be a change. Any sport that demands good cardiovascular, muscular, and respiratory development and that keeps her in sound physical condition should be encouraged. A sport that has some carry-over value—as far as similarity of movement is concerned—for the sport that is her specialty during the competitive season, is excellent for a change, since it gives the athlete added practice while giving her a chance to get rid of any possible mental staleness. For instance, the tennis serve is very similar to the overhand softball throw, while the forehand in tennis is similar to batting and involves hand-eye coordination.

A change to weight training would be beneficial to the athlete whose sport demands strength, such as gymnastics, for example, provided that a program was worked out to develop the muscles needed for this training.

The coach should suggest off-season activities to her players which will give them a chance to remain in top physical condition while relaxing mentally.

The preseason. The preseason is the time to perfect skills, work on fundamentals, ponder strategy, and to strive for a high level of conditioning for a specific sport. Preseason training should aim at improving coordination, putting together a team that runs smoothly, encouraging good mental and physical habits that will carry over during the season, and teaching athletes how to analyze and improve their performances in gamelike situations.

The program should be geared to the specific sport, with other activities put in the background except as relaxation measures. There should be a stepped-up program of conditioning, with emphasis on strengthening the muscles involved in the sport and improving the player's endurance. This program should lead to a gradual improvement in physical fitness, with the peak being reached during the season, preferably at the latter part. Sometimes there is danger that the athlete will reach her top efficiency too early and then slacken off in her ability to perform.

Basic skills should be practiced faithfully. The coach should make it a point to take time to check the athlete often to make sure she is not developing bad habits or is working on a technique incorrectly. Discussion should be encouraged, so if something is bothering an athlete or if there is anything she doesn't under-stand, she will feel free to bring it up and have it clarified before the season starts.

A knowledge of strategy is important. New plays and methods should be worked in and practiced until they are second nature to players. The coach should set up gamelike situations and watch the way her players react under pres-sure. She should simulate close-game situations and teach her players to react with poise and confidence. When a game is lost because of players' indecision or lack of understanding of strategy, the fault lies with the coach, for knowledge that is not handed down to the players for use in on-the-spot situations is know-ledge lost. A coach can't always get a time-out in crucial situations, since she can't stop a competitive meet during a crisis and send in instructions from the bench, nor should she depend on this even if she could. Part of competition is making split-second decisions and keeping a cool head under pressure. These things should be taught before the season begins.

If a coach is working with a team, she should evaluate her personnel before the season, and set up a pattern of play to fit the skill level of her players. The team should be organized into a workable unit that should improve and become even more unified as the season progresses. If the coach is working with a person who must compete as an individual rather than with a team, she must make sure the player has a feeling of loyalty to a cause. A person who competes for some-thing other than herself has a broader goal to compete for, and can usually call on a reserve store of energy when the going gets rough.

Also during the preseason, the coach must be sure her athletes understand specific techniques they may be working on. To tell an athlete to jump higher to get over the bar is not much use to the girl. But if the coach explains the effects of the body's center of gravity and how to get the hips over the bar, this explanation will help her performance. Knowing how to analyze movement and how to apply scientific principles are invaluable aids to both coach and player.

Many players make the same mistake over and over simply because they do not know what they are doing wrong. The coach does not want to make major adjustments in the habits of a skilled athlete, but helping her understand move-ment and strategy will undoubtedly benefit her.

THE COMPETITIVE SEASON

The competitive season is the time when events, meets, and games are held, and includes the period between meets. The coach must plan three things during the competitive season: (1) scheduling of games, (2) the actual playing of the game, and (3) preparation between games.

Scheduling. The scheduling of games depends on the skill level of the athletes the coach is working with. Coaches of junior high, high school, or college girls should consult current guidelines for the length of period for competition, the number of practice sessions per week, etc.

Games should be played against other schools and organizations of approximately the same skill level. The schedule must not be too crowded or too long, since the girls have to have enough time to do justice to their studies and social life. In leagues outside the school system, sound judgment should be exercised in setting up a schedule that is beneficial for the participants, when the season is not regulated by guidelines and standards set up by a governing body.

Good officiating is a must, and the coach must know the type of officials being employed. For any highly competitive meet, officials who hold a national or comparable rating should be obtained. If qualified women officials are available, good. If not, qualified men should be used in preference to unqualified women.

Competing.   The game is the culmination of everything that has gone before, in off-season, preseason, and seasonal training. This is the moment of truth for the coach as well as for the players.

During the contest, if the strategy chosen is not working or if there are some unforeseen circumstances, the coach must be able to face facts and make changes accordingly. Of course, on-the-spot changes do not always work, often because players are unprepared, so the coach must not blame her players if the execution fails when there has been no practice beforehand. It is thus a good idea to set up *two* plans before a contest and to practice both. Then you are prepared for the possibility that plan A may not work, and you can change to plan B.

Depending on the type of meet, the coach may be able to offer suggestions as the competition is progressing. For instance, in track and field, there is enough time between events to enable the coach to talk to her athlete. In games as hockey, volleyball, tennis, etc., there is some time, but very little, and only at specified times. Be careful not to confuse or frustrate the athlete by suggesting changes that have not been tried or talked about before, unless it is a very simple thing that the athlete can do without a lot of thought. Learn how each person reacts in different situations and utilize this knowledge. Some athletes are great when they have a lead, then fold up under pressure. Others fight like mad when they are behind and then relax when they get ahead. Still others are indifferent about the results unless they are spurred by a strong emotion such as loyalty, personal pride, fear, or anger.

When the team or the player gets behind during the competition, the coach must draw on her full powers to keep morale high, for once the athlete has lost heart and is no longer willing to struggle, then the battle has truly been lost.

The means by which a coach gets a team up for a contest and keeps them up during the playing time is strictly up to the coach, for different individuals and teams require different methods. A coach's way of doing this should not be questioned except when the method is harmful to the athlete, either psychologically or physically.

Coaches who can time after time produce athletes who are psyched up for contests are usually the great coaches, for they are able to draw on the full resources of the players. Each coach should try to gain an understanding of her personnel that will enable her to use psychological methods to urge her team on to greater things, while at the same time realizing that some means are not worth the ends because of the negative effects on the athlete.

Some of the more common methods for getting a team or an individual up for a game are:

1. Appealing to their sense of pride as real competitors, even though the odds are against them.

2. Referring to past events which would increase their determination to win. ("Remember last year when we were inexperienced, and this team beat us 40 points by keeping their first team in the whole game?")

3. Reminding players of the importance of a particular contest. ("If we win tonight, we will get to compete in the regional tournament.")

4. Stressing belief in a team's ability to produce, and reinforcing their confidence by telling them they *can do it.*

5. Reminding them that even the top teams in the country are human. ("They wear the same brand of shoes we do.")

6. Pointing out the strengths of the team or the individual. ("We are in much better condition than this team, and we should still be going strong in the last minutes.")

7. Stressing the point that upsets happen every day, and naming some recent upsets that the players are familiar with.

8. Telling the team or player how a particular opponent can be beaten. ("If you keep the ball deep and to the backhand corner, she can't kill you with her forehand.")

Another important function of the coach during the game is to see that players who are injured get immediate medical attention. Some coaches allow injured players to keep on competing because they feel that the outcome of the contest depends on this particular individual. Needless to say, the coach is doing the player an injustice if she lets her go back in when there is a possibility of further injury or increased pain, even though the athlete may beg to continue playing. Follow the advice of a doctor or a person trained in first aid.

If a manager is not part of the team, the coach must see that necessary equipment and supplies are available for the competitive event. This includes any equipment utilized in the meet, as well as towels and sweat suits if each player does not bring her own. In endurance events, cool water or sliced oranges are good for replenishing water that has been lost through perspiration.

Preparation between meets. The period between games or meets is the time for ironing out any rough spots and for making any adjustments in the team's performance. It usually helps to review the preceding game, to discuss what was done wrong, and to point out the good things that were accomplished. If a team is fortunate enough to have films to review, this is the time for checking individual performance and to review the contest play by play. Chalkboard, audiovisual aids, etc., can be used to advantage. Once the previous game has been discussed, it should be put out of mind, and all effort should be concentrated on the coming event. If new plays or strategy are necessary for the upcoming opponent, these should be practiced diligently.

Between contests the coach should be sensitive to the team's morale. A defeat in a previous contest can lead to a negative attitude that can influence the next contest; in the same way a previous victory can lead to overconfidence. For this reason, the coach must stress the importance of the way a team competes, rather than stressing victory alone. A team trained to give its best at all times is conscious only of doing its best, and the fear of defeat is not nearly as great as the fear of playing poorly. This type of team is oriented to playing the game with pride; the joy of accomplishment and self-giving becomes a pleasure of competing. This is not to say that a team shouldn't play to win, for the object of competition is to determine a winner, but winning shouldn't overshadow the methods used. By the same token, a coach should not ask her team to play poorly to keep from running up the score against an inferior opponent. To train a team to compete well and then to ask it to play poorly is an insult to talent. Instead, take care to schedule games against teams of equal skill; in cases of mismatched opponents, substitute bench-warmers in order to keep the score down.

Emphasize things in the order of their importance: *one,* to compete with honor and pride, and *two,* to channel effort constructively so that victory is a natural outcome, but not the only desired outcome.

Between games, the rehabilitation of injured athletes should be undertaken. A hurt athlete should exercise to strengthen the injured joint or muscle, and should try to prevent strain or further injury. If whirlpools, heat treatments, etc., are available, they should be utilized. If trainers are not available to the girls, perhaps they can get help and advice from the men's trainer.

Another objective between games is to see that athletes maintain their conditioning, but do not overwork and become stale. A change in workout procedure and even a day off may be necessary.

PRACTICE SCHEDULE

The way the time is spent during a workout or practice session is an important consideration. Depending on the nature of the sport, there will be some minor differences in the schedule given here. Basically, however, the practice period should consist of: (1) instruction, (2) warm-ups, (3) drills, and (4) practice under game conditions.

Instruction.   Instruction is a very important part of the practice period, for it is at this time that errors in performance, strategy, etc., should be corrected and worked on. Instruction can take place during any phase of the session; it precedes any change in practice routine. The highly skilled athlete needs individual help less often than the novice, but still needs it in a more specialized way.

In instructing the less-skilled person, be specific in explaining the movement to be performed, why it should be done in a certain way, and what results can be expected when it is done correctly. However, the skilled athlete should concentrate more on the overall movement than on movement of a given muscle; she can be confused by a suggestion that she contract a specific muscle in a specific sequence to accomplish a skill. More general suggestions give the skilled girl freedom to concentrate on the total job to be done rather than the step-by-step movement of her body. At the same time, don't be too general in your suggestions. Telling the volleyball player to jump higher to spike the ball, if she doesn't know how to jump higher, is like telling her to create a miracle. But telling her to bend her knees, push hard with her feet and toes, and reach upward with her arms will help her do what you want her to do.

For both the novice and the skilled player, a new movement or a new skill requires understanding. When the athlete is learning a new motor skill, she must be given a clear picture of what she is to do and how to go about doing it. To mention to a diver a new skill such as an inward one-and-a-half somersault can confuse her if she does not know just what it is and how it is to be executed.

In describing a new motor skill, use terms that are familiar to the athlete. In some cases you may be able to relate the new skill to one she has already perfected: for instance, relating the movements for the overhead smash in tennis to the movement made in serving the tennis ball.

The coach who knows something about kinesiology and mechanical analysis is way ahead of the coach who does not. If you know when and how to apply leverage, force, spin, and other physical factors, you can help an athlete to perform better. Even though you may not have had a lot of experience in different sports, if you have a basic knowledge of mechanics, you'll be able to relate this knowledge to areas that are less familiar.

The body build of an athlete should be taken into consideration because it can limit her potential in a particular sport. If she wants to compete in an activity in which her physical makeup is bound to limit her, she should be aware of the fact. The coach who realizes her athletes' limitations due to body build should build her system of play according to the personnel she has. A volleyball team composed of short, speedy players might be more successful playing defense and forcing errors from the opponents, while the volleyball team with plenty of height would be more apt to compile their points from spikes and offensive rather than defensive play.

Another responsibility of the coach during instruction is to see that injuries do not go unnoticed. *All* injuries, regardless of how minor they may seem to the player, should be reported to the coach. Even a small injury can be exaggerated if the activity is too strenuous for the weakened area. The coach should see to it that injuries are diagnosed and cared for by a trained individual. The coach may be held liable if improper care and treatment are given.

Instruction—whether it deals with strategy, safety, motor skills and movement, morale, teamwork, or is simply a result of the coach's interest in the player—gives the athlete a sounder basis for performing well.

Warm-ups.   The effects of warming up are controversial; however, it seems that specific warm-ups done for a specific reason are almost always beneficial. Any activity that involves coordination and timing seems to be helped by a warm-up period that gives the athlete the chance to make minor changes. The girl who shoots free-throws before a game, for example, has a chance to improve her timing. Also, an activity that demands extensive stretching and bending, such as dancing and gymnastics, can be improved by a warm-up period.

If an athlete is competing outdoors on a cold day, or in a cold gym, a warm-up period is especially needed. Activity before competition increases circulation, helps warm up the muscles, and aids kinesthetic awareness. When a sense of touch is involved, such as there is in handling a ball, a warm-up before the game is almost a necessity if a girl is to play her best. If her performance depends on her ability to move quickly, or if excessive strain or tension is placed on the muscles and joints during competition, warm-ups tend to reduce injury and improve performance.

Research studies [5] indicate that warm-ups are beneficial to performance of motor skills, but the effect seems to be influenced by many factors:

1. Type of skill to be performed.
2. Method of warm-up used.
3. Physical condition, age, sex, and psychological condition of the performer.
4. Intensity of the warm-up.
5. Length of rest period between warm-up and performance.

The main reason a person should warm up is to increase the internal temperature of the body, which enables the muscles to function better. When a girl has warmed up, she is capable of a greater range of movement, has better timing and coordination, and is not as likely to suffer an injury [2].

In warm-up, since there is an increase in body temperature, the tonus of the muscles improves; as a result they are more ready to respond to activity. As circulation and respiration also improve, a uniformity of temperature results; therefore the muscles' ability to respond is equalized [1]. There is also evidence that warming up improves the athlete's endurance because it leads to an increase of maximum oxygen intake of approximately 5% [4].

Opinions on the amount of warm-up needed varies from several minutes to an hour or more. The time spent in warm-up exercises varies with the event, as do the exercises used. Basketball players may spend only 15 or 20 minutes warming up; gymnasts, dancers, and track and field participants may take much longer. The amount of time an athlete takes to warm up also depends largely on her conditioning. A warm-up could lose all its advantages if the girl warmed up for so long that she was tired before she actually engaged in competition.

Some athletes have used hot baths, massages, and other means of heating the body, although there is no proof that these means are better than exercise. The exercises used to warm up vary, from bending and stretching exercises to intense practice on the specific skills to be used during the game.

Although most coaches and athletes feel that warm-ups are a very important part of preparing for a contest, the fact remains that many players go into a game or a meet without any warm-up whatsoever, and play exceptionally well without it. At the same time, many who have a sufficient warm-up period perform poorly.

The important thing in warming up is that the athlete should feel sufficiently loose and relaxed. After she has warmed up by running, bending, stretching, and other light exercises, she should do movements similar to those she will be using as she competes, slowly building up her ability to go full speed.

Drills. There are three main reasons for using drills: (1) as a warm-up, (2) for conditioning, and (3) for improvement of skills.

Select drills that will produce the results you want. If conditioning is the main objective, choose drills that will improve conditioning, with warm-up and improvement of skills a secondary objective. Some drills fulfill all three objectives at the same time.

Drills are a good way to improve the skill of an athlete by repeated movement. Be sure that players understand how the drill should be executed, for a drill done incorrectly is a hindrance rather than a help. Keep drills as simple as possible to give the players a chance to concentrate on their execution of it. To prevent boredom, change drills every 5 or 10 minutes.

Practice under game or meet conditions. Practicing skills under game or meet conditions is necessary to good performance. You can achieve this by setting up an actual practice game, or by using drills that contain elements of the competition to be engaged in. Situations that require strategy are especially valuable during practice sessions.

A team or an individual athlete should be trained to react well under pressure. Coaches should not expect their players to play with poise and confidence in a tight game if they have never been trained to react in this manner. Practice sessions that require the athlete to press hard will pay dividends during competition.

Every coach can come up with situations that simulate game conditions, in which the team must be on their toes to win. The volleyball coach might tell team A that they have a one-point lead and need one more point to win the game, but team B is serving. Team A has to get the serve and make the point or else lose the game. The hockey coach might give the red team the ball and tell the blue team they are behind one goal with three and a half minutes left in the game. The track coach might give her number 2 runner a foot lead in the 100-yard dash and tell her number 1 girl she has to make up the difference to win the event, etc.

Another way of simulating game conditions is to set up a team with characteristics similar to those of the opponent to be faced. If a tennis player must compete against a left-handed player who serves well and rushes the net, bring in

Field hockey demands endurance and skill. (Courtesy of Madison Sports Information.)

someone who is left-handed and can rush the net. If the basketball team is to play an opponent that uses a double post on offense and a man-to-man full-court press, set up this type of situation and get the team to practice against it. Some situations cannot be simulated, but the mental attitude can be: Explain the characteristics of the opponent to be faced, and what the players should expect; have an athlete scout her opponent when possible.

In setting up these tight situations, be careful that you give the underdog a chance for a possible victory, provided they keep their heads and react well under the pressure. To set up a situation in which the team knows it doesn't have a chance is to defeat the purpose, and won't result in hustle or determination. Afterward, discuss the reasons why the team managed to win, or why they failed to.

Another advantage of practicing under gamelike conditions is to give the team an idea of how it should pace itself. Many coaches work their players harder during practice than they would have to work during competition, which makes the game seem like play because of the previous conditioning. However, some events require that the athlete pace herself for the best results. The long-distance run, free exercise in gymnastics, and softball pitching are examples of cases in which the athlete must conserve energy or work within a limited framework which should be learned under gamelike conditions.

When an athlete knows that so-and-so-much time is left, or that there must still be a toss of so many feet, or that there are so many yards left to run, psychological factors play a part. Knowing what bounds she must work in gives an athlete added confidence. If the contest is not so different from things she has experienced during practice sessions, things will be much easier for her.

Most butterflies in the stomach result from fear of the unknown or from being afraid one cannot measure up to the competition. Practice sessions that enable a person to recognize her attributes and weaknesses permit her to look at herself under pressure and to know what she can expect of herself and her teammates. Knowing that the world does not fall apart when the bowler doesn't hit a 250 or when the hockey player misses a tackle in a crucial moment helps a girl accept the fact that she can only do her best and hope that it's enough. But when an athlete is thrown into a situation without any previous experience to draw from, she doesn't know what she is capable of doing, and is hampered by fear of the worst unknown area there is: the self.

Therefore, during practice sessions, try to develop leadership in each individual. Especially in team sports, work with the captain to see that she can keep a level head while making quick decisions. This can be done through question-and-answer periods, stress on strategy, and practicing under tight game conditions. Audiovisual aids—such as films, chalkboards, posters, etc.—can be used to help the athlete's thinking. The ability to analyze situations and to make decisions based on an understanding of strategy and personnel are good weapons for coach as well as athlete.

BIBLIOGRAPHY

1. Allen, George H., *Complete Book of Winning Football Drills.* Englewood Cliffs, N.J.: Prentice-Hall, 1959.

2. Capen, Edward K., *et al., Physical Fitness.* Dubuque, Iowa: Wm. C. Brown, 1966.

3. Morehouse, Laurence E., and Philip J. Rasch, *Sports Medicine for Trainers.* Philadelphia: W. B. Saunders, 1963.

4. Taylor, Henry Longstreet, "Exercise and Metabolism," in *Science and Medicine of Exercise and Sports,* edited by Warren R. Johnson. New York: Harper, 1960, Chapter 8.

5. Van Grundy, William, "More about Warm-Up," *Scholastic Coach,* **34,** 44–45, May 1965.

6 Prerequisites for Champions

What makes the difference between the champion and the nonchampion? There is no ready-made formula, no pat answer. There are three factors in athletics—the physical, mental, and emotional attributes of the performer—and the perfection of all three seems to make the difference between excellence and near-excellence. Some athletes are gifted in one or two of these areas, but the real champion, the outstanding athlete, is one who has developed her resources to a high degree in all three areas.

PHYSICAL SKILLS

We all admire the grace and poise of the athlete who has worked until she has perfected her physical skills. The smooth stroke of a tennis player, the spinning action of the diver, the gliding run of a distance runner, the coordinated rhythm of a gymnast, and the powerful strokes of the swimmer are works of art. And like all works of art, they are the result of hard work. Such skills are learned through repetition over a long period of time.

True, some people are gifted with bodies more readily adaptable to sports than others. The sprinter with long legs, the tennis player with height and a long reach, the golfer with long arms and good leverage, and the high jumper with small hips undoubtedly have advantages over people with different body types, provided they have equally developed coordination and strength. However, even athletes with body builds that give them an advantage in a specific sport can be beaten by athletes with less height and less strength when the opponents have practiced more and worked harder on perfecting what potential they have.

Then, too, background and previous experience in the physical world may limit the point some people can reach within a given time. The absolute beginner in bowling will probably be unable to reach winning form in a year; but the bowler who had experience over a period of years and stopped bowling for some reason can probably get back into peak form within a year or less.

Another aspect of a person's physical development is her capacity or potential, or the limits beyond which she cannot go. Some athletes are so physically gifted that there seems to be no limit to what they can do by dedication and hard work. Others reach a point at which further improvement is impossible, regardless of the time and effort they put in. The broad jumper who lacks speed will reach a point beyond which her jump cannot be improved without improving her speed before takeoff. But if she has reached the limit of her speed, willpower alone cannot make her move faster. The high jumper who has short legs is limited in the distance she can jump, even after she has reached her full potential in timing, push-off, and lift. The basketball player who is short may make an excellent guard, but there are limits to her rebounding power because she can jump only so high into the air.

The girl who starts young is more likely to reach her full potential physically than the girl who engages in sports at a later age. This fact is being brought closer to home by the many young athletes who are performing so well in National competition, the Olympics, etc. Examples: Karen Muir, who held the world swimming record at 13, Jim Ryun, who was the fastest miler in the world while he was still in high school, Olga Korbut, who won three gold medals at the 1972 Olympics at the age of 16, and Nadia Comaneci, the Rumanian gymnast who stole the hearts of thousands at the 1976 Olympics while performing to perfection.

Youth has the advantage of speed and endurance, and in events that do not require strength over and above everything else, the young person who develops her talents to the nth degree definitely has the advantage.

Coaching is another important aspect of developing physical skills. The person who has learned to perform correctly and with efficient techniques can accomplish much more than the person who is limited by bad techniques.

So the development of physical skills is determined by several factors. Some of the more important are: (1) age at which the person begins training, (2) body build and physical characteristics, (3) good or poor coaching, (4) time put in on practicing or developing skills, and (5) previous experience which is similar or has carry-over value in the sport.

Champions must have more than physical skills, as we know from the cases of Glenn Cunningham, Ben Hogan, and others who overcame tremendous physical handicaps to become champions in their chosen sports. The combined determination and desire with talent; or one might say that they cultivated their mental and emotional skills along with their physical skills.

MENTAL SKILLS

In sports, the development of mental skills is just as important as the development of physical skills. Yet many coaches neglect this area because it is less tangible.

The athlete who has learned to *think* during practice is a much better player than the one who, during competition, thinks about everything except what she is doing. The subject of mental skill is sometimes covered under the heading of strategy, but the thought process in sports is much more complicated than strategy. To know what one should do and to understand why one should do it are two different things. An athlete can memorize the best angles for shots and the correct way to do a spike, but if she fails to understand why she should perform in a certain way, she does not have one of the most powerful weapons: the ability to analyze movements and make corrections when needed that improves an athlete's game on the spot.

Many athletes make the same mistake over and over. It's not necessarily that they aren't thinking about what they are doing; in most cases it is that they don't really know what they are doing wrong. Therefore the athlete should be taught to be a thinker in the fullest sense of the word, and the younger she learns, the better. She should be kinesthetically aware of her movements. She should be able to break each movement down into parts and analyze them if things aren't going right. If she is able to note an opponent's weaknesses and incorrect movements, this power of observation gives her an advantage. She should be able to make split-second decisions on the spot. She can do this if she has been taught to react with confidence and poise, and if she knows that if she makes a mistake she can figure out what it was and go on from there, applying good principles the next time the same thing happens.

Other mental skills are determination and willpower. If an athlete isn't willing to sacrifice and to work daily on perfecting her skills, she doesn't have much chance of competing against topnotch performers. Many athletes work four or five hours a day, 12 months a year. The girl who can't stick to a schedule and who doesn't have the mental discipline to eliminate anything that might be harmful to her training seldom rises above the level of the average.

The champion athlete must also have self-confidence. Self-confidence comes through self-evaluation. If she has looked at herself objectively and faced her limitations and strengths, she is more apt to believe in herself because she won't attempt the impossible and then weaken her self-confidence by failing to achieve it. Another thing that adds to self-confidence in one's ability to perform correctly in a game situation is to practice a skill over and over so that one is able to perform it correctly in a practice situation.

Another trait well worth cultivating in the athlete is a positive attitude. People are often awed by the tremendous performances of athletes under pressure. Some athletes never seem to perform better than they do when they are backed into a corner. Then they seem to draw on some undeveloped resources. This is usually called "guts," or having an attitude of "I can do it and I will do it." The athlete must feel that she *can* do it and *will* do it.

The athlete must develop the ability to face what seem to be insurmountable odds and refuse to quit until the contest is over. People always admire the scrappy underdog who has heart, for she is the one who can pull off an upset.

People support a certain team or athlete even when they know the odds are against them, simply because everyone knows they are going to battle right down to the wire, and with a few breaks might be able to win, mainly because they are fighters. This ability to stick out a contest even when one is behind, and to fight hard all the way is often the difference between being good or great. How else do underrated teams pull off upsets? In many cases, it is simply that they refuse to lie down and die. Even with the odds against them, they go into competition determined to do their best, to give every ounce of effort they have every second of the game. This ability to never give up, even when the chances for victory seems nonexistent, is pure pride.

The athlete must, in addition, have the mental trait of being able to work with teammates. Teamwork is vital. Most of our great athletes are team players. They are outstanding because of their ability to make the great pass or to set up the perfect play, or to help their teammates out of trouble. This trait of unselfishness is not easily learned. It is a natural impulse for a player to want to make the winning goal, to hit the final spike, to make the outstanding play of the game. But the athlete who is willing to sacrifice this moment in preference to getting the ball to a player who has a better chance for the play is the athlete who should be congratulated. There is as much self-satisfaction—sometimes more—in assisting a player on a goal as there is in scoring. Teamwork is a relative thing. It consists of being aware of the situation when someone else on the team has a better opportunity than you do for making the play. It means being thoughtful of another player on the team who may not be as outstanding nor as good as you are, but who needs help to build up her self-confidence. It involves caring enough for others to work hard for their success as well as for your own.

"Caring for others" suggests another mental trait: empathy. Empathy means putting yourself in someone else's place and being able to understand how he or she feels. There is a great need for empathy on the part of the athlete. To beat a lesser team into the ground just for the sake of a large score shows a lack of empathy. To humiliate an opponent in order to make yourself look good shows a lack of empathy. To rub in the fact that your opponent is inferior shows a lack of empathy.

All athletes lose at one time or another. Therefore the athlete should understand the hurt of the person who is the loser. Athletes should be aware of the pain of going beyond a certain point of fatigue because they too have gone beyond that point. Athletes should know what it is like to face a stronger opponent without a chance of being able to win because of lack of experience, because they too were once beginners. Competition is a wonderful thing when people can compete in a humanistic manner.

Another mental trait the athlete needs is the ability to endure pain. Pain and success in athletics are almost inseparable, especially in endurance events. The great athlete can make the fast break down the court that one more time, can run with a "kick" at the end of the distance run in spite of the pain, can swim the length of the pool one more time when her lungs are aching for air. When she can keep going that extra minute or that extra 100 yards, she suddenly comes into her own. Her body readjusts to the demands and she hits that wonderful plateau known as the "second wind." Then, the next time, the same amount of effort is easier, but she must strive for a still higher plateau, which means more pain, more burning lungs, more fatigue. However, when she has reached the point she has aimed at, she can compete at top efficiency, and she will know that it was worth it.

Finally, an athlete should develop the mental skill of giving. All athletes receive benefits from their participation in sports, but many fail to give anything back to the game. An athlete owes something to the sport that has been good to her. The good athlete can settle her debt by the teaching and coaching of others, and should feel the responsibility of accepting these opportunities whenever possible.

EMOTIONAL SKILLS

Emotions can cause many changes in the body. Fear, for example, can make the heart beat faster, the hands perspire, and the glands shoot adrenaline into the system to prepare it to meet a threatening situation. These physiological changes during stress are the body's way of preparing for a flight-or-fight reaction.

Stress in competition is a result of both internal and external pressures. It forces the athlete to improve her skills and enables her to perform well under highly competitive situations. In fact, the most common pressure on the skilled athlete is the pressure to perform at top efficiency during a competitive event. To do this, she must develop emotional skills that will help her control her feelings, especially the ones that will make her too tense, fearful, or angry to be at her best.

The two emotions the athlete must control are fear and anger. Fear is an instinct that works to protect the individual, from either a real or an imagined danger. In the days of the caveman, it served to prepare a person to run from danger or to stand and fight for his survival. Fear today is usually not fear of physical harm, but fear of something that threatens us emotionally. Threats to our ego or our self-esteem can lead to a feeling of tension, resulting in anxiety and sometimes panic. Some fears of athletes are connected with the pain that results from extreme fatigue, the possibility of failure during a competitive situation, and the reputation of the opponent.

When an athlete is competing, fear that is not controlled can cause her to expend energy that could better be used in the execution of skills. When she can't play well because of fear, she puts herself at a disadvantage before she begins. By utilizing sound emotional skills, however, she can learn to control her fear and make it work for, rather than against her. The excess energy brought about by fear or anger can be used constructively instead of destructively.

Here is an example of positive versus negative reaction. When an athlete is frustrated in her effort to win, her fear of failure may change into feelings of anger: anger at herself because she isn't competing well, or anger at the opponent

Emotions are a part of competition.
(Courtesy of Tommy Geddie.)

because she is the one standing in the way of the victory. Now anger can be useful to the athlete, since it can delay fatigue and may motivate her to an all-or-nothing effort. But temper during competition is usually a result of an inability to accept defeat. Temper causes the athlete to display anger and aggression, which use up needed energy in a negative way.

If the person can harness this excess energy and concentrate on getting even by running harder or jumping higher, the energy aroused by her emotions will make her a better athlete and competitor. When she develops these emotional skills, she can *use* her emotions to combat the frustrations and anxieties she is faced with. The key is to realize that one is afraid or mad, and then to react positively rather than negatively.

Another example of a positive or negative emotional reaction is one's feelings of self-worth or self-confidence. When an athlete meets someone in competition, she may feel confident she can win, or she may feel incapable of holding her own. A basketball player may evaluate her opponent's height, speed, agility, and past performances, judging all these things in relation to what she feels *she* can do. If she thinks she is less skilled than her opponent, she gets a feeling of inferiority. If she feels she can do as well as her opponent, or if she thinks she holds certain advantages, then she may feel superior. Lack of confidence leads to poor performance because the athlete can't concentrate all her energy toward victory; she expends some on thoughts of self-doubt and self-reproach. The unknown athlete has these emotions when she must compete against a well-known one, and even a well-known athlete may have them when she must compete against another well-known athlete.

Regardless of how an athlete feels toward her opponent, she must control her tendency to worry, or to fear the results of a contest. She should reinforce her confidence by concentrating on her strengths and by working on her weak points *before* a competitive situation. She should try to maintain an appearance of confidence and poise, reminding herself that the sport after all is a game and should be enjoyed as such. She should not let the outer appearance of another athlete fool her. Everyone is human. Probably the opponent who looks so self-confident and calm is also experiencing moments of self-doubt and fear of failure. When an athlete thinks of her opponent in this light, it makes the opponent appear a little more vulnerable, and thus subject to defeat like anyone else.

The point is that the athlete can benefit by her emotions, or she can be defeated by them, if she can't channel them constructively. Fear and anger and self-doubt can lead to a better performance or to tightness and lack of poise, and therefore a poor performance. By the same token, overconfidence can hinder her efforts because she is not "up" for the game.

Acquiring emotional skill is hard, and takes practice, but it is necessary if one is to become a great athlete. The athlete must continually remind herself that fear, anger, and self-doubt are common to everyone, while at the same time she must be willing to face up to her emotions and use them to improve her game. Just as she practices a physical skill until she can handle it without conscious thought, so must she practice the emotional skills until she can react to stress without panic.

Habits are learned, and therefore they can be relearned. If the athlete can't handle certain situations well because of her emotions, she must study her reactions, clarify what she feels and why, and then seek reasons for reacting otherwise. If she wishes to excel, doing her best should be reason enough to want more control over her emotions. After she has seen the need for change and has adopted a more positive approach, she must continually picture the type of athlete she *wants* to be. If she is in the habit of falling apart at the seams whenever she is losing and is unable to function well under pressure, she must think of herself as being poised and calm in stressful situations. If she carries a thousand worries and self-doubts into a contest and cannot function well because of tension and fear of failure, she must cultivate the habit of taking things as they come and be content with doing the best she can regardless of the outcome. If she gets mad when an opponent blocks every move or makes a good play, she must try to learn to put her anger to good use by becoming more determined to get by her opponent, or at least to outthink her.

The sky is the limit for the athlete who can exercise self-discipline when others around her are experiencing panic and anxiety, and are reacting accordingly. If she can win the battle with herself, there is no such thing as defeat.

BIBLIOGRAPHY

1. Corbitt, Ted, "The Emotions in Athletics," *Track Techniques*, **21**, 662–663, September 1965.

2. Harris, Dorothy V., "Research Studies on the Female Athlete: Psychological Considerations." *JOPER*, Jan. 1975, pp. 32–36.

3. Neal, Patsy, and Thomas Tutko, *Coaching Girls and Women: Psychological Perspectives*. Boston: Allyn and Bacon, 1975.

7 Title IX and Athletic Programs for Women

Even though the social climate for women athletes has been gradually improving over the last decade, the one major development that has resulted in the greatest improvement in women's sports programs has been Title IX of the 1972 Education Act.

Once women had to utilize bake sales, car washes, and various other projects to raise money for their athletic programs and trips. In 1974, the women's volleyball team at West Georgia College ran the concession stand at all home basketball games to raise money in order to play in the national volleyball tournament, and the women's crew team at Boston University won two national championships without receiving one cent from their school's athletic department. They accomplished this by practicing at six in the morning, borrowing boats from other schools, and sponsoring bake sales, raffles, car washes, and a rowing marathon. At the same time, the men's crew team was alloted $35,000 and two full-time coaches. Most women now have access to budgets, facilities, equipment, travel means, and meals they never dreamed were possible.

Big money has come to women's athletics as a result of Title IX (not necessarily good, but a fact). In 1973, the University of Washington was spending $18,000 on the women, but in the 1974–1975 budget, the amount went up to almost $200,000. At about the same time, UCLA jumped its women's budget from $60,000 to $180,000, and Arizona State set aside 60 scholarships to be used for the women's athletic program [6].

Today, it is not uncommon for big schools to be working with more than a hundred thousand dollars in their budgets for the women. Even small colleges have had tremendous increases in their budgets as a result of Title IX.

PURPOSE OF TITLE IX

Schools and administrators have not always been so lenient in allowing for the expansion of women's sports. Nor have coaches always been as careful to see that girls and women have the opportunities that men have to participate in interscholastic and intercollegiate athletics.

Title IX has increased opportunities for women to participate in sports.
(Courtesy of Indiana University News Bureau.)

The miracle that has resulted in the sports explosion for women in the last few years has resulted from the law, signed into effect by President Ford on July 21, 1975, that states that " . . . no person in the United States shall, on the basis of sex, be excluded from participation in, be denied the benefit of, or be subjected to discrimination under any education program or activity receiving Federal financial assistance."

The regulations of Title IX ban sex discrimination in educational areas such as admissions, counseling, course work, financial aid, faculty jobs and salaries, after-school activities and sports. Of course, it is the inclusion of sports in Title IX that has created so much controversy.

Some of the rules and requirements of Title IX for interscholastic, intercollegiate, and intramural athletic programs are: (1) a school may have separate teams for contact sports, (2) if a school already has a team that excludes one sex, individuals of that sex must be allowed to try out for that team, unless it's a contact sport (Title IX doesn't eliminate the right of a girl to try out for a contact sport team, however), (3) if there is enough interest on the part of women, schools must offer the same sport for women that already exists for men (or a sport comparable to that already offered to men. For instance, football for men and field hockey for women), (4) women must have equal opportunity as far as equipment, travel, medical services, training, facilities, coaching, and publicity, and (5) a school doesn't have to spend equal funds for men and women's programs, but it must provide the women enough funds for equal opportunities.

All schools were required to evaluate their athletic programs by July 21, 1976. This evaluation was to include a comparison of the school's current practices with Title IX requirements, an evaluation of the interest and abilities of men and women in the school, and the development of a publicized plan for a sports program that would meet the needs of the men and women.

As far as classes are concerned, Title IX requires all physical education classes to be co-educational, except for contact sports and sex education classes. However, within the classes, students can be grouped by ability. Separate toilet, shower, and locker room facilities may be provided as long as they are comparable for men and women.

Although schools were expected to take firm steps toward compliance to Title IX in the first year, elementary schools did not have to comply fully until July, 1976, and secondary and post-secondary schools were allowed until July, 1978 to meet the requirements to Title IX.

OPPOSITION TO TITLE IX

The National Collegiate Athletic Association (NCAA) especially fought the rules of Title IX. Their opposition was based on a belief that the men's athletic programs would suffer greatly, and would possibly even go under in some instances because of the extra financial drain on their budgets as women's programs expanded. One of the NCAA's main concerns was that the revenue-producing sports such as football and basketball was not exempt under the regulations.

Michael Scott, the attorney who represented the NCAA in its fight against Title IX said: "Excessive revenues from football and basketball at many colleges have defrayed the costs of men's and women's programs in other sports, and regulations which do not make it clear that revenues from a particular sport may first be used in that sport eventually means the erosion of the strength of that sports program and consequent loss of revenue"[9].

Another concern expressed by other coaches in regards to the effects of Title IX was that intercollegiate athletics as we know them today would be changed. J. Neils Thompson at the University of Texas expressed it this way: "We've said repeatedly we're for women's athletics, but we have to take in $3.2 million a year right now to break even. It's getting harder. There's inflation. There's competition for the entertainment dollar. If we're required to divert too much of this to certain programs, it could be disastrous" [17].

The sad thing in the struggle to weaken Title IX was that very little argument was spent on whether the principles of Title IX were right or wrong. Almost all opposition to Title IX was based on financial issues, which does not speak very highly for the commercialized role sports plays in our society today. Once the regulations of Title IX made it clear that equal opportunity did not necessarily mean equal expenditures on the women's programs, much of the panic displayed by the opponents to Title IX disappeared.

HEW Secretary Caspar W. Weinberger, in trying to dispel the fears of the NCAA in regards to financial problems they were foreseeing in their men's programs, said: "I can't see anything in the provisions to put intercollegiate athletics out of business." Weinberger went on to say that the regulations were written "to eliminate the very evident and obvious discrimination that has taken place against women in athletics over the years, most unconsciously." He pointed out that the regulations had been written to end sex discrimination without disrupting the "entire pattern of American college life" [9].

FINANCING PROGRAMS

Many of the severe financial problems predicted by the NCAA have not materialized as women's athletic programs have expanded, partly because most women have not demanded outrageous budgets overnight, and partly because sources of income have been utilized other than the previous athletic budget of the school (universities spent more than 99% of their total athletic budgets on men's sports in 1971, and approximately 98% on the men in 1976 [7]).

In order to comply with Title IX, schools have resorted to three means of getting money for the expansion of the women's programs: (1) by cutting funds in other areas of the school program, (2) by cutting men's athletic funds, and/or (3) by finding other sources of money to use in the athletic programs. In 1975, the high schools in Chicago planned to increase their women's athletic programs from three to twelve sports by raising property taxes. In other situations, help for the women's programs have come from the general school fund, from student fees, alumni contributions, state grants, and increased gate receipts.

Rather than look for additional funds, some schools have chosen to eliminate some of the "minor" sports for men, such as golf, skiing, tennis, swimming, and baseball, in order not to have to finance teams for women in these sports. This was done, of course, so that a lower number of women's teams would have to be included in the budget, and so that the revenue that previously went to the men's "minor" sports could be rechanneled to the women's programs without having to cut back on the major or revenue-producing sports such as football and basketball. Evidently, in cases like this, the overall program for the students has suffered since not everyone enjoys watching or participating in football and basketball.

Most coaches would be the first to admit that the men's sports programs were in financial trouble long before Title IX. However, some administrators and coaches saw Title IX as the chance to cut back of sports programs that had gotten out of control while trying to keep up with other colleges in their conferences.

In order for cutbacks in the men's programs to work, everyone must cut back the same amount and in the same sports so that the fine line of competitiveness is not destroyed. If one school must work with fewer scholarships, less money for recruiting, etc., the opinion of most coaches is that that school would not have a chance in tournament play, or even in the season's schedule.

Elroy Hirsch, Athletic Director at the University of Wisconsin, said: "It doesn't bother me at all that money is being taken away from the men. If everybody does it, then it wouldn't hurt anyone. As long as there is equality within the conference, that is fine"[1].

However, many men coaches have resented the rapid escalation of women's programs after having worked for years to build up the men's programs. Some would prefer that the women prove themselves first before getting to eat from the pie . . . not realizing that one must have a pie first in order to eat from it.

SECONDARY SCHOOLS AND TITLE IX

Administrators and coaches in high schools have found it easier to comply with Title IX than colleges and universities, mainly because there has been less money involved and not as much pressure to produce winning teams, national champions, etc. However, the National Federation of State High School Association has always taken a more liberal and fairer approach to the female participating in sports.

Perhaps society's acceptance of the young female in play activities, but its more negative attitude toward the older woman in strenuous activity have helped the high schools to include the girl in sports activities more readily than it has allowed the colleges and universities to do so. At any rate, even the high schools are seeing a tremendous increase in interest in athletics for the female.

In 1971, there were 300,000 girls competing in sports at the high school level [6]. In 1973, over 800,000 girls were participating in sports at the high school level, while in 1974, this figure jumped up to over 1,300,000 [18].

Some states, such as Iowa, have found that their girls' programs attract a larger number of spectators than their boys' programs.

Even so, administrators and coaches are having to re-evaluate their budgets, use of facilities and equipment, salary scale, and coaching supplements to eliminate sex discrimination at the high school level.

WOMEN'S PROBLEMS WITH TITLE IX

All complaints at the high school and college level has not come from the men in regards to the reprecussions of Title IX.

Some women educators have felt that the women's programs have progressed too fast too quickly, and that the women are now accepting all the financial benefits without seeing the long-term problems that come with big money in athletics.

Another complaint has been that after years of negative criticism against the men coaches and their programs geared toward winning, the women are now gearing their programs in the same direction and placing the same emphasis on winning as the men have.

One woman coach who took a long, hard look at the new trend in women's sports was Dorothy McKnight, coordinator of women's athletics and the

Women are also experiencing the pressure to win. (Courtesy of UTA News Service, James Russell.)

women's basketball coach at the University of Maryland. When her school started considering athletic scholarships for women, she decided she did not want to be a part of high pressure recruiting and the "win at all costs" philosophy. "I figure we'll be into the buying and selling business," she said, "and I can't do that. . . . I've had pressure already, without scholarships. Pretty soon they'd be telling me I have to win, or that I better get that guard or that pitcher. I don't need it." In explaining further why she did not want to continue coaching, McKnight said, "I just don't believe what's happening. I mean, we finally have the men cutting back on financial aid, and now they want to get women into it. To me, it's asinine" [13].

Other women coaches have become upset with the increased pressures of more intensified programs for girls, and have sought teaching jobs without coaching responsibilities. Increased athletic programs for women, however, have led to another problem. There are few teaching positions today that do not include coaching responsibilities.

OTHER COMMENTS ON TITLE IX

Title IX has resulted in expanded sports programs for girls and women. It has also made women more aware of their rights in regard to educational opportunities, especially in athletics.

But it has not solved all the problems by any means. In some cases, it has created many new ones. The rules and regulations have been so vague and confusing in some instances that many still do not understand them.

However, it is evident that women's programs are increasing and receiving more financial support at the secondary and college level, and that sports programs for women will never be the same since Title IX came into being.

Increased salaries, coaching supplements, officiating fees, and better job opportunities are just a few of the positive results of Title IX.

BIBLIOGRAPHY

1.   "Athletic Directors See Title IX as an Enemy," *Asheville Times* N. C., Tuesday, Nov. 12, 1974, p. 14.

2.   Bock, Hal, "Small School Programs Suffering, Too," *Asheville Times*, N. C., Wednesday, May 14, 1975, p. 33.

3.   Cash, Sara, "Athletic Title Wave," (Part 1), *Atlanta Journal and Constitution*, Sunday, Sept. 22, 1974, p.12-G.

4.   Cash, Sara, "Athletic Title Wave," (Part 2), *Atlanta Journal and Constitution*, Sunday, Sept. 29, 1974. p. 1-G.

5.   "Fair's Fair," (Scorecard), *Sports Ill.*, May 20, 1974, p. 17.

6.   Gilbert, Bil, and Nancy Williamson, "Women in Sport: A Progess Report," *Sports Ill.*, July 29, 1974, pp. 28–31.

7.   Hogan, Candace Lyle, "Fair Shake or Shakedown?", *WomenSports*, Sept., 1976, pp. 50–54.

8.   "Many College Athletic Programs Are in Big Trouble," *Asheville Times*, N. C., Thursday, Feb. 20, 1975, p. 20.

9.   "New Rules Concern NCAA," *Asheville Times*, N. C., Wednesday, June 4, 1975, p. 25.

10.   "New Rules for Women," *Newsweek*, June 16, 1975, p. 50.

11.   Parkhouse, Bonnie, "The Destiny of Women in Sport: Alpha or Omega?", *JOPER*, January, 1975, pp. 52–54.

12.   "Public School Sports Program Killed; Problems Predicted," *Asheville Citizen*, N. C., Thursday, Feb. 6, 1975, p.5.

13.   "Reverse Revolt," (Scoreboard) *Sports Ill.*, Nov. 3, 1975, p. 16.

14.   "Sex Bias Proposals Challenged," *Asheville Times*, N. C., Wednesday, June 4, 1975, p. 42.

15.   "Sex Separate Departments: OCR Interpretation of Title IX Regs," *AAHPER Update*, Dec., 1976, p. 6.

16.   "Shedding Light on Title IX," *WomenSports*, February, 1976, pp. 44–48.

17.   "Title IX Law Changing Women's Role in Sports," *Asheville Times*, N. C., Monday, Nov. 11, 1974, p. 13.

18.   "What Research Tells Us about the High School Girl," *AIA-GWS News*, Spring, 1975, p. 1.

8 Problems of Competition

Today's widespread interest in women's athletic programs, and the financial backing resulting from the passage of Title IX, have given women coaches and players support and motivation unknown in previous decades. However, so much has happened so quickly, that most coaches and administrators have not been prepared to handle effectively the great increase in funds and the change in direction of the women's programs.

Several problems are now evident. Some of the problems do not have answers as a result of our overall cultural patterns, and the pressures exerted by the society we live in. Other problems can be solved only on an individual basis, depending on the value system and objectives of particular areas, schools, and coaches. And some problems being faced in the women's programs are outgrowths of overnight expansion which did not allow for adequate leadership and foresight to keep pace with the sports explosion.

Some of the more important decisions facing women coaches and athletes revolve around: (1) big money and athletics, (2) scholarships, (3) recruiting, (4) pampering of athletes, (5) pressures to win, (6) officiating, and (7) sportsmanship and ethical behavior.

BIG MONEY AND ATHLETICS

Probably the one major thing that has affected the direction of professional, collegiate, and many amateur sports is the influx of huge amounts of money into sports. Just for example, the 1976 Olympic Games were originally estimated to cost $310 million, but actually ran into a $1.5 billion extravaganza. Security alone cost $100 million [6, p. 34].

In professional hockey, it was reported that 7 out of the 20 New York Rangers' players were making between $100,000 and $200,000 a year in 1975 [28, p. 96].

In 1976, the *average* salary for a professional basketball player was $109,781. In comparison, the average for professional hockey players was $72,000, and for professional football players, it was $55,000 [2, p. 8].

Also, in 1976, six baseball players from the Oakland As signed contracts for a total of $9.2 million dollars, to be payed over a 5–6 year period. One player, Joe Rudi, received a $1 million bonus for signing [8, p. 46].

The men are not the only ones experiencing big money in sports. In the last few years, the women have seen tremendous jumps in the purses for professional sports, and in the budgets for college athletics. (See Chapter 7.)

After winning a gold medal in the 1976 Olympics, it was estimated that Dorothy Hamill would sign for a contract of $1 million or more to perform in the professional ice show world. Previously, another beautiful ice skater, Peggy Fleming, had signed a $4 million-plus contract with Bob Banner Associates; Janet Lynn, a bronze medal winner at Sapporo had signed a $2.8 million contract with the Ice Follies [11, p. 19].

In 1971, everyone thought it was unbelievable that Billie Jean King had won over $100,000 in professional tennis. However, in 1973, five women won more than $100,000. One of those five, Margaret Court, pulled in over $200,000. In 1973–1974, professional women skiers had only one event they could race in, worth $7000. The next winter, they had four races worth $40,000 in prize money [9, p. 29].

In 1974, women golfers were competing for $1.8 million dollars, while Jo Ann Prentice won $32,000 for one event (the Colgate-Dinah Shore tournament). The same year, women tennis players competed for $695,000 worth of prizes [27, p. 51].

As the budgets of professional and college teams have gone up each year as a result of increased salaries, higher costs of scholarships, lawsuits, labor problems, and more and more frills, the pressures of inflation have dug even deeper into the available money—making it impossible for some teams to continue to exist.

The fans and spectators and supporters of the sports programs have been the ones to suffer. In 1970, the Washington Redskins sold tickets to their games for $6, $7, $8, and $12. In 1975, the tickets had jumped to $9, $11, $12, and $18 [1, p. 20].

Robert Schmertz lost approximately $1 million on the WFL's New York Stars' franchise, and supporters of the New Orleans Jazz of the National Basketball Association lost $1 million also in 1974 [28, p. 95].

In 1975, when the 10-team World Football League went out of existence, it had lost $30 million. During the 1974–1975 season, it was estimated that 15 out of the 28 pro basketball teams had lost more than $1 million [1, p. 20].

Many other professional sports would be going under if it were not for the underpinning of high-priced ticket sales and huge television payments.

But professional teams are not the only teams in financial trouble. As deficits increase, many schools have found it necessary to trim back their expenses, and in some cases to drop particular sports, such as football, in order to make ends meet—or at least, in order to survive financially.

Stonehill College, in Easton, Mass., has experienced the deficit in athletics that has become common for many schools. In 1975, it was estimated that the school spent $137,000 on athletics and took in only $2000. In 1972, Loyola University of New Orleans eliminated intercollegiate athletics because it could not support the costs of the program [3, p. 33].

It is not unusual for budgets at some of the major colleges to run from $2–3 million. Some of the real power schools, such as Ohio State, have budgets of $4 million [26, p. 108].

As Calvin Hill, professional football player, pointed out, "Collegiate sports are a business—there's no doubt about it." [19, p.3].

If it were not for the revenue from television, most professional teams, and many college programs, could not meet the huge financial burdens they have created through escalating salaries, billion-dollar arenas, etc.

In 1975, the 26 teams of the NFL split $55 million as a result of network coverage [28, p. 96].

Many male athletes have benefited from television commercials for years, but it has only been recently that female athletes have been used to advertise products on TV, and that women's events have been given television exposure to any great degree.

Cathy Rigby drew $50,000 a year for commercials with the Florida Citrus Commission, while Colgate-Palmolive, which has backed women's sports extensively on TV, increased its 1973 budget of $4.5 million to about $7 million in 1974. ABC, the most active network in covering sports, won the bid to cover the King-Riggs tennis match with an offer of $750,000 (the next closest bid was from NBC for $450,000) [9, p. 29].

Other big money has been poured into televising the women's superstar competition and into the Dinah Shore LPGA golf tournament, as well as for a couple of ABC specials on women athletes.

One does not realize how much sports and athletics have gotten out of perspective until one looks at some of the money figures being paid out to keep professional and intercollegiate teams afloat. This fact is brought home even more when one realizes that a member of the President's Cabinet only earns $60,000 a year, and a United States Senator earns $42,500. It makes one wonder about our value system when high school stars go into professional ball with million-dollar contracts.

As a result of the big money being poured into athletics, the pressures on coaches and teams to produce have become tremendous. One sports executive, in speaking of the greed and selfishness of many athletes in grabbing what they can financially without any regard to the effect it has on sports as a whole, said, "It is a madhouse." In pursuing the subject further, Bob Briner said, "Sport does not have to be reformed so much as it has to come to its senses. Players must be paid what can be afforded, not what is wanted, and they must start paying their dues to the fans instead of to their agents. I may be old-fashioned but I still believe that special position brings special responsibility" [4, pp. 36, 42].

Since women's programs are now following the same route as the men's programs, and as women's budgets and prize money increases, players and coaches must be aware that big money brings its own objectives and its own pressures.

On the college level, these pressures can be felt in the necessity for scholarships and recruiting. At the high school, college, and professional level, pressures have resulted in the pampering of athletes, the drive to win, the increasing lack of sportsmanship, and a change in ethical and moral decisions.

SCHOLARSHIPS

Until 1973, the AIAW (Association for Intercollegiate Athletics for Women) did not allow scholarships for women.

When Title IX went into effect, it not only gave women the right to equal opportunity in athletic participation but it also gave them the right to receive the same type of financial aid in athletics that men are receiving.

In the last few years, the number of scholarships for women athletes has increased at a rapid rate. In 1974, Arizona State had approved 60 scholarships in women's athletics, and as early as 1973, 700 girls had applied for one of the 20 scholarships offered by the University of Miami [9, p. 29].

Although AIAW has attempted to keep the emphasis down on scholarships by limiting recruiting means, some coaches have bent the rules to obtain topnotch high school women athletes.

Scholarships have been a status symbol for the women, just as they have been for the men . . . possibly even more so for the women at this point in the development of the women's programs. Many women athletes coming from sound financial backgrounds seek out schools offering scholarships, even though that particular school might not offer the courses most desired. Today, schools not offering scholarships to women athletes are finding it hard to compete against schools which do give free rides by way of scholarships.

Although the AIAW has set limits on the number of college athletes who can receive scholarships or financial aid for their athletic ability, few schools presently have the money in their women's athletic budget to offer the maximum number of scholarships, such as 12 in basketball, field hockey (soccer), gymnastics, lacrosse, softball, swimming–diving, track and field, and volleyball.

The schools which do have large budgets have not shown any great advantage in their added financial advantage, mainly because the women's programs have not become firmly established. Therefore, prospective athletes have sought out the "name" coaches, rather than specific schools. Since smaller schools, such as Immaculata College (Pa.), had the same advantages as larger schools before scholarships were legal for the women, some of the national champions were small schools with small budgets, and very knowledgeable coaches.

However, as more and more money in the larger schools becomes available to the women, it is only a matter of time until the extra number of scholarships being awarded will create powerhouses in the larger and wealthier universities, just as in the men's programs.

At that time, good athletes will seek out the number one teams, making the strong even stronger, and the weak teams even weaker. Good coaching will not be the important factor it is today, but rather the ability to recruit and to offer financial help through scholarships will often distinguish between runners-up and champions.

Colleges are now faced with a problem that seems unique. Some professional women athletes, finding that they could not make it in professional leagues, or that they were not enjoying the long seasons of professional leagues, or else finding that the leagues were not financially stable, have regained interest in playing out their four-year eligibility at the college level. Since AIAW allows a professional player to play in any other intercollegiate sport besides the one in which she was a professional, some professional volleyball and softball players have qualified for college play under this rule, and are either playing with university teams, or are in the process of trying out for college teams.

One professional basketball player, Karen Logan, wishing to play basketball at the college level, has attempted to get permission from AIAW to compete in this sport. As of this writing, the permission has not been granted. Players switching back and forth from professional to amateur could prove to be a real headache under our present-day system. Whether AIAW can maintain their stand under increased pressure from sports groups and name individuals remains to be seen.

Some coaches have found the headaches and the added pressures connected with scholarships are just not worth it (see Dorothy McKnight, Chapter 7), and have preferred to get out of coaching altogether.

A former coach of Calhoun Community College in Decatur, Alabama, Carol Worrell, expressed it this way: "The girls didn't value the scholarships like the boys do. They quit, they missed practice. . .they just had an intramural attitude toward the whole thing. Yet, I was putting my whole life into my coaching. It was totally time consuming. When it got down to it, I just didn't feel like all the effort was worth it."

Other coaches feel that scholarships for women are a great thing, partly because they reward women for excellence in the physical realm, and partly because "if the men have them, the women should."

Some coaches are enjoying the benefits of scholarships. They make coaching much easier because only the highly skilled women receive financial aid and coaches no longer have to contend with the "walk-on" athlete they were required to coach a few years ago.

One paradox is that while the women are enjoying the addition of scholarships to their programs, the men have been talking about reverting to scholarships based on financial need. The economy, and the problems of recruiting, may force men and women to meet at a middle ground which would allow reasonable programs to exist without threatening the entire college with financial deficit.

As in most problems, whether scholarships and recruiting are negative or positive experiences depends greatly on the ethics and philosophy of the individual coach.

However, when a coach's job depends on his or her win–loss record, priorities change greatly, and are not always good—or right.

RECRUITING

AIAW has attempted to keep recruiting from getting out of hand by limiting what a coach can legally do to interest an athlete in her particular school. As stated on page 45 of the 1976–1977 AIAW Handbook (published by AAHPER, Washington, D.C. 20036), "Active recruitment of prospective student–athletes may not include a member of the university or its delegate being paid or given release time for the purpose of athletic recruitment."

This rule, making it illegal for a college to pay anyone to recruit prospective women athletes, was passed in the hope that it would keep competition more even regardless of the amount of money a college had in its budget.

Even so, some women athletes have found their recruitment by women coaches to be not much different from that experienced by men athletes. In 1974, Shirley Babashoff, a swimmer, was contacted by more than seven big schools, even though she had never indicated any interest in attending them, [9, p. 29] and Nancy Lieberman, the youngest member of the 1976 Olympic women's basketball team, was pressured by college alumni, coaches, and influential people connected with colleges and universities. She was also offered a car and an apartment [13, p. 37]. Nancy finally went to Old Dominion, a school that has been trying to build up its women's basketball program for years.

The problem of recruiting has been intensified in the women's programs as more and more pressure has been put on a school and the coach to come up with a good team. Some women, and some men, coaches have not wanted to take the time to go through a long building process. They have found it easier to go out and lure the super talent. Super talent makes them look good as coaches because skill on the part of the player has already been developed, and their coaching does not affect the team's record either way to any great degree.

One criticism leveled at the AIAW has been that their enforcement of rules is weak since it depends upon its member institutions to investigate infractions of the rules on recruitment and to assume the responsibility of enforcing those rules [13, p. 39]. Lack of a strong investigative organization has, in some cases, given the unethical coach unfair advantage over the conscientious and honest coach.

Billie Moore, coach of the 1976 Olympic team, has always emphasized that athletes should take a good look at the academic program of an institution and should base their decision to attend or not attend a particular school solely on the educational values found there. She has also been strongly against bending the rules to recruit the good athlete. "I hope that if a student is approached with offers that fall outside of what the regulations permit that she will report it," she said. [13, p. 39].

Volleyball action. (Courtesy of Carol Olson.)

Since active recruiting is forbidden by AIAW, some schools are making their programs more enticing by bringing in women as coaches with whom players can immediately identify and for whom they would want to play. At the same time, the institution receives a great deal of publicity because these well-known individuals are connected with their athletic program. An example of this is Utah State (Logan, Utah). In the fall of 1976, Marily Weiss, women's athletic director, hired Mary Jo Peppler as coach and Marilyn McReavy as assistant coach of Utah State's volleyball team, and Karen Logan as assistant coach of the basketball team. Having the two former professional players and superstar competitors (Peppler in volleyball and Logan in basketball) and McReavy (an Olympic and national team member and former coach of Sul Ross State which won two national collegiate championships under her coaching) has given Utah State publicity it could not have obtained in other ways.

One fear many women coaches have is that the recruiting of female athletes will become as unethical and high pressured as that used in recruiting male athletes. One very successful coach, Frank Broyles of Arkansas, in speaking of recruiting and the many infractions connected with sports, has said that "if something isn't done, the lid is going to blow off" [26, p. 107.]

The same thing might be said of the women's programs in the next ten years or so if the first priority in the women's programs is to win by any means and by any methods. Again, many decisions must be made by individual coaches as to the ethical aspects of recruiting and enticements of the woman athlete.

PAMPERING OF ATHLETES

The athlete is one of the most envied and admired persons in our society. Consequently, many times the athlete has been set aside as one of the special few, receiving privileges and special attention that are sometimes undeserved.

For years, special dormitories and eating tables have been reserved for athletes in men's intercollegiate programs and individual help and private tutoring, unavailable to the average academic student, have been the privilege of the male athlete.

Almost every professor and teacher at some time or another has been pressured to keep athletes in school by "fudging" a little in their grades (and in some cases, even falsifying their grades). And news of special offerings to star athletes of under-the-table benefits, such as free cars and housing, and sometimes even sex, have surfaced time and again in the men's programs.

Professional athletes, pulling in hundreds of thousands of dollars a year, strike for more pay, or refuse to sign their contracts. During games some professional athletes exhibit cruel and violent behavior that would not be tolerated in normal circumstances. When criticized, they attribute their actions to the "nature of the game."

Some extreme brutality, such as that exhibited in ice hockey, has been pinpointed for what it is, and brought into courts of law. Even in court, the athlete has almost always received preferential treatment.

Many individuals have questioned the exceptions and the pampering almost all athletes receive during their competitive life. Others ask why coaches and officials continue to tolerate the temper tantrums of superstars who have manifest psychological problems.

Questions are raised concerning why there is one set of rules governing the athlete, and another set of rules, far more stringent, governing the non-athlete.

Ideally, sports should allow the individual the opportunity to develop the body and the mind, and to coordinate social values and common civility. However, in many cases, while the body is developed to the highest possible degree, the mind is allowed to remain at subhuman levels.

There is no doubt that sport has become one of the most important things in our society today. It has larger audiences than the best art shows or dramas or the most exciting concerts. However, it is questionable that sport has become important enough to permit athletes to adopt a code of ethics completely different from that endorsed by the rest of American society and to receive privileges and exceptions that the average person does not.

One must also question whether the attempt at excellence by the athlete is any different from the attempt at excellence by the writer or the housewife or the construction worker, and whether the small segment of our society made up of athletes should be permitted to ignore the rules and common courtesies observed by the rest of us.

One goal of athletics is excellence. But one cannot claim success if that excellence is confined only to physical development to the detriment of mental and social development. Our society is too complex to allow one-sided individuals to become the heroes and heroines, and to gain individual benefits at the expense of the majority.

If we design our programs to develop outstanding athletes who have complete command of their bodies, but little regard for individual and social responsibility and ethical conduct, then we can only expect more problems in our society.

It is true that big-time athletics is greatly intertwined with the economy of our country. But it is also true that sensitivity and concern for others is equally vital to our social well-being, and that individuals at all levels of life must learn to live with others if our society is to function properly.

It is hoped that women athletes will not be pampered and freed of their individual responsibilities by coaches, alumni, and fans who are pushing them toward physical perfection. And hopefully, in the coming years writers such as Ron Clarke cannot speak of the results of the women's programs as he did of the men's when he said: "Today, the fun in big sport is fast vanishing, with athletic careers being blueprinted so thoroughly that champions seem in danger of becoming robots manipulated by biologists, chemists, and computer specialists"[5, p. 142].

PRESSURES TO WIN

Almost every phase of our lives is built on the desire to excel and to be on top—whether in our chosen professions or on the athletic field. Competition is ingrained into the American way of life, and this fact is not likely to change.

However, this enthusiasm for competition and coming out number one does not always have positive effects. Many schools and colleges have found the drive to excel in a particular sport, or in several sports, has its price.

Society as a whole puts intense pressure on coaches and players to produce. Add to that the status a coach receives for building a winner, and the money and financial support given to a program by an institution or its alumni, and you have a cycle that has no end.

This great American obsession with winning has probably done more harm to athletics than any other one thing. As winning has become the prime objective of most programs, the other values have become unimportant.

"The single most destructive element that has emerged in sports in this country over the past 15 years," Thomas Tutko said, "is the philosophy that winning, and annihilating your opponent in the process, is the only dimension to playing the game." [22, p. 74].

The drive to win has made the athletic department one of the most powerful departments on campus. Even presidents of most colleges and universities feel incapable of coping with the mania to win "at all costs." It led one president of a Southwest Conference college to say, "I'd like to get rid of sports recruiting and big-time football. If I did, though, I couldn't stay in this state for two days" [26, p. 108].

Realizing the problem of having winning as the first priority, George Hanford said, "We've got to slow down this drive on campuses to be Number One. Something needs to be done to break the cycle"[26, p. 111].

Television, magazine, and radio coverage of outstanding teams and athletes increases the need to be on top. The more publicity a team or player receives, the more is expected of the group or the individual. This tremendous exposure creates psychological pressures to continue to excel, which is correlated with winning.

Dr. Bruce Ogilvie explains, "This quest for excellence has become the neurosis of our times. The casualty rate is extremely high" [19, p. 3].

What most coaches don't realize is that there is nothing wrong with winning or with losing. Both processes hold an educational experience. However, winning becomes negative when the means for winning are no longer ethical. Winning also becomes negative when the victory is not earned. Winning takes care of itself when a team performs well, and is a by-product of physical and mental excellence.

"I think Americans are too preoccupied with winning," Mary Jo Peppler said, "Winning should be a by-product of a perfection-oriented pursuit" [16, p. 29].

Unfortunately, many women are finding themselves more and more concerned with their win–loss records as greater amounts of money are being channeled into their programs. All of the problems of big-time athletics that women for years have criticized the men for are now at their doorstep. "Everybody thought that when women came on the scene, they'd clean up the act a bit. But show biz is show biz . . ." [13, p. 38].

It may be impossible now to change our cultural expectations and our list of priorities in regard to athletics—men's or women's. We have created a way of life that will not easily be changed.

But if the women really want to develop a model for their programs that will be different from that for the men's, they must change their emphasis from winning to playing well, from victory at all costs to enjoyment of the sports experience; and they must make it a point to develop the total individual, not just as a *playing* individual, but as a *social* being.

Al McGuire knew what he was talking about when he said, "Winning is overemphasized. The only time it's really important is in surgery and war." [23, p. 55].

Playing with determination. (Courtesy of BYU Sports Information.)

Officiating

Women have found in many areas that as the quality of play has improved, the quality of officiating has not kept pace.

Part of the problem has grown out of the hesitancy of universities and colleges to offer officiating classes at the time programs for women were first getting off the ground, and part of the problem is that many women and men do not wish to take the verbal and physical abuse that has become a part of officiating today.

If coaches, players, and spectators were more aware of the "separation of power" necessary to run a game smoothly, there would be less friction between the officials and the participants. As a result, more individuals would probably consider taking the time and effort to become qualified officials. Now that officials have become the victims of continual harassment, it is a wonder that there are so many left.

In a game situation, it is the responsibility of the official to officiate, the coach to coach, and the player to play.

Coaches would be very resentful if the officials came over and criticized their strategy or their player substitution. At the same time, players would be upset if the officials told them how to set a screen and when to shoot the ball. Just as it is not the officials' responsibility to tell the coach or the players how to participate in the game, it is not the coaches' or the players' responsibility to tell officials how to officiate.

It is human to make mistakes. Officials are not perfect—but neither are players or coaches.

Unless spectators and coaches and players learn to accept the decisions of the officials (right or wrong) as part of the game, and to do the best they can under the circumstances, officiating will continue to lag behind the quality of play. Coaches and players must learn to show more respect for the officials. Until more status and respect is given to those calling the game, the number of individuals qualified to officiate will decline rather than increase.

SPORTSMANSHIP

The sad thing about athletics in America is that as the skill and strategy level of coaches and players has improved, the level of sportsmanship has declined.

It is not uncommon to read of spectators throwing objects onto the field, or at players and officials. At the same time, the conduct of many players and coaches has become even more obnoxious and offensive.

Gamesmanship and psychological readiness have taken on a different meaning today. Many players, in getting "psyched up" for a game, no longer limit their mental preparation to performing well physically—but instead mentally prepare themselves to hate the opponent. This intense buildup of hate lessens the guilt players feel when they actually go out to "wipe out" the opponent.

Winning has become such an overwhelming objective that care and concern for others have become irrelevant. Competition no longer includes cooperation. It has become a life and death battle—on which jobs depend, scholarships hang, salaries hinge, and status comes and goes. As a result, sportsmanship has fallen by the wayside. Good deeds and courtesy are not worth hundreds of thousands of dollars. Kindness and fairness are not rewarded with Superbowl rings and new cars. In our money-oriented society, one cannot live comfortably on good sportsmanship.

However, as sportsmanship has declined, sport has lost much of its true meaning. The "spirit of sport" is now seen rarely. Instead, we witness teams performing like machines; we watch pageantry without meaning trying to replace things of significance; and we wonder how to control the monster we have created.

Frightening changes are already taking place in the sports world as a result of the lack of respect of human life and unsportsmanlike conduct displayed during competition. Many high schools are scheduling their games in the afternoon rather than night, in order to increase security. In 1975, the National Football League sent out a demand that security become tighter to prevent spectators from throwing objects at officials and players.

Violence has become so common during sporting events that a sociologist has predicted that spectators going to see football games will soon have to go through the same type of security screening that airlines use to detect dangerous

(Courtesy of UTA News Service, James Russell.)

weapons. Dr. Irving Goldaber from Brooklyn College said: "You have to assume there is potential for assassination in a football stadium" [24, p. 36].

This behavior would have been unbelievable ten years ago. However, today, after years of allowing unsportsman-like behavior to go unchecked and ignoring the unethical practices used to obtain winning teams, we should not be surprised at the violent potential of our sports.

"Kill the umpire" has been tolerated part of our sports vocabulary for years. Hockey players try to kill each other almost every game. Football players know all the techniques for maiming each other, while baseball players consider it a "part of the game" to throw a deadly missile at a player's head.

What started off as mental intimidation through the "psyching up" process has now crossed the fine line into physical intimidation. Fans and players are no longer content with verbal abuse. Physical abuse has also become "part of the game."

As an athlete, I know that once one has lost the enjoyment, the prime reason for playing has also been lost.

It is possible that it is too late to change the direction our sports have taken the last few years which has lead to lack of respect for others and too much emphasis on winning. It is this total disrespect for others that has taken away from the "spirit" of the rules, and left disorder and brutality in its place.

But if we cannot change the direction of our programs and restore some value to sportsmanship and ethical behavior based on concern and respect for others, we can expect sports to become a military operation in the next few years rather than the great American pastime.

What can be done to create a change in the sports environment? Coaches can teach ethical behavior as they teach physical skills. Coaches can demand emotional control along with physical discipline. Administrators can spell out what they expect from the crowds attending their games and enforce these expectations. Television commentators can stop complimenting athletes on how much they were able to "get away with," and point out the rules of the game that should be followed. All the media, television, radio, magazines and newspapers, can make the spectators and participants more aware of the importance of the "spirit of the rules," and make sportsmanlike conduct the rule and not the exception.

Everyone connected with sports can emphasize the importance of respect for the officials, and for the skills of the opposing teams as well as for the skill of the home team.

We must learn to be more tolerant of the mistakes of others. We must especially learn to respect the talent and hard work of others, regardless of which team they represent.

And impossible as it may seem, we must encourage honesty on the field regardless of the penalty resulting from fair play. Mary DiStanislao, coach of Northwestern's field hockey team, had the right idea. When told that one of her players (Barbara Roche) had reversed the official's ruling that she had scored a goal by admitting she had hit the ball on the wrong side of the stick, Mary commented, ". . . I love to win, but you've got to be honest. She did the right thing" [Sports Ill., Nov. 22, 1976, p. 23].

We can continue our sports programs as they are, with a definite lack of sportsmanship on the part of the fan, players, and coaches, or we can choose to try to change the emphasis from winning "at any cost" to respect and concern for others as human beings.

Our only other alternative in the next few years is to have our games officiated by machines, and our stadiums protected by extreme security.

And then the cycle would be completed. The big problem then would be changing the name of the game. There is no way it could still be called "sport."

BIBLIOGRAPHY

1. Ammerman, Graig, "Bloodletting Far from Over in Pro Sports Crisis," *Asheville Times*, N.C., Thurs., Nov. 13, 1975, p. 20

2. "Basketball Players Are Top-Paid Professional Athletes—Earning Average $110,000 Yearly," *National Enquirer*, Jan. 20, 1976, p. 8.

3. Bock, Hal, "Small School Programs Suffering, Too," *Asheville Times*, N.C., Wed., May 14, 1975, p. 33.

4. Briner, Bob, "Making Sport of Us All," *Sports Ill.*, Dec. 10, 1973, pp. 36–42.

5. Clarke, Ron (with Alan Trengove), "Are We Creating Super Athletes—or Monsters?", *Reader's Digest*, Oct., 1975, pp. 141–145.

6. Deford, Frank, "More Dark Clouds over Montreal," *Sports Ill.*, July 19, 1976, pp. 32–39.

7. Felshin, Jan, "Sport Style and Social Modes," *JOPER*, March, 1975, pp. 31–34.

8. "Finley Shakes Baseball World," *Asheville Citizen*, N.C., Thurs., Dec. 9, 1976, p. 46.

9. Gilbert, Bil, and Nancy Williamson, "Women in Sport: A Progress Report," *Sports Ill.*, July 29, 1974, pp. 28–31.

10. Gilman, Kay, "Sports Chatter," *WomenSports*, Dec., 1976, pp. 28, 42.

11. Grimsley, Will, "Hamill's Imminent Gold Medal Worth $1 Million,"*Asheville Times*, N.C., Feb. 12, 1976, p. 19.

12. Harris, Dorothy, and Jane Condon, "Home Gym," *WomenSports*, Dec., 1976, pp. 38–41.

13. Hogan, Candace Lyle, "The Confusion of the College Recruit: Who's Pulling the Strings?", *WomenSports*, Aug., 1976, pp. 36–39.

14. Lapin, Jackie, "Trailblazer," *SportsWoman*, June, 1976, pp. 44–45.

15. Larned, Deborah, and Cheryl McCall, "Mighty Mead Strikes Out at Sports," *WomenSports*, Aug., 1976, pp. 40–41.

16. Lawrence, Evelyn, "Utah Gets Another Golden Spike, Mary Jo Peppler," *Sports Woman*, Nov., 1976, pp. 24–29.

17. Lipsyte, Robert, "Pleasures of the Flesh," *Newsweek*, June 23, 1975, p. 13.

18. Michener, James A., "Women Who Win," *Ladies Home Journal*, March, 1976, pp. 71, 82–85.

19. Mongelluzzo, Bill, "Organized Athletics as Much Big Business as Sport—Panel," *The Times-Picayune* (New Orleans), Thurs., March 13, 1975, p. 3, section 1.

20. Neal, Patsy, "Women Athletes and Coaches—Are You Really So Lucky?", *Woman Coach*, Nov.-Dec., 1975, pp. 36–37, 39, 41.

21. Parkhouse, Bonnie, "The Destiny of Women in Sport: Alpha or Omega?", *JOPER*, Jan., 1975, pp. 52–54.

22. Rutan, Samuel, "Does Sex Affect Your Game?", *Bazaar*, May, 1975, pp. 74–75.

23. Sabol, Blair, "On the Sunny Side of Defeat," *WomenSports*, Aug., 1976, pp. 54–55.

24. "Sociologist Says Sports Have Violence Potential," *Asheville Citizen*, N.C., Wed., Sept., 1976, p. 36.

25. Smolkin, Shelley, "Sport Shy: How Real Are Your Fears?", *WomenSports*, November, 1976, pp. 62–65.

26. "Sports Recruiting: A College Crisis," *Reader's Digest*, July, 1974, pp. 107–112.

27. "Sportswomanlike Conduct," *Newsweek*, June 3, 1974, pp. 50–55.

28. "The Pro-Sports Boom Is Going Bust," *Reader's Digest*, Sept., 1975, pp. 95–98.

9 Analyses of Sports and Strategy

To be able to analyze her athletes' strengths and weaknesses is one of the greatest assets a coach can have. Every situation demands that the coach be able to do this, and that she then be able to work out a plan of action so that she can obtain better results from her athletes. And she has to be able to make these decisions on the spot— for example, during a crisis in a game—when a wrong decision can lose the contest.

The coach who is good at *analysis* can, so to speak, take a movement apart and study it, and understand the separate parts that make it up. The coach who is good at *strategy* can put this knowledge into practice to get desired results. Basically, analysis concerns physical characteristics and movement, while strategy concerns mental readiness. The two factors are complementary.

Better equipment, increased knowledge of movement, new techniques in performance, weight training, better diet, and many other things have brought about an improvement in sports performances. However, as opportunities become equalized, and as all individuals gain the chance to engage in athletic programs, the factor that is going to make the difference in performance is the coaching. Good coaching must combine an accurate inventory of potential (analysis) with a plan of attack compatible to the personnel (strategy).

STUDYING AND ANALYZING MOVEMENT

In studying movement to determine potential, a coach may use many methods. It is up to the coach to select the method most appropriate to her needs. Films, photographs, charts, plotting, and videotapes can be useful. The money and time available are major considerations for those wishing to utilize these methods. Simple observation is one of the easiest and most often used methods, although naturally it is subjective, and therefore not always valid.

In analyzing the player in action, the coach should: (1) watch the performer's overall movement, (2) follow one specific part of the body (for example, the hand) as the girl performs the movement, (3) take film or photographs when possible (so that she can study action by means of stills or slow-motion film), (4) record action through plotting when possible, (5) discuss her findings with the athlete, and (6) suggest the movements that the athlete should practice. When specific measurements such as plotting are used, the coach should: (1) find the center of body movement (center of mass is slowest-moving part, and easiest to see), (2) know the distance from this center to the base, (3) know the extent and direction of hip movement during the action, (4) determine where the body weight is at start and finish of action (weight shift is usually at climax of action), (5) look at position of head, (6) check to see how wide the base of support is (wide stance usually means stability), (7) determine direction of feet during the action, (8) look for sway, dip, and unusual twist during the performance, (9) note the extent, direction, and pattern of the follow-through of the arm, hand, and leg, (10) try to see a picture of the total range of movement, (11) follow the movement of the hand or foot, paying special attention to the hand, wrist, and fingers, and (12) write down her impression of the performer.*

The coach who is dealing with skilled athletes will find analysis much easier if she knows the components and movements that make up the sport. For instance, basketball is composed of running, jumping, throwing, catching, etc. The coach can get hints for improvement in the overall game by looking at some of the other fields of motion, and then transferring this knowledge to her specific sport. Hints on how to achieve speed on the fast break, for example, can come from observation of sprinters in track; aids in teaching catching and throwing can be transferred from softball.

Working with left-handers and right-handers is not nearly as complicated as some teachers and coaches make it seem. In most cases, the only comment that needs to be made to left-handed players is that left and right should be transposed in the directions. (Most left-handed people do this automatically because they have learned to adjust to an environment that is geared to right-handed people).

Being left-handed is not nearly as much a handicap as playing against a left-hander. For instance, in tennis, the receiver must adjust to the spin of the ball going in the opposite direction on the serve and other strokes, and in basketball, the defensive player must remember to overplay the left side of the left-handed person, which is normally the weak side of a right-handed person.

The coach should observe left- and right-handed players from the ball side in some sports (for instance, in bowling), and should give added attention to left-handed individuals during the learning of a new skill to be sure they have transposed left and right given during the instructional period.

CHANGING AND IMPROVING PERFORMANCE

The coach should not try to change the overall performance of the skilled athlete (for often this would throw off all her movements and reactions), but should try to bring about minor changes which could improve the athlete's performance

---

* From notes taken in class on Analysis of Sports, conducted by Dr. John Cooper at the University of Utah; used by permission.

without ruining the confidence, pattern of movement, and coordination that has been built up through the years. For instance, in analyzing the movements for a broad jumper, the coach might suggest a longer approach to help build up speed rather than insisting that the athlete go back to the basics of running. Or in the case of the tennis player, it might be a wrist snap late in the serve that needs comment, rather than a complete overhaul of the swing.

Any major changes necessary should be made in the off-season to allow the girl time to master the skill before the competitive season. Regardless of the extent of needed changes, once an analysis has been made, the next step is improving the athlete's performance. What works with one individual may not work with another. The psychological factors involved in sports are immeasurable and in many instances uncontrollable. The coach must always exercise tact and not go beyond a point that will cause the athlete to lose self-confidence. Some people respond physically when the coach explains what should be done and why. Others find it easier to verbalize what the coach has tried to get across. Others may respond more readily to written notes that the coach has made during observation. Some react best if they can see the film or photographs, so that they can follow their own movements step by step. Others need to be encouraged every step of the way, humored, or prodded by other psychological means. At any rate, the coach must work within the limitations of the athlete, using the athlete's weaknesses to her advantage when possible.

People at different skill levels react to changes in movement in different ways. In coaching the beginning player, the coach must give the athlete a chance to see *how* a movement is performed. But once she is past the beginning stage, the girl must know *why* a movement is performed in a certain way. At first, visualizing an action makes learning and change easier, but when athletes are skilled, it is insight that makes performance more effective. So it is with the coach: She must be able to see the movement in its entirety, understand how it is accomplished, and as a result have an insight as to what changes are necessary for more efficient performance.

Sometimes a coach can improve performance just by changing some of the implements used in competition. Balls in most instances are standardized, but uniforms can be varied to help a team's vision and peripheral perception. If a girl is afraid of hustling after a ball on the floor, knee pads or knee socks can eliminate the fear of floor burns. Examples of changing the implement used in competition and thereby changing performances are the fiberglass pole in high jumping and the steel racket in tennis.

For a skilled athlete, one of the best means of improving performance is to compare her movements with those of a champion. Top athletes have perfected minute details, and the athlete wishing to improve can learn from the champion. Reading about outstanding athletes, watching movies of top teams and individuals, and observing performances firsthand can certainly aid the aspiring athlete, provided she will take her own limitations and unique movements into consideration.

When playing, one should remember that once a motion has been started, it is hard to stop it. Getting an opponent to commit her body weight in the wrong direction is the key to faking in basketball, and can be utilized in other ways when competition depends on balance and timing. In order to counteract an opponent's move, a defensive player must move quickly, and through a greater arc. Because of this, the offense has the advantage; this advantage can be equalized only by anticipation and speed in reaction time on the part of the defense. If the defense uses correct positioning, and keeps plenty of space between herself and the opponent, this can prevent the opponent's having an advantage in speed before the defense can counteract the offensive moves. On the other hand, this gives the offense a different advantage in that it allows her greater choice of movements in the added space.

Another thing to remember is that an athlete cannot make a movement in one plane without first moving in another. Flexion cannot be accomplished without extension first, nor can you extend without flexing. To extend the legs on a jump, a person must first flex the knees. To get wrist action in shooting or throwing, a person must first cock the wrist.

UTILIZATION OF STRATEGY

Strategy involves a plan of action, and demands that a player be mentally ready to move in a prearranged direction to extract a desired reaction from the opponent. With strategy, an athlete can out-think the opponent and counteract her plans. Every plan of strategy must take into consideration the weaknesses and strengths of one's own players, as well as the opponents'. If the athlete is simply competing against her own time or record, coaching strategy will involve getting the most from her psychologically as well as physically.

UNANSWERED QUESTIONS IN COACHING

Coaching cannot be summed up in exact statements. There is no set formula for coaching because there are too many variables connected with it. Each coach brings unique contributions to the coaching field. The coach has to work with individual players, each of whom has unique mental, physical, and emotional skills, and then pit these players against opponents, each of whom also has a unique combination of skills.

We do not yet know—in fact, we'll probably never know—the *best* way to coach an individual or a team. There are so many untried methods that the field is relatively wide open for the coach who is willing to try new methods of getting the most from the athlete.

There are so many questions the coach and teacher must answer in order to tap the full potential of athletes. Some answers to the questions below can be revealed through research and experience. Others we may never know the complete answers to.

1. Why do some people perform better under pressure, while others perform worse?

2. How do you teach poise under stressful situations?

3. How do you teach self-confidence while at the same time giving the person a true picture of her strengths and weaknesses?

4. How can you detect staleness, and what is the best way to prevent it?

5. Should coaching for sports in which implements such as rackets, bats, etc., are used be different from coaching for sports which do not require implements?

6. Should coaching for sports such as golf, bowling, archery, etc., be different from coaching for sports which involve body contact, such as hockey and basketball?

7. How does coaching individual sports differ from coaching team sports?

8. How do you teach aggression?

9. What personality traits are best suited for particular sports?

10. How do you teach a person to react faster in a competitive situation?

11. At what age should competitive programs be started?

12. How do you get an athlete "up" for a contest?

13. How do you motivate a person to practice on her own?

14. How can you improvise equipment for better teaching and coaching results?

15. Why is it that when a player is in the best frame of mind, she sometimes gives the poorest physical performance (and vice versa)?

16. How can the athlete control tension to achieve the best results?

17. What is the best means of teaching a person to (1) jump higher, (2) throw farther, (3) catch better, (4) swing harder, (5) run faster, (6) endure longer?

18. What it the best progression for teaching physical education, and why isn't this progression reasonably uniform in our school systems?

19. How do you teach people to compete in a humanistic way?

20. What are the *real* values of sports?

21. Are the same values inherent in sports for girls as in sports for boys? If so, why has the girls' competitive program been so limited?

22. Are athletes less prone to crime and other antisocial behavior than nonathletes?

23. What psychological traits do top athletes have that average athletes do not have?

24. What is the pain threshold for the athlete training for an endurance event?

These are only a few of the questions that need to be answered. We very much need research on the subject of competition, as it concerns the athlete and the coach.

To be useful, analysis and strategy must be specific. Therefore this chapter will discuss some intermediate and advanced techniques and strategy needed by the skilled player, rather than the basic fundamentals, which the advanced player should already have mastered, and which are fully described in many other textbooks. It is impossible to cover all the refinements of technique in this book. Thus I have tried to select ones that ought to be useful to most coaches working with girls who have progressed beyond the beginning level.

ARCHERY

Coaching Emphasis

1. Use same anchor point each time. Establish the anchor best suited for control.

2. Draw arrow back same distance each time.

3. Check aim for accuracy each time before releasing the arrow. Never rush the release.

4. Be sure stance is correct, body is aligned with the target, chest is lifted, and abdomen is flat.

5. Practice consistency in moves; for best results, archer should operate like a machine.

Mechanics

1. Corner-of-the mouth anchor; see Fig. 9–1. Often used in field archery.

   a) Any one of three fingers (usually forefinger) drawing arrow may be anchored at corner of mouth. Same finger should be used each time.

   b) To give firmness, anchor finger should be braced against tooth. Mouth should remain closed, with teeth clenched.

   c) Thumb should be turned down and hooked under jaw when arrow is at full draw.

2. Under-the-chin anchor; see Fig. 9–2. Usually used in target shooting.

   a) Arrow is drawn back directly under chin.

   b) String cuts across the center of chin, lips, and nose.

   c) Thumb is relaxed and close against neck.

   d) Use kisser button or ball of serving on the string at a point above the arrow nock so contact with the lips will result. To ensure consistent movements, button or serving should contact lips at same spot each time. See Fig. 9–3.

3. Methods of aiming (sight, point-of-aim, and instinctive).

 a) *Sight:* most accurate. Sights can be made or bought. To make one, take cork or sponge, adhesive tape, and large-headed pin. Use tongue depressor or popsicle stick for marking the point of aim. (See Fig. 9–4.) Attach cork to bow with adhesive tape; stick pin in cork to left of bow. Experiment at different distances, moving pin until distance can be accurately marked in yardage on the stick. In adjusting a bought sight, move the sight bar in the same direction as the error: If arrow hits high, push the sight up; if arrow is to the right of the target, push the sight in, etc. Either keep both eyes open, or close left eye and use right one to line up the target.

Fig. 9–1 High anchor. Finger braced in corner of mouth to keep draw and aim consistent.

Fig. 9-2 Low anchor. Some hold string slightly to side of center of face; others bring string back to touch center of nose and chin.

Fig. 9-3 Use of button to increase accuracy.

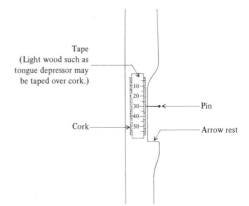

Tape
(Light wood such as
tongue depressor may
be taped over cork.)

Pin

Cork

Arrow rest

Fig. 9-4   Homemade sight for back of bow.

b) *Point-of-aim:* indirect method. Sight with the use of some object, such as golf ball or stick, placed in position on the ground according to the range you are shooting from. In adjusting the marker or the point-of-aim, move it in the direction opposite to that of the error. If the arrow goes high, the point-of-aim should be placed lower or closer to the archer; if the arrow goes to the left of the target, the point-of-aim should be moved to the right, etc. In this method, you are looking at the point-of-aim but seeing the point of the arrow as a secondary object.

c) *Instinctive:* Look at the target and shoot according to visual reckoning rather than lining the target up with something else.

4. Shooting Aids

a) Select a bow that one can handle well (average woman archer will usually use a 32-pound bow, although it may vary from 28–35 lb). Bow length for a woman is usually from 62–64 inches.

b) A nocking point attachment on the bowstring will establish consistency and increase accuracy (this can be made by wrapping the string with 1/2" adhesive tape, or with nylon serving thread). Tape or thread should be wrapped to allow an easy release of the arrow from the string.

c) Foot markers may be used to ensure the same stance each time.

d) A full-length mirror may be used during practice to check archer's form.

e) A kisser button may be used on the string to aid the archer in obtaining the same draw and anchor point each time (button touches lips in same place each time).

f) A click device may be attached to the bow to determine the release point.

g) An arm guard aids in the protection of the forearm and holds the clothing close to the body to prevent arrow being thrown off target.

h) Finger tabs give protection to the fingers and allow the string to slide easily and quickly off the first joint of the fingers.

i) Selection of arrows is very important. Arrows should be rated for "spine" or stiffness of the shaft. Select well constructed arrows of (1) aluminum (the most accurate but also the most expensive), (2) fiberglass (more accurate than wooden arrows), and (3) wooden arrows. Stiffer arrows are needed for heavier bows.

Other Factors

People have won national tournaments and meets by using both the under-the-chin anchor and the corner-of-the-mouth anchor, so you can take your choice. Many think that the under-the-chin anchor is best for long-range shooting and that the corner-of-the-mouth anchor is best for short-range shooting, because of the angle of the arrow at the draw.

Since the arrow leaves the bow on a curved path, the farther the target is away from the archer, the higher she must aim the arrow. It is easier to aim high when you are using the under-the-chin method.

Shooting from a short distance requires that the archer point the arrow straight ahead or even toward the ground. The corner-of-the-mouth position makes this easier and also places the arrow closer to the sighting eye.

Archers who are consistent in their point-of-aim, their draw, and their anchor point often still miss the target because they do not hold their aim steady before the release. For steadiness, keep the left shoulder firm, eliminate creeping, relax the fingertips, use the shoulder and back muscles to keep the tension in the right arm, and hold the aim long enough to get set (4–6 seconds upon full draw). Exercises to build up strength in the arms and shoulders should be used.

Problems	*Corrections and Coaching Hints*
Arrow goes too high. Possible causes: arrow nocked too low, anchor point too low, archer's mouth open.	Place serving on string so arrow may be nocked at right angle to string; adjust anchor point by placing first finger under chin if using low anchor, or index finger to mouth if using high anchor; keep teeth together.
Arrow falls short. Possible causes: underdrawing, creeping, holding aim too long, dropping bow arm, wind blowing toward archer.	Draw arrow completely before release; hold hand steady on anchor point; hold aim just long enough to get set; don't allow bow arm to drop, but keep arm parallel to ground; allow for wind by lifting point-of-aim.
Arrow goes left. Possible causes: anchor hand moving away from face, string hitting clothing or arm, tightening grip on bow too much, hyper-	Keep finger on anchor point; keep hand holding bow relaxed; rotate bow arm so elbow is turned outward; allow for wind blowing from right

extension of bow arm, failure to judge wind, sighting with left eye.

Arrow goes right. Possible causes: relaxing grip on bow too much, lifting of elbow on drawing arm, turning head more than usual, failure to judge wind, bow tilted to right.

side by aiming more to right of target; aim with right eye.

Adjust grip on bow by pointing fingers of bow hand straight toward target. Bow rests on V formed by pointed fingers and thumb; drawing elbow should not be higher than arrow and drawing arm should be parallel to ground; allow for wind blowing from left by aiming more to left of target; keep bow level.

Arrow goes over target. Possible causes: overdrawing, only two fingers of drawing hand on string, leaning away from target, wind coming from behind archer.

Draw arrow back to pile; keep three fingers on string; keep body in alignment, with shoulders level; lower point-of-aim when wind comes from behind.

Hand or forearm is hit by string. Possible causes: hyperextension of wrist of bow arm, allowing upper limb of bow to tilt to left, putting too much pressure on string with first and second fingers.

Keep wrist in straight line with bow arm; keep bow upright; distribute pressure equally among three fingers on string; keep arm on straight line from elbow to nock.

Arrow slides off arrow rest. Possible causes: squeezing the nock, flexion of wrist of drawing arm, pulling bow arm too high.

Relax fingers while holding nock and pulling string for draw; hold wrist in straight line with elbow.

Arrow flies in erratic line. Possible causes: unsteady hand at anchor point, not opening fingers simultaneously to release arrow, too much strain from pull, holding aim too long (which causes drawing arm to shake), unbalanced arrow, torn fletching.

Keep drawing hand steady at anchor point; relax all three fingers simultaneously; release arrow as soon as aim is found; check arrows before shooting them.

String hits wrist. Possible cause: string not tight enough, hyperextension of elbow, improper release.

Check distance between string and braced bow (*fistmele*); this distance should be approximately 6–7 inches. Do not hyperextend elbow and release smoothly.

Inconsistency of results even when all movements up to release of arrow have been correct. Possible causes: poor follow-through; body or bow moves before arrow hits target.

Hold shooting position, with anchor point and stance steady, until arrow hits target.

Going for the bull's eye. (Courtesy of Madison Sports Information.)

Strategy

Strategy in archery is not as complicated as it is in most sports. Mental readiness is important. One must also allow for environmental elements such as wind, sun, and rain. The archer naturally does not have to counteract opponents' moves, but must concentrate only on what *she* must do to get the arrow into the target. She must not worry about her opponent's score or let the opponent's accuracy upset her. The archer who can close out everything from her mind except her own movements and her own score has the battle half won. Concentration is necessary; so is consistency, which depends on concentration.

The archer should remember exactly where she aimed on the previous shot in order to make any needed adjustments for error. Once she decides on her point-of-aim, she must be determined and confident as she shoots. To hesitate is to ask for trouble, because strain in muscles builds up.

Wind is one of the most frustrating factors to an archer, especially at long ranges; if the wind comes in gusts, it is hard to determine how to allow for it. The degree of adjustment depends on the direction and strength of the wind. The archer should make it a point to practice on windy days in order to learn how to allow for the wind.

Some archers prefer to use plastic vanes instead of feather ones when the wind is blowing hard or it is raining. The plastic gives more accuracy, since wind drift is reduced to a minimum and rain does not affect the plastic as much as it does feathers. Because plastic vanes are all identical, the archer does not run the risk of the arrow going off course, which can happen when the feather fletching has become damaged. However, the archer, before using arrows with plastic vanes in competition, should practice with them, since the flight of plastic-vaned arrows differs from that of feather-fletched ones.

BADMINTON

Coaching Emphasis

1. Wrist snap (important for power, speed, and deception).
2. Deepness of forehand and backhand clears as defensive strokes.
3. Accuracy of forehand and backhand drives down the sidelines as offensive strokes.
4. Placement of shuttle for the serve.
5. Power and deception on overheads.
6. Pinpoint accuracy on drop shots.
7. Development of the round-the-head stroke.
8. Strategy.

Mechanics

1. Wrist snap: Cock wrist prior to the hit and then rapidly flex the wrist as the racket contacts the shuttle.
2. Clear: Snap wrist vigorously and shift body weight forward. High, deep clear should be used to allow player time to get back into position, to force opponent back from net, and to allow player to slow the pace when she is tired. As an offensive stroke, the clear follows a path just high enough to go over the opponent's head without allowing her time to drop back into position for the return shot.
3. Drive: Most effective when shuttle is hit at shoulder height, since path of flight should be nearly parallel to floor and as close to top of net as possible. Excellent for quick placement when opponent is out of position, or to draw opponent from side to side. Take care that the shuttle does not rise upward after it passes net; otherwise opponent may have chance to smash it back.
4. Serve
   a) Hold shuttle in same position in relation to the body each time. (The higher the point of contact, the flatter the arc as the shuttle goes over the net. Must be contacted below waist to be legal.)
   b) Cock wrist to same degree each time, allowing for soft touch on short

serve and enough power to execute long serve by a powerful flexing of the wrist.

c) Degree of flexing determines the distance the shuttle will travel; angle of racket head determines trajectory of shuttle flight.

d) Slight rotation of the wrist immediately before contact of racket with shuttle can, with practice, send shuttle to any desired spot on court.

e) Mark off specific areas on the court for player to aim for during practice. Example: Draw a semicircle about a foot in radius in the deep corner of the singles service court on the opponent's backhand side, or a circle with a 6-inch radius for the short serve in the corner of the doubles service box on the opponent's forehand side, etc. (See Fig. 9–5.)

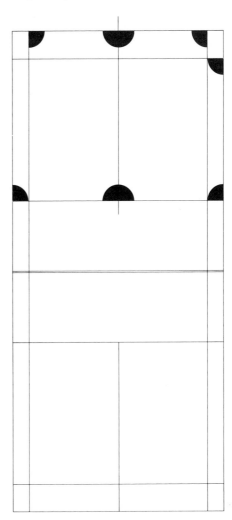

Fig. 9–5 Marked off areas of court for practice in serving singles and doubles.

Problems with Serve	Corrections and Coaching Hints
Short serve: hitting shuttle too high. Possible causes: too much wrist flexion; racket face angled up too much on contact with shuttle.	There is little wrist action on the short serve. When contact is made racket face should be angled to send shuttle just over top of net. Tie a string about 6 inches above the net and practice hitting between net and string.
Short serve: serve goes into net. Possible causes: shuttle drops too low before contact; wrist is extended too much when shuttle is hit.	Racket should contact shuttle just below waistline; *guide* shuttle over net with a gentle flexing of the wrist.
Lack of accuracy. Possible causes: shuttle held at a different position for each serve; racket head angled differently. Increasing or decreasing arm swing.	Use same service position on all serves; racket head should be angled in direction of desired flight. Only difference between one serve and another should be in amount of force applied on contact with shuttle.
Long serve: shuttle doesn't go deep enough. Possible causes: too little power; too little wrist action; failure to follow through; shuttle held too close to body.	Hold shuttle away from body by extending arm; cock wrist and snap it through rapidly on contact; allow natural follow-through by continuing upward swing.
Illegal serve. Possible causes: racket head is above wrist on contact; both feet do not remain on the floor; racket is higher than waist when shuttle is hit.	Swing underhanded rather than sidearm; be sure both feet are in service box; let shuttle drop lower to keep racket head below hand and waist before contact with the shuttle.

5. Smash or overhead. (See Fig. 9–6.)

   a) Use motion similar to the smash in tennis (except that in badminton the wrist does more work).

   b) Bring racket to a position behind head, with wrist cocked.

   c) Allow shuttle to drop slightly in front of body.

   d) Reach up and contact it at its highest possible point, snapping wrist as contact with the shuttle is made and following through.

   e) Make follow-through motion down and across left side of body.

   f) Just before racket contacts shuttle, shift weight from rear to forward foot.

(a)   (b)   (c)

Fig. 9-6 Overhead stroke.

g) Ordinarily, keep feet in contact with floor, even though you rise up on toes to get most height and best body weight shift. However, at times, you may leave the floor just before hit in order to gain more height on the reach, allowing better angle from which to hit shuttle down into opposite court.

Problems on Smash

Corrections and Coaching Hints

Lack of power and speed. Possible causes: body facing net; improper weight shift; feet leaving floor when not necessary; too little wrist action.

Body should be at about a 45-degree angle to net; begin with weight on rear foot and then shift to forward foot, with feet remaining on floor to help in transfer of weight; cock wrist when racket is brought behind head; snap it through as contact is made.

Smash is too flat rather than angled down. Possible causes: shuttle allowed to drop too low; not enough wrist snap; elbow bent when racket contacts shuttle.

Extend arm upward for shuttle; snap wrist to get downward angle; make contact as high as possible.

Smash is hit too deep or flight is too high. Possible causes: shuttle allowed to drop too far behind head; poor positioning of body; late wrist snap.

Get under clear quickly; allow shuttle to drop slightly in front of body. Snap wrist immediately upon contact.

Smash goes into net. Possible causes: shuttle dropping too far in front of the body; hitting at too much of an angle when overhead is taken from deep in the court.

Bring body more directly under the shuttle; when smashing from deep in the court, do not use as much angle; reduce acuteness of wrist snap.

Inaccurate placement. Possible causes: incorrect follow-through; lack of practice.

Allow racket and arm to follow through on left side of body; during practice, concentrate on placing shuttle. Place baskets on court and try to hit into them.

6. Drop shot
   a) After a smash or deep clear, use a drop shot for change of pace or to get opponent off-balance.
   b) You can take a drop shot on forehand or backhand side, with either underhand motion or overhead swing.
   c) Try to make shuttle cross as close as possible to net and then drop vertically on opponent's side.
   d) Generally speaking, use same movement for a drop shot as for a more powerful stroke such as the smash; same backswing, transfer of weight, etc. However, at moment of impact, use little wrist action, so that you hit shuttle softly and it barely goes over the net.
   e) Use delicate touch, with little follow-through.

f) Use deception: a powerful smash or a deep clear one moment, the next moment a drop shot starting with the same motion.

g) When you have an advantage on an angle for placement of a stronger stroke such as the smash, always take the stronger in preference to the slower stroke or drop shot, since a slight inaccuracy can allow opponent time to make the return.

h) Aim drop shot to force opponent to hit up.

i) Use hairpin shot to return drop shot. Effective because opponent has usually taken a couple of steps backward to regain her position in middle of court, and can be caught with her weight moving away from net.

j) When opponent is playing deep, use cross-court drop shots, with shuttle angled from one side of court to the other.

k) Expect drop shot when opponent must run fast to play a short shot that has dropped below the top of the net. Opponent must hit up, forcing her to hit a return drop shot or a deep clear.

Problems with Drop Shot	*Corrections and Coaching Hints*
Lack of deception. Possible cause: player does not go through preliminary motions of a more powerful shot.	Use same backswing, shift of weight, etc., as for a more powerful stroke, differing only in follow-through and in force applied by wrist action.
Shuttle goes into net. Possible causes: shuttle has dropped below top of net before player contacts it; racket not angled up enough to clear net on return; incorrect wrist action and lack of "touch."	Racket face must be angled according to position of shuttle in relation to net; wrist must guide shuttle and stroke must be firm and soft. Touch is developed only through practice.
Shuttle goes too high when crossing net. Possible causes: too much force from wrist; angle of racket face improper with respect to relation of shuttle to net.	Use gentle wrist action and "tap" shuttle over; adjust angle of racket face on contact to send shuttle just over net; very little follow-through. At times, the racket face will "recoil" on contact to take force from hard hit by opponent. Tie string 4–6 inches above net and practice hitting drop shots between string and net.

7. Round-the-head stroke (see Fig. 9–7).
   a) Use this stroke to hit a shuttle on left side of head.
   b) Bring racket back behind head with elbow bent and wrist turned to allow contact on forehand face of racket.

Fig. 9–7   Round-the-head stroke.

c) Stroke forward, with forearm brushing top of head.

d) As contact is made with shuttle, extend arm and snap through with wrist.

e) Make slight follow-through, coming down on right side of body.

f) Remember that this stroke is possible only in badminton, because the light-weight racket and shuttle put little strain on arm and body during execution.

g) Use this stroke in place of backhand at times; it allows more power and speed.

h) You should limit your use of this stroke because of weight shift to left, which can leave right side of court open to fast return by opponent.

i) The greater the distance the shuttle is from your left side, the more you must lean to left, keeping weight on left foot.

j) If shuttle is close to left side, you can obtain greater speed and power from the round-the-head stroke than from the backhand stroke. However, if there is time, move under shuttle and hit the smash, since this is an even more forceful shot.

Problems with Round-the-Head Stroke	*Corrections and Coaching Hints*
Lack of power. Possible causes: player keeping elbow bent during stroke; too little wrist action.	Reach up and out, extending arm on stroke; wrist should be cocked and snapped quickly as contact is made.
Shuttle goes into net. Possible causes: letting shuttle drop too low before contact is made; shuttle too far in front of body.	Start stroke sooner; reach for shuttle; position body in line that will allow shuttle to drop to left of head.
Lack of deception. Possible cause: player uses same placement shots, allowing opponent to anticipate stroke.	Cross-court shots should be varied with shots down the sideline and with drop shots.

Strategy

Strategy in badminton is similar to strategy in tennis in the sense that the object is to hit the shuttle where the opponent can't reach it, and to get her moving and off-balance before attempting the put-away shot. Especially in playing singles, it takes a lot of patience to keep the shuttle in play until the opponent makes a weak return.

However, too much aggressiveness can pull the player out of position and leave part of the court open. Hitting the shuttle away from the opponent or to a place where there is a large unprotected area can be effective, since the opponent must move to get to the shuttle. Most players can't hit as well on the move as they can from a stationary position, so placing the shuttle can force the opponent into errors.

Learn to use a variety of shots. A clear, followed by a drop shot or a smash—or a combination of drives, clears, smashes, drop shots, and sharply angled cross-court shots—can thoroughly confuse the opponent. In badminton, variety of shots and the ability to think while moving is as necessary as speed and quick reflexes.

Strategy for Singles

Serving

In singles, the serve must either be short and low, or high and deep. To keep the opponent from gaining an advantage that would allow her to go on the attack, the deep serve is usually used. The deep serve forces the receiver back, and, if placed properly, is very hard for the opponent to smash. The receiver usually has to use a defensive stroke such as the clear to return the well-placed deep serve.

The short serve should be used as a change of pace to keep the receiver honest, and is effective against a player who is slow or who has shifted her weight backward in anticipation of the deep serve. A short serve that is too high or a deep serve that is too short is disastrous.

Server's Position and Placement

When serving, stand approximately 4 feet from the short service line, and near the center line. This distance may be varied according to the height and speed of the server and her ability to cover the court. After serving, and after the return of shots, move to the approximate center of the court, since this puts you in the best place to cover all possible shots. (This position should be slightly closer to the net than the exact center, since clears must cover a greater distance than drop shots; this gives the player a little more time to move back than to go forward.) This center position may vary about a foot on each side of the center line, according to the possible angles of the opponent's return.

The best placement for the serve is to a deep corner of the service box; best of all is a serve that is high and deep and near the center line, because this cuts down the angle of the opponent's return. If, after serving, you return to your defensive position in the middle of the court, the only way the receiver can pass you on the return of a long serve at the center line is to try to get the shuttle down one of the sidelines. However, if you are alert, you can easily intercept any sideline passing shot. A serve to the sideline corner rather than to the center-line corner allows the receiver a greater angle for her return, since she may return it down the sideline or cross-court. (See Fig. 9–8.)

In any situation in which you have sent the shuttle to the sideline corner, wait about a foot to the side of the center line in the direction of the shuttle in

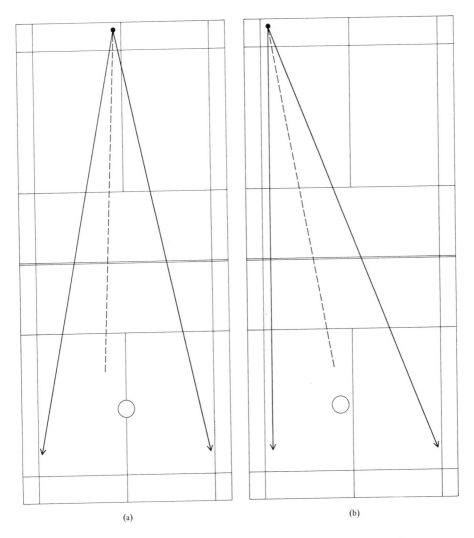

(a) (b)

Fig. 9–8 Angles of return on the serve. (a) Placing the serve deep and to the center line makes possible the angle shot to either side. If server moves into position correctly in middle of court, she should be able to cut off either of these returns. (b) Placing the serve deep but to the sideline makes possible a cross-court or a sideline return. The server must move slightly toward the sideline to cut off the shortest return down the sideline.

order to reach the shortest-angled shot, which would be the return down the sideline. If she were to send it back with a cross-court shot, the shuttle would have to travel a greater distance, and this would give you more time to move across court to cut off the return.

Receiver's Position

If you are the receiver, wait for the serve about 5 feet behind the short service line. Your position in relation to the center line depends on which service court you are in. When possible, take a position that will enable you to take the shot on your forehand side and which will allow you a slight advantage in being able to get into position for the deep serve to the center line corner. If you are receiving in the right-hand court, stand near the center line; if in the left-hand court, stand about 3 feet from the center line. However, be careful not to overplay.

When you are the receiver, you must be able to anticipate the direction of the serve, but not move before the shuttle has been hit, because the server may detect the shift in your weight and place the shuttle accordingly. Since the long, deep serve is most often used in singles, you must be prepared for this type of serve without putting yourself at a disadvantage if the serve goes short instead.

Keeping the body weight low, with one foot forward, and the weight evenly balanced will help you get a good push-off in either direction. Once you have determined the direction of the shuttle, you must get into position at once, arriving within hitting range before it can drop. If you can move quickly and get into position, you have a chance to smash the service return, although most returns are clears or drops. Learning to move backward, sideward, and forward at full speed and then coming to a controlled stop is a must for the skilled player. Once the serve has been hit, the receiver must move quickly back to the center of the court.

General Strategy

Some good returns of the high serve are: a drop shot just over the net but to the center of the court (to cut down the possible angle of return), a clear to the opponent's backhand, or a smash. One of the best returns on a short serve is a high clear, deep into the backcourt, preferably to the backhand of the opponent, or a drop shot if she has already started moving back and you see her shift her weight backward.

Strategy in badminton is a little like strategy in chess: you plan a couple of shots ahead and try to get your opponent to move and react to your advantage. Many players tire if the opponent runs them constantly, and begin to make errors as a result of fatigue. Others can't hit the shuttle as well moving backward as forward, or vice versa. Others have one definite weakness such as inability to handle a drop shot to the backhand. You must pick out these weaknesses and incorporate them into a plan to attack. For every shot that is sent across the net, there are specific angles of return open to the opponent, so you should overplay slightly in the direction of these hits in order to cut down the angle of return as much as possible. When the shuttle is close to the net and near the sideline, the opponent has the widest possible angle for her return, while shots in the center of the court allow the smallest angles of return. Ordinarily, when you must play a shot that has been hit down your sideline, your best return is back down the opponent's sideline on the same side of the court, because the shuttle takes less time to travel on this straight path than it would cross-court. When you must come in close to the net to play a shuttle, a high clear deep in the opponent's court is usually the safest, although a hairpin drop shot, well placed, can often catch the opponent asleep. Drop shots are always effective when the opponent has been forced back to her endline or is off-balanced. Cross-court shots are effective if the opponent has been pulled out of position toward the sideline, or has started her move toward the sideline to cut off a possible sideline shot.

If you can get your opponent moving from side to side, and then place a shot to the side she has just left, you can usually catch her moving in the wrong direction. Because of the speed of a smash, cross-court smashes are always effective. A drop shot as a return to a smash from deep in the court is also a good shot. Always try to get into good position before hitting the shuttle, rather than trying to reach back for a shuttle that has dropped behind your head, or that has fallen too far in front of your body.

Strategy for Doubles

Serving

A good doubles team must have an accurate serving game because every shot that enables the opponents to hit downward gives them a definite advantage. In doubles, because of the shorter service courts, the deep serve is more dangerous to the serving side than the short one. The short serve to either corner is better than the long one. A serve that is short and near the center line is the best, because it allows less angle for the opponents' return. The player serving should stand about a foot back of the short service line and approximately 3 feet to the side of the center line.

Sometimes the server can gain an advantage by hitting the shuttle toward either shoulder of the receiver. The receiver will react by reflex; her most natural movement is to lift her racket at an angle that returns the shuttle cross-court, which server and partner should anticipate. As a result, the return will often go out-of-bounds or to one of the waiting players [3].

If the receivers are moving forward on each serve because they are expecting the short serve, use the long serve as a change of pace. In this case, if you are serving into the right service court, the long serve toward the center line is best. If you are serving into the left service court, the long serve toward the sideline will place the serve to the opponent's backhand. However, the return down the sideline should be anticipated.

Receiving

The receiving position in doubles depends on the speed and height of the receiver, although most women prefer to stand approximately 3 feet behind the short service line. The receiver has a definite advantage if she can rush the net on the short serve and make contact with the shuttle while it is still above net height, because this enables her to hit downward.

The whole objective in doubles is to gain an advantage so that the team can go on the attack. When a team can hit downward on the shuttle or when they have the opponents working defensively to keep the shuttle in play, they are the offensive or attacking team. A team that must hit the shuttle upward or return shuttles weakly as a result of poor positioning is considered to be on defense.

You gain an advantage by hitting the shuttle as soon as possible, both because you may hit it before it drops below the level of the net and because the sooner it is hit, the less time the opponents will have to get ready for the return. One of the best times for starting an attack is when the serve is received. The reason is that all serves must go slightly upward in order to clear the net, since the racket head must be kept below the waist and wrist until contact is made on the serve. Once a team goes on attack, they must keep their opponents under pressure and on defense until the point has been won. You can do this only by using speed, deceptive techniques, and accurate placement of shots through a variety of angles.

Placement

In doubles, the three important weapons are the smash, the clear, and the drop shot. Placement depends on the opponents' weaknesses and methods of play. Sometimes a shot placed directly between the opponents creates confusion as to who should hit it. Some teams have trouble with sideline shots or shots hit directly at them. Often a smash hit at the body of an opponent will result in a weak return because she can't move out of the way quickly enough and must hit with her arm and swing cramped. Any shot hit at the feet of the opponent is hard to return, especially if she is moving forward or backward at the time.

Systems of Play

The best defensive formation for doubles is usually side-by-side. On offense, a team can usually attack better with one up and one back, but the system of play depends on the personnel. There are four different systems commonly used in doubles. Two of these—the parallel and the up and back—are fairly simple and are usually used by beginners, while the other two—the diagonal and the rotation—are more complicated and are usually only used by highly skilled players. (The players usually slide in and out of the side-by-side system as they go from defense to offense, while using the diagonal, the up and back, or the rotation systems.) The advantages and disadvantages of the four systems of play for doubles are as follows:

1. *Parallel.* Easy system to understand, but some confusion may result when shuttle is hit between the two players. Agree beforehand that all shots in the middle will be taken by the girl on the left, since she will be able to use her forehand. Both girls must cover full length of the court, which means that both girls must have a variety of shots and be capable of moving well. If one girl is weaker than the other, a team will "play" that one girl, creating a game of singles against two opponents.

2. *Up and Back.* Weak when used by players on the defensive, since it leaves much of the side area uncovered. Also poor system when the weaker player is forced to take the back position. Good system for cutting off weak returns at the net, and for getting sharply angled shots.

3. *Diagonal.* Allows for protection against clears to the deep backhand corner, especially if the team consists of one right-handed player and one left-handed player; however, leaves the left-hand corner near the net open for drop shots, and the right-hand deep corner fairly open for well-placed clears. At times the weaker player may end up playing the backhand clears.

4. *Rotation.* Difficult and complicated to execute properly, especially if a team is made up of one right-handed player and one left-handed player. The players are continually moving and thus can move into their shots, using their forehands to best advantage. Demands that both players do a great degree of running and react smoothly as a unit. Leaves some areas open and vulnerable.

In the parallel system, each girl covers one half of the court, the division line being the center line. The girl on the left takes all shots hit down the middle, since it is her forehand, and each girl must cover all deep and short shots on her half of the court.

In the up-and-back system, one player must cover approximately one-third of the court from the net back to the short service line (sideline to sideline) and the other player must cover the rear two-thirds of the court. The player at the net sets up in the middle of the court just inside the short service line (heels usually on this line), while the girl in the back of the court positions herself about 5 feet inside the back boundary line, also in the center of the court. Who plays the net position and who plays the deep position is determined in three ways: (1) The server becomes the front player while her partner becomes the back player. Then, when the team receives, the receiver becomes the front player and her partner plays the back. (2) When serving, the girl serving is the front player and her partner the back player. But when they receive, the type of serve sent over by the opponents determines who goes up and who goes back. On short serves, the receiver becomes the front player and her partner drops to the back; however, if the serve is long, the receiver becomes the back player and her partner must come up to the net. (3) If one player is stronger than the other, she takes the back position at the first possible moment, while her partner plays at the net. (See Fig. 9-9.)

In using the diagonal system, a team combines the parallel and the up-and-back methods. An imaginary diagonal line separates the court. This line runs from about six feet from the back boundary line (right-hand court) to a point at which the short service line and the left sideline meet. The girl playing the right-hand court must take all shots along the net and down most of the right sideline, while her partner playing on the left must handle shots along all of the back boundary line and down most of the left sideline. This system is much easier if the team happens to be made up of one girl who is right-handed and one who is left-handed. In the unlikely event that both players are left-handed, the imaginary

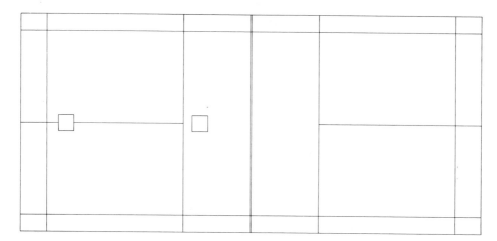

Fig. 9-9 Playing up and back in doubles.

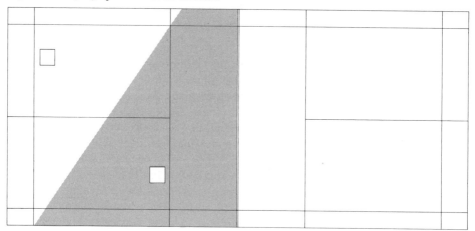

Fig. 9-10 Diagonal positioning in doubles.

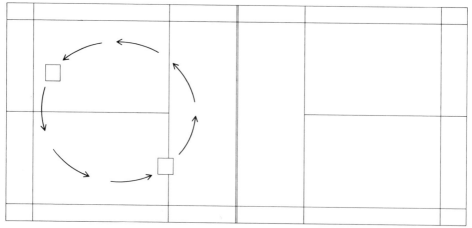

Fig. 9-11 Rotation method.

diagonal line would run from right to left. When both players are equally skilled, whoever is in the right area covers that area, while the other one takes the left. However, if a team has one strong player, the better player should take the left diagonal whenever possible in order to return the backhand shots more effectively. (See Fig. 9-10.)

Probably the hardest system of doubles play to understand and execute is the rotation or revolving method. It is a modification of the diagonal system, and involves coverage of the two areas while players are moving in a counterclockwise direction. This rotation evolves from a side-by-side defensive position to a one-up-one-back position when advantageous on offense. The player on the right covers short shots, while the player on the left covers deep shots. The position of the player on the right-hand side of the court is usually about two feet closer to the net than that of the player on the left-hand side: this makes it easier for the right-hand player to take all drop shots. Ordinarily, the player on the right-hand side does not back up more than one step to hit an opponent's shot. Instead, the player on the left will come over to take the shot on her forehand side, while her partner moves over to the left-hand side position. When the player on the right-hand side must move over to take a shot at the net in the left corner, her partner moves over to the right side and replaces her in the right-hand net position. As soon as the first girl makes her return, she drops back to the left-hand corner. If both players were left-handed, the movements would be made in a clockwise direction, to allow them to use their forehands to the best advantage. If the team were to consist of one right-handed and one left-handed player, it would be very hard to use this system effectively. (See Fig. 9-11.)

BOWLING

Coaching Emphasis

1. Perfection of timing and balance.
2. Accuracy in picking up spares.
3. Consistency in scoring.
4. Working within established patterns of movement that bowler already has.

Mechanics

1. Timing
   a) Remember that timing depends on coordination of arm swing and steps.
   b) Check a bowler's timing by standing to side and watching ball and feet of bowler.
   c) In four-step approach, if ball isn't back to left foot on second step, ball will go into backswing late. Bowler will have to cut backswing short or slow down approach during last two steps to allow ball to catch up.

Correction: (1) start ball higher to gain momentum for swing, or (2) hold ball lower to give it a head start on the first step.

d) If ball has gone past left foot on second step, ball will go into backswing too early, causing bowler to hesitate at top of backswing or to carry the ball back too high on backswing to allow feet to catch up. Correction: (1) lift ball slightly on first step so fall won't start until second step, or (2) hold ball closer to body so there will be less momentum on the downswing.

e) Speed of approach can be controlled by pushaway. For a slower approach: (1) hold ball lower, (2) hold ball out farther from body, or (3) step before starting the pushaway. For a faster approach: (1) hold ball higher, (2) hold ball closer to body, or (3) start pushaway before first step.

f) Let your sliding foot stop just before the lift.

2. Method of aim

a) Avoid changing from pin bowling to spot bowling or line bowling indiscriminately; choose one method and stick to it.

b) Spot bowling seems easier to most bowlers, because the spot they are aiming for is closer to them. Advanced bowlers usually select a specific board to roll their ball over (anywhere from 8-12 boards in from the gutter, depending on the type of ball thrown and the speed of the lane).

c) Regardless of the method of aim, concentration is necessary.

3. Picking up spares

a) Principles of angle and ball roll are important.

b) Pin movement is based on force and angle of ball when contact is made: (1) If you hit pin dead-center, it goes straight backward. (2) If you hit pin on side, it moves diagonally and backward. (3) If you barely touch pin on side, it moves to opposite side with very little backward movement.

c) Movement of ball depends on its weight and the speed it has been thrown: (1) The heavier the ball and the faster it has been thrown, the less it deviates from its path when it makes contact with pins. (2) Given equal force, the path of a heavy ball varies less than that of a light ball. (3) A fast ball is deflected less than a slow ball. Therefore a bowler should select a heavy ball that she can throw with a reasonable amount of speed.

d) To increase pin action, approach should allow ball to roll toward pins from as great an angle as possible.

e) When pins are left on a side, the ball should be rolled from opposite side to allow more alley for error and to increase angle at impact.

f) If only one pin is left, aim ball at center of pin to allow for slight error to either side.

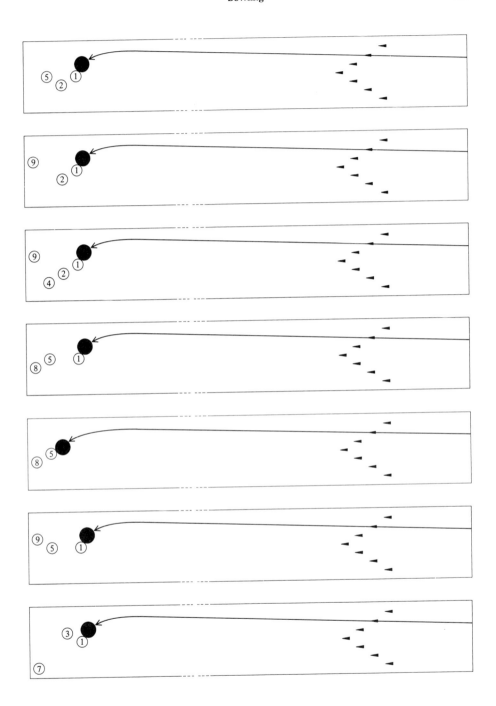

Fig. 9-12 Angles of picking up spares with hook ball. (a) Pins can be knocked down by hitting 1–3 pocket.

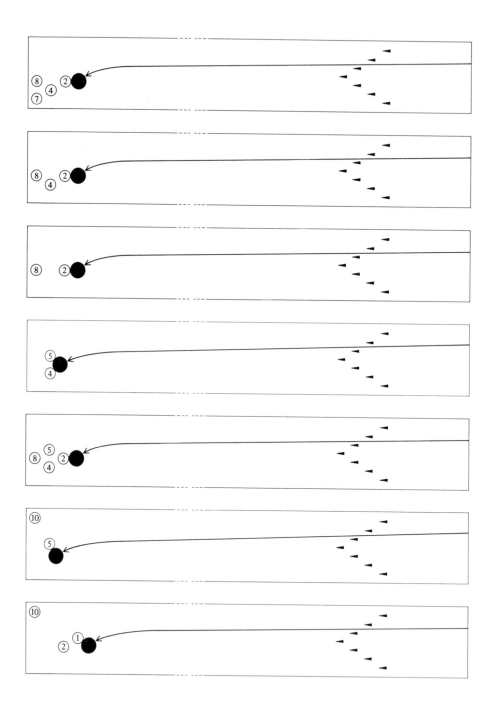

Fig. 9–12 (b)   Pins can be knocked down by hitting 1–2 pocket.

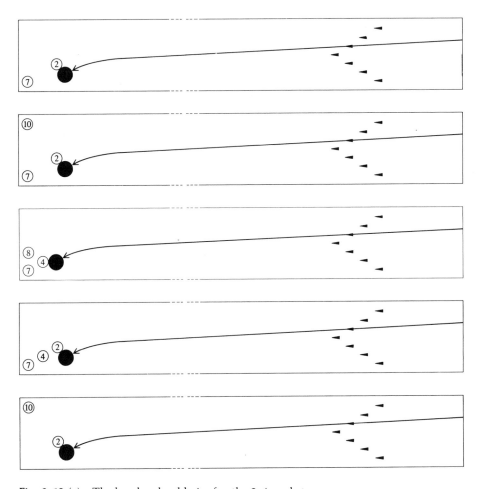

Fig. 9–12 (c) The bowler should aim for the 2–4 pocket.

g) To pick up sleeper (one pin directly behind another pin), aim ball at center of first pin to force it straight back into second pin.

h) When several pins are left standing, use the principles of force and angle to deflect the first pin so that it will hit into the other pins.

i) See Fig. 9-12 (a–e) for angle in picking up spares. Keep in mind that this angle will vary slightly depending on the type of ball being thrown.

j) If you are using the heaviest ball you are capable of controlling but can't get enough speed to knock pins down after hitting in pocket, you can increase speed of ball by: (1) holding ball higher to gain more momentum on swing, (2) using more pushaway, (3) taking ball higher on backswing (up to shoulder level), and (4) improving timing on footwork and swing.

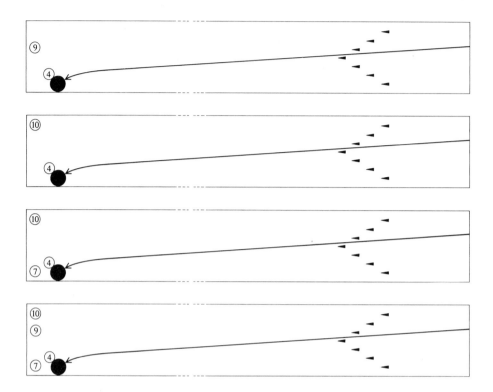

Fig. 9-12 (d)   The bowler should aim for the 4-7 pocket.

4. Grips

    a) *Hook ball.*   The V between thumb and first finger does not rotate. The thumb points toward 9 o'clock and fingers toward 2 o'clock position (some prefer to place thumb at the 10 o'clock position). Thumb comes out first; then, as fingers come out, the ball is lifted and a counter-clockwise spin is created (when bowler is right-handed). Wrist should not be turned to get spin; spin will automatically result if bowler has correct grip on ball.

    b) *Curve ball.*   Grip is the same as for hook ball, but a greater arc is obtained by rotating hand and wrist from right to left as ball is released. On the curve ball, the turn or lift should not be started until ball has passed left foot at foul line.

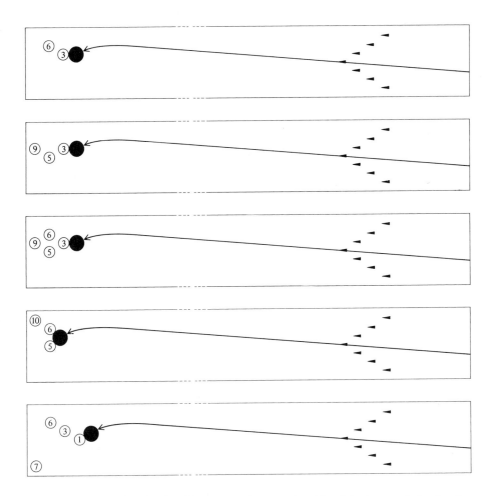

Fig. 9-12 (e) The bowler should move to the opposite side of the lane and aim for the 1-3 pocket.

c) See Fig. 9-13 for the stance, approach, and roll of the ball for the straight, hook, and curve ball. Note that this figure shows the straight approach and an approach with a "drift." The "drift" is not usually taught, although some prefer this type of approach because in some cases it allows an easier arm swing. Also, keep in mind that the stance, approach, and ball roll shown in Fig. 9-13 vary according to individual preference, spin on the ball, and the conditions of the lane.

d) Back-up ball is not recommended since the angle of entry into the 1-3 pocket forces the ball away from the strike impact points.

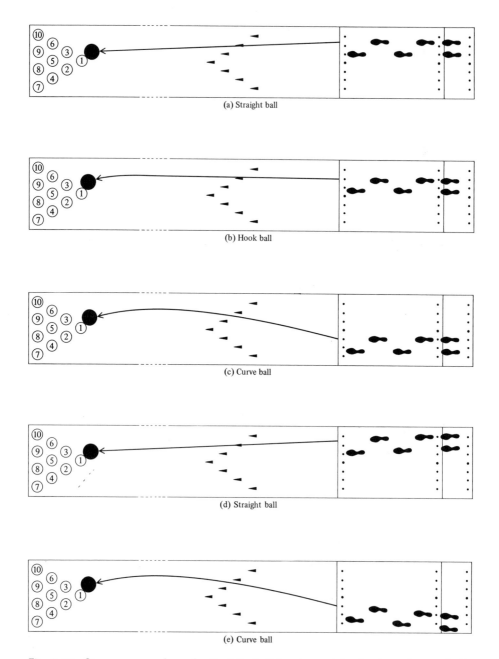

(a) Straight ball

(b) Hook ball

(c) Curve ball

(d) Straight ball

(e) Curve ball

Fig. 9-13 Stance, approach, and roll of the ball for the straight, hook, and curve ball. Parts (a), (b), and (c) show a straight approach. Parts (d) and (e) show a slant approach.

Problems	Corrections and Coaching Hints
One shoulder ahead of the other. Possible results: sidearm motion; ball being angled off to side.	Start approach with both shoulders parallel, facing pins. Check this position after delivery to see if parallel position has been maintained.
Uneven approach. Possible cause: first step taken out to side of approach line.	Concentrate on first step. Point toe toward approach line. Place piece of tape on floor where first step should be taken.
Sidearm swing. Possible cause: right shoulder behind left shoulder; ball held too far to left before approach is started; arm too far from body on the swing.	Keep head, shoulders, and body in straight line; hold ball more to right to allow swing to go straight backward; swing arm close to hip.
Backswing too high. Possible cause: incorrect pushaway. Results: too much speed, poor timing, and inaccuracy because of lack of control.	Don't force ball down alley in attempt to get more speed; hold ball closer to body; shorten pushaway.
Not enough backswing. Possible cause: incorrect pushaway. Results: lack of speed, little pin action, poor timing.	Hold ball higher; push ball out more on pushaway.
Lack of smooth movements at foul line. Possible causes: lack of balance or poor timing. Results: inaccuracy; too much spin.	Make slide smoothly, with weight balanced on left foot; don't apply turn until ball has passed left foot (curve ball); check grip before starting approach.
Wrong position during follow-through. Possible causes: right foot may be too far to side; hand may not be pointing toward pins. Result: poor balance.	Balance weight on left foot; point left toe toward pins; keep shoulders squared to foul line; right leg should be back, right arm and hand extended toward pins.
Releasing ball too soon. Results: lack of speed, lack of control, hard bounce.	Take ball past left foot before release; pick out spot a few inches past foul line and "reach" out toward spot before release.
Releasing ball too late. Possible cause: weight staying on rear foot. Results: "lobbing" of ball and lack of control.	Balance body weight over sliding foot; bend from the waist; release ball when it is just past the left foot.

Poor timing. Possible causes: footwork too fast or too slow; backswing too low or too high; first step too long or too short; approach too fast; skip part of approach.

Take deliberate steps; build up speed slowly; if backswing is too low, use more pushaway; if backswing is too high, keep ball in closer to body.

Inconsistency in movements. Possible causes: failure to start from same position each time; holding ball too far to left side of body; lack of pendulum swing; incorrect pushaway.

Line up the same each time for the first ball; hold ball at center of body or to right side before pushaway; take ball straight back and straight forward; push ball away before first step in three-step approach; push ball away on first step in four-step approach.

Pins are left because of poor pin action. Possible causes: ball rolled with too much speed or too slowly; too much skid or slide on the ball, pocket not hit correctly.

For more speed, increase pushaway to gain height on backswing and momentum on approach; if ball is too fast, keep pushaway close to body, and use a shorter approach or a heavier ball; try to get more lift and follow-through with hand toward pins.

Strategy

Strategy in bowling involves using a point of aim, understanding angle and force, consistency in picking up spares, ability to adjust to differences in lanes, and mental readiness, especially when pressure is present. Mental readiness consists of concentration and self-confidence, as well as the ability to adjust the point of aim until accuracy is obtained.

Pressure affects different people in different ways. If you are usually a relaxed bowler, you should be aware that you are feeling pressure when you begin to feel tense and your muscles tighten up. If you usually take your time and do everything deliberately, you are feeling the pressure when you begin to lose your concentration and vary your pattern of execution. Pressure especially affects the bowler who does not have self-confidence and determination. This type of person can cope with tension only by re-evaluating and accepting her own skills.

The most tension-prone person is the one who has had no competitive experience and who is not prepared for the pressures of competition. The only way she can cope with the pressure is to enter into competition every chance she gets, until she knows what to expect. The inconsistent bowler, because she must push herself to maintain a high score, also feels the pressure of competition.

Reasonable goals and concentration on the game, however, can lead to a relaxed competitor. The athlete prone to pressure should compete only against her own score and not that of an opponent. It goes without saying that there is no substitute for practice.

GOLF

Coaching Emphasis

1. Perfecting swing for accuracy and power.
2. Changing grip for deliberate slice or hook.
3. Hitting effectively out of poor lies.
4. Putting and reading greens accurately.

Mechanics

1. Swinging for accuracy
   a) Work to "groove" swing, so that movements are same each time.
   b) Check grip, stance, weight shift, swing, etc., to see that you do them consistently.
   c) Concentrate on hitting ball to a specific spot each time.
2. Swinging for power
   a) Remember that power depends on position of ball in relation to feet, leverage applied on swing, and timing on wrist snap.
   b) For woods and long irons, play ball opposite left heel; for medium irons, center it between feet; for height and less roll (usually short-iron shots), play ball farther back toward right heel.
   c) The more power you want, the more you should move ball toward forward foot and the wider the base of support should be (feet should seldom be farther apart than shoulder width).
   d) In the complete motion of the swing ("waggle," forward press, backswing, downswing, and follow-through), when you want extra distance, concentrate on two phases: (1) bracing or pushing with legs, and (2) good wrist action at right time.
   e) For proper leg action, shift weight to rear leg on backswing, then to forward or left leg on downswing. Just before contact, complete shift by pushing strongly against ground with toes of right foot, giving more power from legs.
   f) For proper wrist action, cock wrists on backswing. For maximum power, uncock them in the hitting area, just before actual contact with the ball.

Problems in Getting Distance	*Corrections and Coaching Hints*
Shifting weight to forward leg on backswing. Causes: trying to keep head too steady; moving body forward as club goes backward.	Shift weight and turn in same direction as club moves on backswing; rear or right foot should "press" against ground as you shift weight.
Body sways slightly. Cause: improper body turn of shoulder and hips. Results: less than maximum use of muscles in back and left side.	Maintain address position, but backswing should result in a coil or turn of the body. This turning should stretch muscles of the left side. In practicing, turn back to sun and watch shadow to see if body sways as you make backswing.
Left arm bent, right arm not cocked at start of downswing. Results: Poor use of muscles on left side of body; straightening of arm on start of downswing, which may lead to uncocking of wrists before getting to hitting area.	Shift body weight to forward foot immediately at start of downswing; move right elbow in close to side. Keep left arm firm and straight. Strengthen left arm by practicing backswing with club in left hand only.
Lifting up in hitting area. Cause: improper weight shift; uncocking wrists too soon; straightening legs.	Weight shift must come on downswing; do not uncock wrists until they enter hitting area; hit down and through the ball; flex legs until the follow-through.

3. Hitting the slice
   a) Slices are caused by: (1) hitting ball with an "open" club face, and (2) hitting ball on an outside-to-inside path.
   b) For deliberate slice, change grip. This "weak" grip consists of turning one or both hands too far to the left of the shaft. Usually, in a normal grip, you can see two or three knuckles of left hand, and one on right hand. However, in slicer's grip, only one knuckle shows on left hand and two or more on right hand. (See Fig. 9-14 for slice grip.)
   c) In slicer's grip, the V of right hand points toward chin, or even toward left shoulder (in normal grip, it usually points toward right shoulder).
   d) As a result of this grip, wrists turn to right at start of backswing, opening club face; almost impossible to turn club face to a square position for the hit.
   e) Stance is open; right foot is approximately three inches ahead of left foot; this forces club head to start back outside line of flight, helping to produce spin needed for slice.

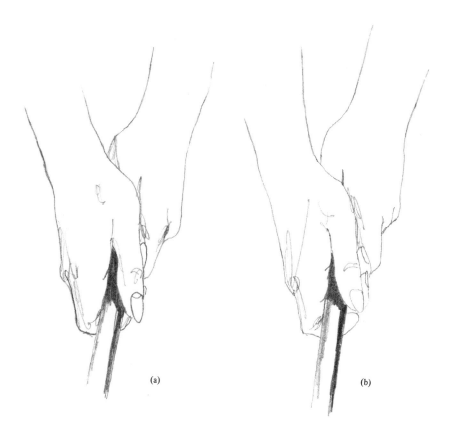

(a)

(b)

Fig. 9-14 Slicer's grip and normal grip. (a) Weak position of hands, which leads to slice. (b) Grip corrected to eliminate slice.

f) Sometimes people slice unintentionally; see helpful hints below.

Problems in Eliminating Slice

Slice as result of weak grip. Causes: incorrect grip; hands too far to left on shaft.

Slice as result of open stance. Result: club face goes back outside intended line of flight.

Corrections and Coaching Hints

You should be able to see 2 or 3 knuckles on left hand, and 1 on right hand. V should point toward right shoulder. Make grip stronger by turning hands more to right of shaft.

Use a square stance, with shoulders and hips square and on line with target.

Slice as result of swaying. Causes: too much weight shift to right foot, making it almost impossible to return weight to left foot on downswing. Results: an open club face or an outside-in swing.

Keep right leg firm, and turn hips on backswing; transfer weight to left leg on downswing.

Hands too far ahead of club face before contact. Causes: hips leading too much; failure to uncock wrists soon enough. Result: open club face at impact.

When hands have passed shoulder height on downswing, accelerate club head; uncock wrists immediately before contact. Shift weight properly to get right hip movement.

4. Hitting the hook
   a) Use hooks to get ball around dog-leg or other obstacle on left.
   b) Hooks are caused by: (1) hitting ball with closed club face, and (2) hitting ball on inside-to-outside path.
   c) For deliberate hook, change hands to "strong" position on shaft. Move hands more to right. You should see three or more knuckles on left hand, while back of right hand may be turned so far that no knuckles can be seen. (See Fig. 9–15 for hook grip.)

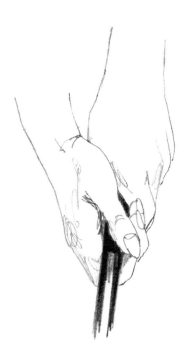

Fig. 9–15   Grip to perform a hood shot.

d) In hook grip, the V of right hand will point to right shoulder or even beyond. As result of this grip, club face is closed at top of backswing and at impact.

e) Use closed stance, with right foot about 3 inches behind left foot, forcing club face to start back inside line of flight.

f) On the hit, the wrists pronate; on the follow-through, left palm faces up and right palm down.

g) The hints given below offer some help in getting rid of an unintentional hook.

Problems in Eliminating Hook	*Corrections and Coaching Hints*
Grip too "strong." Cause: hands turned too far to right of shaft.	Turn hands more to left, and grip shaft in palm and fingers. V of right and left hands will point between chin and right shoulder.
Standing too far from ball. Results: hook, as player has to reach out to hit ball, causing club head to go back on an inside path.	Move closer to ball; stand in more upright position. Take club head straight back.
Compensating for hook. Player anticipates hook and aims to right of target. Results: closed stance; club head forced back inside target line.	Use a square stance, with feet, hips, and shoulders parallel with target line; take club head straight back. Practice by placing piece of tape or yardstick on ground lined up with target. Then place feet in line with tape, and make club head follow tape back in straight line.
Lack of firmness with left hand at top of backswing. Results: too much domination of swing by right hand; club face turned to left.	Keep grip firm with left hand; may be necessary to use a shorter backswing. Strengthen left hand by squeezing tennis balls and by isometric exercises.

5. Pushing the ball

   a) Pushing causes ball to go to right of target.

   b) Pushed ball does not have a spin or slice, but is usually result of: (1) incorrect alignment when addressing the ball, (2) club face closed at address or during downswing, (3) lack of hip turn, and (4) overemphasis on keeping head down [7].

   c) After ball has been hit with a fairly square club face, swing is usually inside-out rather than straight.

Problems Causing Pushing of Ball

Corrections and Coaching Hints

Incorrect alignment and aim. Causes: shoulders, hips, and feet are on line to right of target, forcing hands and arms to swing on a path to right of target.

Open stance from previous address, allowing shoulders, hips, and feet to line up with target. Place club down on ground to line up address position if necessary.

Closing club face at address or early in backswing. Causes: golfer "feels" this incorrect club face position during swing. Tries to compensate by opening club face at top of backswing; ends up pushing ball to right.

Be sure club face is square to ball at address, then carry club straight back.

Incomplete body turn. Causes: hip rotation is incorrect. Results: it blocks movement of hands and arms, causing swing to go to right.

Coil hips when turning to left; this allows arms to swing along target line.

Keeping head down too much during follow-through. Result: may force restricted turn of hips and shoulders.

Allow head to move and turn naturally during follow-through. This will let hips and shoulders make a natural turn.

6. Pulling the ball
   a) Causes ball to go to left of target.
   b) Pulled ball goes on a fairly straight line, and is caused by: (1) incorrect coil of body on the backswing, (2) incorrect weight shift, and (3) uncocking of wrists too soon on downswing [7].
   c) After ball has been hit with a fairly square club face, swing is usually outside-in rather than straight.

Problems Causing Pulling of Ball

Corrections and Coaching Hints

Swaying to right on backswing. Possible result: forcing club head outside of target line.

Maintain a fixed point around which you coil body, keeping right leg firm.

Weight does not shift to right side on backswing. Possible result: forces player to fall back on right foot on downswing, causing club head to go outside target line.

Shift weight to right foot on backswing in order to allow proper weight shift to left foot on downswing.

Uncocking wrists too early on downswing. Results: breaks up natural shift of weight to left side, forcing club head outside target line.

Don't rush hit; allow wrists to uncock naturally as they enter hitting area.

Hitting out of a trap. (Courtesy of Madison Sports Information.)

7. Hitting effectively from poor lies

  a) *From sand traps:* Most effective means is explosion shot. Wedge is best club for this shot. Plant feet firmly in sand in an open stance, with ball off left heel. Use swing similar to pitch shot. Club head must not touch sand, should be open for best results in cutting through sand, and squared with target line. Concentrate on spot club will hit sand, hit sand one to two inches behind ball, and continue motion of club until it has cut through sand. Follow-through is important to prevent club head from stopping in sand and leaving ball in trap due to lack of force. If too little sand is taken, ball will go too far. If ball is not buried in sand, regular shot may be used instead of explosion shot.

Problems of Hitting from Sand Traps	*Corrections and Coaching Hints*
Ball still in sand after shot. Causes: taking too much sand; lack of follow-through.	Hit closer to ball; be sure club head comes out of sand on follow-through.

Ball goes too far. Cause: taking too little sand.

Hit at least an inch behind the ball; watch *spot* you are going to hit, rather than ball. If sand is wet, decrease distance between ball and spot of contact with sand.

Ball is topped and knocked deeper into sand. Causes: looking at ball rather than spot behind ball; lifting up on hit.

Concentrate on spot one to two inches behind ball; keep knees flexed; hit down through sand.

Poor balance. Cause: not getting good foothold in sand. Results: club can hit too far behind ball; can hit on top of ball if weight isn't shifted properly.

Move feet around in sand until they are planted firmly.

   b) *From uphill lie:* Ball should be opposite left foot with weight on downhill leg. Club should follow slope of hill on backswing and follow-through. Hook or pull usually results from weight being concentrated on rear foot, so aim ball to right of target. More height and less distance will also result, so use a lower-numbered club than usual. If you cannot shift weight normally, choke up slightly on grip, take a shorter backswing, and pivot less than usual.

   c) *From downhill lie:* Ball should be opposite uphill or right foot, with weight on downhill foot. Slice or push shot usually results from weight shift to downhill foot too early in swing, so aim ball to left of target. Open stance slightly, with swing following slope of hill. If possible, shift some weight to uphill foot on backswing. Ball will fly lower than usual and roll farther, so higher-numbered club should be used to get more height on ball.

   d) *From side-hill lie:* Swing depends on whether ball is lower or higher than feet. In either case, ball is usually positioned in center of stance, so use a square stance. If ball is above feet, flex knees slightly, keep weight on balls of feet, and choke up on club (ball is closer to body than usual). Hook usually results, so aim to right of target. If ball is below feet, flex knees and keep weight more on heels to prevent too much lean forward. You may need to widen stance to help balance. Use lower-numbered club and three-quarter swing to compensate for need to reach more for ball. Slice or push usually results, so aim to left of target.

  8. Putting

   a) Method of putting varies according to personal preference and comfort.

   b) You can use hinge swing (wrist action) or pendulum swing (arm action).

   c) Bring club face back with left hand square to putting line; keep club face as low and close to ground as possible. Then bring club face straight through ball and follow predetermined line of putt.

Lining up a putt. (Courtesy of Madison Sports Information.)

d) When you stroke a putt, you keep club face in contact with ball longer than you do when you tap a ball, so this usually gives you greater accuracy.

e) Place ball off toe of forward foot with head over ball. Ball placement, stance, and head and body position vary greatly with different golfers. Consistency is the key.

f) Reading the green is an important part of putting. (See Strategy for information on this.)

Strategy

The golfer does not have to counteract her opponent's moves, as one does in team sports, but must be able to react to the golf course, environment, and opponents' shots in a confident and a controlled manner.

Reaction to pressure. Many golfers, although they do well during practice rounds, score higher in a tournament because they can't handle pressure. Strategy in golf demands control of the emotions.

On the tee, in the rough, and on the putting green: these are three places where pressure becomes particularly intense, usually because the player lacks confidence in his or her ability to hit the ball to a specific area (such as down a narrow fairway), or feels anxiety when faced with an unusual situation, such as a bad lie in the rough.

Relating the unusual situation to a common one can often relieve the tension. For instance, a golfer can form a mental picture of a green in the middle of a narrow fairway and aim for the middle of the "green," rather than thinking about the hazards of the fairway. It also gives the player more confidence to select a club she knows she can control even though she may not get as much distance on the shot with this club as with another.

On the green, the same principle can be applied if the golfer forms a mental image of the hole as being the center of a larger area about the size of a bucket. Aiming for the "bucket" rather than for a small hole gives the player confidence, and takes her close enough to the hole to make the second putt effective even if the first does not go in. Another image frequently used by golfers is an imaginary line or path about an inch wide that goes from the ball to the cup; the player tries to roll the ball down this imagined line.

Hitting from the rough.   When playing the ball from the rough, a person's first objective should be to get out of the rough and back on the fairway. The second objective is as much *distance* as possible. The player should select a club that she knows will take the ball out of the rough, regardless of the distance that must be sacrificed. In thick rough, a lofted club should be used. If there are overhead obstacles such as tree limbs, a lower-numbered club should be used to keep the flight low.

When playing the ball, the player should take everything into consideration: the wind, the terrain, the hazards, the distance, the best position to land if a second shot must be taken, the skill of the player making the shot, etc. The player should take risks only when the circumstances justify it.

Placement of shots.   The golfer should cultivate the habit of thinking positively, and of visualizing the shot she wants to make. On long shots, she has a better chance if she aims for the center of the green rather than for the pin, since a slight error can result in the golfer missing the green if the pin has been placed to the side. On close shots, she should aim for the pin, but play toward the low side of the hole if the green is not level.

She should aim the ball short if the hazards are behind the green, and long if the hazards are in front of the green. She should select a club that will give the desired distance without her having to overswing.

Hazards present a special problem, not only in concentration and confidence, but in club selection. If the hazard is close, players should select a club that will give adequate distance and enough loaf to send the ball over safely. If the player is not sure she can hit the ball far enough to clear the hazard, she should play the first shot to the front of the hazard so that the second shot can clear it.

When a golfer is approaching a green which has no hazards in front of it, she should use a lower-numbered iron for a pitch-and-run shot. She should aim the ball at the edge of the green and allow it to roll toward the cup. The wetness of the green determines the amount of roll obtained; a dry green gives the ball a faster and longer roll than a wet one.

Playing the grain and slopes.   The speed of the roll for pitch shots and putts is also determined by the type of grass growing on the green. Most courses in the southern and southwestern states use Bermuda grass, which gives a very slow-rolling surface. Courses in the east, midwest, and along the west coast mainly use bent grass. Bent grass allows the ball to roll fairly fast, since its blades are narrow [31].

Another factor in the roll of the ball is the direction of the grain of the grass. If the grain goes toward the cup, the ball rolls faster than it does when the grain is going away from the cup.

You should stroke the ball with less force when you are putting with the grain, and stroke it harder when you are putting against the grain. To determine the grain: (1) look at the edge of the cup, (2) look at the fringe of the green, and/or (3) look at the reflection of the sun on the green. Inspect the cup for an area that is ragged-looking, and then stand on that side and look across the cup. You will then be looking into the grain. You may also rub your hand over the grass at the fringe of the green to determine the grain, since all the grain on the green usually runs in the same direction. The easiest method is probably to look for a reflection of the sun off the grass. You can detect more of a sparkle or a shine when the grain is running in the same direction you are facing.

Before you putt, look at the ground and try to determine whether there are any rough spots or divots that need to be repaired. Also check the cup for any rough edges. If there are spots that can't be repaired, stroke the ball a little harder than usual to prevent it from being bumped out of line by these spots.

Get a good picture of the slopes on the green by stepping back from the ball and looking at the entire green. Some golfers prefer to look at the ball from the opposite side of the cup also. As it gets closer to the hole, the ball tends to break more because of its slower speed. When you are putting uphill or up a slope, tap the ball firmly. When putting downhill, stroke the ball gently.

Stance.   In the fairway, positioning of the ball in relation to the feet depends on the distance to be covered and the type of shot to be executed. Usually, when hitting the ball hard, a player uses the square or slightly closed stance (with the ball placed off the left heel). For shorter shots, such as chipping and pitching, she uses an open stance. An open stance is usually also used for trouble shots, such as shots from traps and from the rough. For chips and pitch shots, the ball is usually more toward the right foot, while for trap shots the ball is off the left heel.

Playing the wind.   A golfer must always consider the wind when making a shot. She should keep the ball as low as possible to reduce the effects of the wind, except in a tee shot, when the wind is coming from behind her. In such a shot, the objective is to get the ball high into the air so that the wind can carry it a greater distance. She can achieve this by: (1) teeing the ball up higher than usual, or by (2) playing the ball more toward the forward foot.

If the wind is blowing toward the golfer, she should: (1) use an iron that is 2 or 3 numbers lower than usual, (2) move the ball back slightly toward the right foot, and (3) choke up about an inch on the grip. These factors help keep the ball low.

If the golfer is using an iron and has the wind to her back, she should again keep the ball low, to keep the wind from affecting its flight. However, the wind will usually add some distance to the hit even when the ball is kept low, so she should use a higher-numbered club or less swing.

If the player is hitting the ball into the wind from the tee, she can keep it low by moving it more toward the center of her stance or by teeing it lower.

When a player is hitting the ball into a crosswind, she should apply the same principle of keeping the ball low. If the wind is coming from her left, she should aim the ball to the left of the pin; if the wind is coming from her right, she should aim the ball more to the right of the target.

Adjusting to climate.   When a golfer is playing on a cold day, she should keep both her hands and the ball as warm as possible (a cold ball won't travel as far as a warm one). She can keep her hands warm by wearing gloves in between shots or by keeping her hands in her pockets. When the ball is not in use, it will stay warm if she puts it in her pocket.

On hot days, a golfer should take salt pills before the round. If water is not available on the course, she should carry a thermos of water in her bag. She should try to maintain a leisurely pace to prevent fatigue from the heat, and if she perspires freely, she should carry an extra glove or a rosin bag so that she will always be able to get a firm grip on the club.

Competing.   In medal play, the golfer shouldn't gamble, but should take the safest shots to get out of a trap or the rough. In match play, she can afford to take chances on a hole. Of course, even in medal play, there are situations in which the player must play boldly if she is to win. For instance, if she is down one stroke on the last hole and her opponent is in good position to chip on, she may have to gamble everything on her second shot.

A golfer should warm up properly before playing an actual round. She should sharpen up her timing in putting, use her irons to increase her accuracy, and hit a few balls from the tee. During these practice shots, she should concentrate and aim at something specific; this enables her to make last-minute adjustments before the round starts.

GYMNASTICS

Coaching Emphasis

1. Complete body awareness (kinesthetic), control, and tightness.
2. Rhythm, beauty, poise, expression, and variety of gymnastic and dance moves for floor exercise and balance beam.

3. Composition of steps, runs, jumps, turns, acrobatic skills, and tumbling with balance for balance beam.

4. Strengthening program for upper arms and shoulder girdle and abdomen, and development of a routine involving swing with changes in hand grips, and fluid patterns of movement from one bar to the other as well as over and under each bar while performing on the uneven bars.

5. Development of leg strength and timing for long flight, perfection in execution of specific vaults, and complete control of body during performance in vaulting.

Mechanics

1. Floor exercises

   a) Composition consists of exercises within 1 to 1½ minutes.

   b) Music should complement all movements.

   c) Composition should cover entire area (12 meters by 12 meters or 39′4.44″ by 39′4.44″ at the minimum), with both curvilinear and straight line floor patterns.

   d) Composition usually starts with sequence of tumbling, followed by the main part of the routine, consisting of dance, jumps, turns, spins, balancing movements integrated with additional tumbling, and ends with another tumbling sequence.

   e) The skilled competitor must blend tumbling, dance, and acrobatics—exhibiting or demonstrating balance, agility, and coordination.

   f) When one is composing a floor exercise routine, the possibilities are unlimited. A few skills that might be utilized are: front and back tumbling, leaps, jumps, locomotor movement, pivots on hands and feet, trunk movement, and various forms of dance.

   g) Probably the most basic skill to be learned for all gymnastic events is the *handstand.* The body position in the handstand can be described as "stick" or straight. The hands, shoulders, and hips should be in alignment. The head is neither extended or tucked; the hands are placed in a shoulder width position with the fingers pointing straight ahead; the body is stretched upward so that the toes are forced upward (toward the ceiling). The whole body is in as tight and controlled a position as possible. Spotter stands on side of gymnast to spot or catch legs.

Problems with Handstand	Corrections and Coaching Hints
Lack of control. Causes: loose body, body arch, head extension, and hands too far apart.	Contract major muscle groups, practice skill by walking feet up a wall—with mat under body.

h) The *front walkover* requires flexibility as well as strength. Start in standing position; lift arms over head as the leg is lifted, and step forward to the foot, placing hands on floor as for a handstand. The head should be up and the eyes focused forward, while the first leg is "kicked" over and the second leg pushes. The kicking leg should lead, while the arms and fingers help with the push. As the first foot lands, the other leg should be out and stretching forward to help pull the upper body up to its original position. A forward push of hips occurs, and then the body immediately returns to upright position with arms up and shoulders and head back until complete upright position is regained. Spotter stands to side, one hand on small of back and other on shoulders.

Problems with Front Walkover	*Corrections and Coaching Hints*
Inability to get completely over. Causes: not enough "kick" with leading leg and push with second leg; not enough strength in abdominal muscles.	Kicking leg should lead throughout; second leg pushes against floor; muscles should be kept tight, especially those in the abdomen.
Jerky movements. Causes: poor timing; not enough muscle control. Poor split position, improper shoulder drive.	Motion should be fluid, with one leg following other leg; do not hesitate; strengthen muscles in hands, arms, legs, and abdomen. Use spotters to help with feel of timing.
Inability to come up to standing position. Causes: not enough push with arms and fingers; second leg not stretching forward; abdominal muscles not contracting enough; poor inverted body stretch, poor thigh strength.	Use muscles of hands and fingers to aid in pushing body up; stretch out second leg to help lift upper body; keep abdominal muscles firm; contract abdominal muscles as hands and fingers push from floor; use spotters.

i) On the *back walkover,* start in a standing stride position (one leg forward and one back), lift one leg, bend backward, and reach with the arms. The first leg should be kicked up and over while the extended hands are placed on the mat, and the other leg follows. Land with first foot and then the other, and end up in a standing position. The performer should have a spotter until she has perfected the movement. Spotter stands to side, one hand on small of back, other hand on back of shoulders.

Problems with Back Walkover	*Corrections and Coaching Hints*
Inability to get over. Causes: not enough lead with head and extended arms; not enough kick with leading	Lead with head; try to arch upper back; reach with the arms; use "kick" on lead leg; push with second foot.

Back walkover on a beam. (Courtesy of Sundby Publications.)

leg and push with second leg; not enough back arch or abdominal strength. Poor split position, poor shoulder extension.

Inability to stand up. Causes: not enough push with shoulders, hands and fingers; feet spaced too far apart or too close together when they hit floor; lack of amplitude.

Use spotter to give added lift. Contract stomach muscles as lead leg goes over.

As legs go over, push hard with arms, hands, and fingers; place feet in comfortable stride position.

j) To perform the *aerial cartwheel* or the side aerial, start in a lunge position, with back perpendicular to floor. Rear leg lifts up quickly, followed by an extension of and push from the floor with the bent leg (front leg). Direction of force is upward and forward. The body rotates through the air, landing on first leg and then second. Spotter stands on side of front leg, hands on front of hips to help lift.

Problems of Aerial Cartwheel

"Dumped" or low cartwheel

Corrections and Coaching Hints

Push more from legs. Don't pike at hips or bend forward at the waist. Don't throw arms down. Focus eyes up.

Striving toward perfection. (Courtesy of Paul Jackson.)

2. Balance beam
   a) Composition consists of basic locomotor movements, sitting and lying positions, tumbling, dance, and acrobatic rolls, showing balance in all skills.
   b) Mount and dismount should be perfected.
   c) The routine composition should be perfected within the alloted time.
   d) *Forward roll.* Start in squat position, lift hips slightly, place back of neck on beam with head to side while hands grip beam. Bring hips slowly up and forward as roll is executed. Hands help regulate speed of the turnover. Stomach muscles help control movement of legs as they come over head and then lower to the beam. Legs remain extended as they are brought up and over the head, with toes pointed. To come out of this roll, drop legs down on each side of the beam and let body come up into a sitting position; or go to a single-leg squat, pose, and then to a stand.

Problems with Forward Roll	*Corrections and Coaching Hints*
Inability to get over. Causes: insufficient push with toes; failure to move hips forward to start roll.	Push toes against beam; move hips over head.

(Courtesy of Paul Jackson.)

(Courtesy of Sundby Publications.)   *(Courtesy of USU Women's
Sports Information.)*

The beauty of performing on the balance beam.

Lack of balance. Causes: body not aligned with beam; going over too fast; not enough abdominal strength to control movements of legs; loose body.

Be sure roll is in a straight line. Start hips up slowly; allow body to roll over slowly, keeping hips and legs under control by contracting abdominal muscles. Use spotter to guide hips and body in a straight line, with hands around waist.

     e) *Backward roll.* Start in back-lying position; pull everything to midline of body and be tight and grip upper part of beam with hands. Contract abdominal muscles to lift hips and legs over shoulders. As hips are above shoulders, hands push down to lift body and allow head to pass between hands.

3. Uneven parallel bars

     a) Routine is primarily swings, kipping, circling, and gliding moves, with grasps and regrasps in maneuvers from bar to bar.

     b) Movements should be continuous, and gymnast should strive to establish an even and steady sense of rhythm.

     c) The gymnast must have excellent abdominal, arm, and shoulder girdle strength.

     d) In a *kip between the bars,* * the gymnast sits on the low bar and grasps the high bar (overgrip). The body is piked forcefully at the waist; legs then extend backwards as the arms pull down. Spotter takes station between bars, with hands on performer. Hips are given a slight upward push as extension phase begins.

     e) In a *glide kip,* * stand behind the low bar, pike the hips, and lift back and upward while the arms reach forward and catch the low bar. Glide forward starts with the body in a piked position. Feet are kept as close to floor as possible, until the end of the glide (at which time the body is completely extended).

     f) In a *kip from a glide,* * pike the body forcefully at the end of the glide (bring ankles up to low bar). As hips start to drop back under the low bar, extend legs and simultaneously pull arms forcefully down straight.

     g) To perform a *straddle sole circle turn cast wrap,* * stand on low bar facing high bar. Take an overgrip on high bar, then jump so that feet are straddled outside of the hands with soles of feet against the bar. Begin backward momentum. As hips begin to ride up back side of high bar, forcefully extend the legs and bring them together. Then 180 degree turn is

---

* Information on kip between bars, glide kip, kip from a glide, straddle sole circle turn cast wrap, back seat circle, and front hip circle taken from paper, "Intermediate Level Uneven Parallel Bars," by Mimi Murray, Springfield College. Information on handspring vault based on paper, "Side Horse Vaulting," by Mimi Murray.

Watching the action. (Courtesy of Indiana University News Bureau.)

initiated. Hands may be changed one at a time or both at the same time (more difficult move) as turn is initiated. If turn is to be to performer's left, the performer may desire to place the left hand in an overgrip position on the high bar before beginning the move. Right hand crosses behind the left and assumes an undergrip. Body then approaches the low bar in a long hang. Bar pikes the body and a "wrap" results. Spotter stands between bars and on opposite side from direction the gymnast is turning toward. Spotter's hands are placed under gymnast's hips and small of back to help her complete the turn and to help carry the body into the low bar.

h) The back seat circle underswing on the low bar can be used to progress to the *back seat circle.** In a sitting position, the gymnast falls backward, while maintaining a pike with the head tucked. When under the bar, performer changes direction and begins to ride back up the bar. Extend legs, pushing down on the low bar, release the low bar, and grip the high bar. Spotter stands between bars, places both hands on small of gymnasts back in the second phase of the move.

i) In the *front hip circle,** body is in a thigh rest position on low bar, (bar is low on thighs, with body extended over and above it). Pike body forcefully at waist while torso and head drive out and down. Legs extend from their piked position as body rotation about bar is almost completed. This leg action lifts body up back side of the low bar. In performing front hip circle, gymnast must get body high, and initiate the move with a great deal of impetus.

j) In the *back hip pullover mount,* stand between bars, with body turned toward low bar. Place hands on low bar in an overgrip, then swing one leg outward and upward (leg straight in piked position) while pushing off with the other to bring both legs up and around the bar. At same time, pull with arms, keeping body in close to bar. As legs swing over bar, arms should be extended to complete the move to a straight-arm support. Point toes. Lift head.

k) *Back hip pullover mount.* Stand between bars, with body turned toward low bar. Place hands on low bar in an over-grip, with arms bent, and then swing one leg outward and upward (leg straight in piked position) while pushing off with the other to bring both legs up and around the bar. At same time, pull with arms, which are still bent, keeping body in close to bar. As legs swing over bar, arms should be extended to complete the move to a straight-arm support. Point toes. Lift head. (See Fig. 9-16.)

Problems with Back Hip Pullover Mount	Corrections and Coaching Hints
Inability to get hips and legs up and over bar. Causes: allowing body to drift too far out from bar; too little swing with legs; too little pull with arms.	Arms should remain flexed to keep body in close; swing leg up forcefully (keeping it straight) while other leg pushes hard from floor to aid swing; *pull* with hands and arms. Use spotters.

---

* Information on kip between bars, glide kip, kip from a glide, straddle sole circle turn cast wrap, back seat circle, and front hip circle taken from paper, "Intermediate Level Uneven Parallel Bars," by Mimi Murray, Springfield College. Information on handspring vault based on paper, "Side Horse Vaulting," by Mimi Murray.

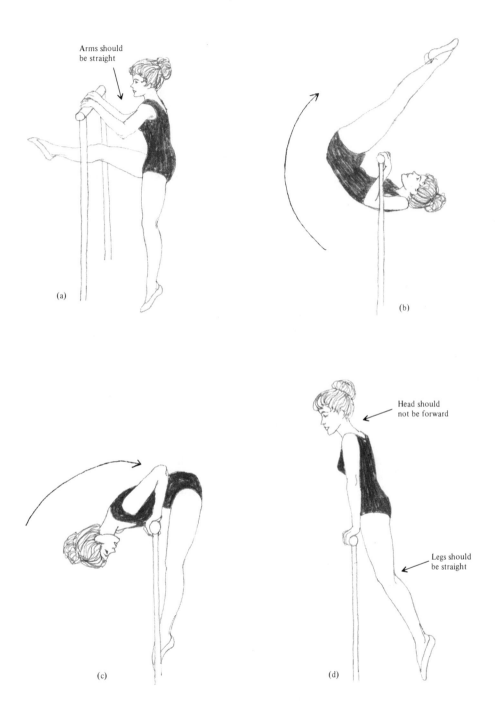

Arms should
be straight

(a)

(b)

Head should
not be forward

Legs should
be straight

(c)

(d)

Fig. 9-16 Back hip pullover, showing common problems.

Inability to end up in straight-arm support. Causes: not enough strength in arms and shoulders; incorrect hand position.

Work on even parallel bars to build up strength in arms and shoulders; concentrate on straightening arms when legs go over bar; use overgrip.

4. Side horse vaulting

   a) The scoring is based on length of flight, execution of vault, and general control of body throughout the vault.

   b) The *handspring vault* is essential to the correct performance of most other competitive vaults in gymnastics. The most critical part of vault is the preflight phase (period from takeoff board until arrival upon the horse). For a successful approach, one should run hard (knees high in beginning), and use long and low strides as one approaches the Reuther board. When 5–8 feet away from board, take one long step and hit middle of board, "popping off" the board with both feet (knees forcefully extended in an explosive action). As legs "pop" off, arms are thrust fore-upward to add lift, sending body into a completely straight and stretched position, (this stretching allows the preflight to be as high and long as possible). As the hands touch the horse (approximately shoulder width apart), elbows are locked, and body is in a stick handstand (without arch and stretched). As hands contact horse, let shoulders relax slightly, and afterflight phase begins (hands are on horse only momentarily). As body starts to pass a 90-degree inverted position, shoulders and wrists exend and stretch to push body in an upward and outward direction (again, a "popping off" motion). As body moves freely through air, body is completely extended and head is between arms. (See Fig. 9-17.) When feet hit floor, bend knees slightly to absorb shock (feet should be hip width apart), keep arms out to side and up with palms facing forward. Extend legs and come to an upright standing position.

Problems with Handspring Vault

Corrections and Coaching Hints

Inability to get over on handspring. Causes: incorrect takeoff; elbows bending; shoulders in front of hands, head tucking; arched or piked body on horse.

Don't slow down approach, push hard with toes, balls of feet, and ankles against board, use arms to aid legs in "popping off" board, keep elbows locked, let hands touch horse when shoulders are almost directly above; pushoff with shoulders and hands should be forceful.

Landing off-balance. Causes: too little or too much turn as body goes over horse; lack of flexion in knees and failure to use arms to aid balance when landing on floor.

Practice timing; let knees give when touching floor. Bend slightly forward at hips; outstretch arms to help maintain balance.

Fig. 9-17 Handspring vault.

Strategy

Strategy in gymnastics is defined by one's physical conditioning, and mental preparedness. The girl who practices her routine enough to be confident in her ability to execute it has prepared herself to perform well. A gymnast should not attempt a new stunt during competition, or include one in her routine that she has not perfected during practice. The competitive situation fosters tension and anxiety; if there is a lack of confidence, this can lead to a poor performance.

The gymnast, for her protection, should have adequate mats and spotters. A warm-up period should precede any strenuous work on the equipment. If her hands tend to perspire, she should use a powdered magnesia chalk. She should adjust the uneven parallel bars, within the limits of the rules. Since she is allowed a takeoff board for mounting the uneven parallel bars and the balance beam, and for vaulting, she should take advantage of this added height and bounce when she needs it.

When the gymnast is doing a difficult stunt on the bars, beam, or horse, she should have a spotter who knows the timing involved and who can handle her full weight if anything goes wrong. Knowing that she will be saved from a bad fall if she has a mishap will add to her confidence in performing. The gymnast must develop her mental powers and discipline in order to perform with self-control, poise, self-confidence and creativity. At the same time, she must have a certain amount of daring and courage in order to "attack" the apparatus when needed. Mental toughness, a strong and agile body, and an artistic approach is needed by the gymnast if she is to perform well.

FIELD HOCKEY

Coaching Emphasis

1. Develop thinking players with a sound understanding of the fundamentals of the game
2. Train confident players. Players must have confidence in: a) teammates, b) own skill, and c) conditioning—mental and physical
3. Speed of thought and execution
4. Accuracy—more important to perform a few basic skills well than to have a large repertoire of half-learned, poorly executed skills.
5. Consistency and adaptability.
6. Possession.

Mechanics

1. The push pass.
   a) One of easiest and most accurate passes.
   b) Can be made quickly in any direction with either foot forward.

c) Easier for beginning player to push right than to drive right. Less demanding footwork skills than drive.

d) Stick remains in contact with ball throughout stroke. Easier to disguise the pass until last moment thus avoiding "telegraphing" play to opponents.

e) Side-on position left shoulder faces toward target.

f) Feet approximately shoulder width apart, knees slightly bent.

g) Ball in front of body approximately midway between feet.

h) Power comes from arm action as well as push from back foot to front at time of stroke.

i) Stick remains in contact with ball as long as possible.

j) Follow through in direction of target.

Problems with Push Pass	*Corrections and Coaching Hints*
Stick tilted back. Ball rolls over stick.	Angle stick forward, follow through.
Lack of power. Arm action and weight transfer not performed at same time.	Step through onto front foot at same time as push with arms.
Lack of power. Shoulders square, body not in side-on position Follow through impeded.	Get feet around so left shoulder is facing target. Follow through.
Ball lifts because head is raised on push or weight is back on heels.	Head over ball throughout stroke. Weight moving forward throughout follow through.
Player pokes at ball.	Keep stick in contact with ball for entire stroke.
Ball behind feet or too far in front of feet. Cause: inaccurate or weak pass.	Get feet in position to play ball at comfortable distance from body.

2. The drive
   a) Powerful, accurate drive reduces chance of interception.
   b) Drive valuable when switching fields and changing direction of play.
   c) Ability to move the ball about quickly with a drive gives the attack more time to make the next constructive play.
   d) Execution of the drive involves: (1) Feet approximately shoulder width apart. (2) Side-on position, left shoulder pointing toward target. (3) Ball should be at comfortable distance from body, generally midway between center of body and left foot. (4) Hands together on stick. (5) Firm left

wrist. (6) Quick backswing. (7) Follow through on hit. (8) Transfer weight to front foot—head and weight should be over over ball at time of contact. (9) Concentrate. Eyes should watch the ball.

Problems with Drive	*Corrections and Coaching Hints*
Failure to transfer weight. Results in loss of power. Ball undercut and chopped when too close to right foot on hit. Ball sliced when in front of left foot on hit.	Errors usually due to poor footwork preceding hit. Concentrate on getting feet in proper relation to ball. Step onto front foot and follow through on the hit.
Looking up while hitting. Topping of ball.	Keep head down over ball throughout stroke.

3. The stop
    a) Good player has the ability to receive balls of varying speed, from any angle, without deflection.
    b) Ability to stop ball dead on stick is great advantage for receiver—increases amount of time to make next play.
    c) Footwork crucial. Should anticipate next play—get feet in best possible position to field ball and send on quickly.
    d) Stop requires concentration as well as skill.
    e) Players should think of stop as "catching" the ball.
    f) Stick down.
    g) Relaxed wrists and hands allow player to "give" with stick.
    h) Stick angled forward into ground, facing direction of oncoming ball.
    i) Stick angled so that, should a deflection occur, ball will be in most advantageous position for receiver, not opponent, to play.
    j) Full length of stick behind stop enables player to stop ball which unexpectedly bounces.
    k) Head over ball on stop.

Problems with Stop	*Corrections and Coaching Hints*
Lack of concentration. Worried about opposition or already thinking about next play.	Direct total concentration on ball and making dead stop.
Stick rigid; poke forward at ball. Ball deflects ahead or pops up. Stick in air results in missed ball.	Correct stick angle. Relax, and give on the stop. Keep stick on ground.
Feet, ball, stick get tangled together.	Concentrate on moving feet and receiving ball well away from feet.

Moving the ball downfield. (Courtesy of Madison Sports Information.)

Strategy

Systems play   In recent years there has been a growing emphasis on "systems" play. One can no longer look out on a field and expect to find two teams opposing each other in the "traditional" 5-3-2-1 formation. Any number of variations, from 4-2-3-1-1 to 3-3-3-1-1, may be found. A controversy over which system is best has grown along with the increased experimentation with various attack and defense formations. Individual skill and team unity are more important than the actual system being played. Plays break down more often due to a lack of mastery of the basic receiving and hitting skills rather than due to poor tactical plans.

Today there is more emphasis on interchanging of positions than ever before. Less position restrictions are set, and greater freedom of movement is encouraged. Players, instead of regarding themselves as one set position, must now have a greater knowledge of the game and must be ready to quickly assume any position.

While current systems play allows for greater freedom of movement and creativity on the part of the individual, it also places greater demands on each player. All-round players with good understanding of attack and defense are required. With the emphasis on interchanging of positions, and constant movement off the ball by attack, players must be more sensitive than ever to the positioning of their teammates and opponents. Greater adaptability and individual skill is required as each player must now be able to play any position in which she finds herself on the field.

The "traditional" role of the fullbacks has changed somewhat in recent years due to the growing dissatisfaction with the amount of midfield freedom allowed to inside forwards, and the inefficiency of the up-back fullback interchange. Midfielders or links (position title is irrelevant—actual function is important) now attempt to break up the attack earlier in the defense's own half. Midfielders aggressively mark man-to-man while the sweeper behind assures cover and depth on defense.

A rapid changeover from defense to attack is important. The midfield must be crossed quickly and the attack mounted immediately in order to allow the opposing defense little time to recover. Once a team has possession, all players are members of the attack. Players from behind may overlap, receive back passes, and move rapidly through on attack at any time. Awareness of the opposition and teammates is essential in distributing play and making the most constructive use of space. The ability of all players to see the spaces, and to seize opportunities to initiate the attack at any time, adds an element of surprise and prevents the opposing team from settling into their accustomed style of play.

Offense   It is important for forwards to learn to think off the ball and make an intelligent appraisal of the possibilities. Forwards should be aware at all times of the spaces on the field positioning of their opponents as well as their own teammates. The time to decide what to do with the ball is not *after* one has received the pass. Rather, the player must size up the opposition *before* she receives the ball. Anticipating the play, she should move her feet in the best possible position to field the ball and quickly carry out the next play. The flow of the game depends, in large part, upon each player's sensitivity to the movement of her opponents and teammates, and upon her ability to adjust and react spontaneously to the situation at hand.

There can be no set, mapped-out plan of action for each situation that arises in a game. Each player must learn to assess for herself the strengths and weaknesses of her opponents and teammates. Successful attack play requires skill and lots of hard work. Successful plays, in most cases, do not just happen. For every play that works there are ten that fail. To a certain extent each player creates her own "luck." Players must *want* the ball enough to create passing and scoring opportunities. Each player must be determined and tenacious enough to cut, recut, tackle back, and constantly be moving or ready to move, so that she is mentally and physically prepared to immediately seize any attacking opportunities which arise. The ability to fail, regroup, and try again is the mark of a good attack.

Width in attack is important. Forwards should avoid bunching as this makes it easier for one defender to guard two attackers. The forward off the ball is responsible for getting free. Sometimes it is best to pull away from the teammate with the ball and delay movement into the space until she is ready to pass. Other times the player without the ball will move only as a decoy, cutting to create a

Concentration—a big part of athletics. (Courtesy of Madison Sports Information.)

space for a teammate. Intelligent movement off the ball can be distracting to the defense. Diagonal cuts and interchanging of attack positions makes it more difficult for defenders to concentrate on both the forward and the ball, and effectively cut off the passing angles. It forces each defender to make a decision: should she follow the free player or play the space. Depending upon whether the defender decides to play the space or the player, the forward making the cut will be free to receive a pass, or her teammate will be free to receive a pass in the space she has just vacated.

Many times defense are beaten but the forwards fail to take advantage of the situation because they have not anticipated the play before it occurred. Too often free players pass to marked teammates or carry the ball too long themselves, allowing the defense to recover. Dribbling the ball tends to slow down play, while a quick pass downfield to a space or teammate, followed up by an all-out rush by the attack, can often result in numerical superiority for the attack. Forwards should attempt to penetrate quickly midfield and within their attacking 25 yards. Otherwise the defense will have time to set up, leaving the forwards a small space in which to maneuver. There is little room for error within the 25-yard line and goal. This is why attack play so often breaks down here and so few goals are scored. Most players lack the precise stickwork which would enable time to dodge within a small area, maintain body and ball control, and follow up quickly with an accurate shot at goal.

It is not always possible for forwards to get off a clear shot at goal once they are inside the circle. Rather than working toward the "perfect" shot, forwards should sometimes take the earliest shot possible, confident that their teammates will be rushing and ready to redirect their shot into the goal. It is often possible to draw a penalty corner in the circle by pushing the ball behind the defender on her nonstick side, forcing her to obstruct.

It is desirable to have depth in attack, with one wave after another putting sustained pressure on the opposition. "Hunting in pairs" is an effective tactic which puts a great deal of pressure on the defense. Forwards should be encouraged to support each other and tackle back if possession is lost. Although the individual tackling back might not get the ball, she is playing an important role by forcing her opponent to pass or dodge quickly. Hopefully the pressured defender will make an inaccurate pass or uncontrolled dodge which can then be intercepted by alert midfielders on the attack player's team.

Defense   Much of defense, once the basic skills have been learned, involves common sense and reacting quickly and decisively to the situation at hand. Organization is important on defense. The defenders must act as a coordinated unit in order to be effective. Each player must understand her own basic defensive responsibilities and those of her teammates in order to prevent confusion in marking and picking up free players. Beginning defenders must learn to resist the temptation to wander and follow the ball. A cohesive defensive unit with sound positional knowledge can many times calmly and confidently dictate the play of the opposing forwards (provided the teams are not greatly mismatched in skill level).

The defense, by assertive positioning, attempt to restrict the amount of space available to the attack. They hope to force the attack to travel the least dangerous and most time-consuming path toward goal. Defenders should narrow the angle of attack and force the opposition away from the funnel toward goal. Their aim is to prevent the forwards from taking a shot a goal. If a shot is to be conceded, it should be at the worst possible angle for the attack.

Defense requires control and patience. Many times it is best not to hastily rush in to tackle the forward with the ball. Few forwards have the ability to beat a defender in a one-on-one situation. The longer the forward dribbles the ball, the greater her chances of losing it. A patient defender will stall and hold her ground between the forward and her desired path toward goal. This allows the rest of the defense time to set up and possibly intercept a loose dodge or inaccurate pass. Very often the opponent with the ball will telegraph her intentions. An alert defender will learn to read the feet, eyes, stick of the forwards, and anticipate the pass or dodge. Reading the play, the defender then moves her feet and stick in the best possible position to intercept the ball.

While defenders need to exercise restraint in their tackles, they should beware of playing too defensively and being overly cautious. Whenever possible, the defenders should break up the attacking moves early, before a coordinated attack has time to develop. Each defender must have confidence that her team-

Defense! Defense! (Courtesy of Madison Sports Information.)

mates will react quickly, and will readjust their positioning to lend defensive support.

Whether a defender rushes through for an interception or holds back depends upon a number of factors: the speed of the ball, the speed of the defender, the speed of her opponent, the angle of the pass or dodge, and which player has the most favorable chance of getting to the ball first. If the defender feels it is probable that she can get to the ball first, she should not hesitate but should make an all-out effort to do so. If, however, she feels the chances are good that she will not be successful, she should hang back in a stable defensive position which will enable her to immediately pounce on the ball should it be deflected by her opponent.

Tight marking inside the circle is crucial. When marking the defender is denying possession to her opponent. She positions ballside and goalside of her opponent. The forward cannot be permitted to shoot or deflect the ball. Midfield it is sometimes more important for the defender to play the space rather than tightly mark her opponent. Here a through ball, sent behind the defender, is more dangerous than a flat pass to her opponent. Depth in defense is essential. Before a defender commits herself to closely mark her opposing forward, she must be assured that she has defensive support. The players behind protect against the through ball or dodge. The closer the play gets toward goal, the less space available to the forwards, and the easier it is for the defense to cover both the player and the space.

As a general rule, when forwards outnumber defenders, the defense should quickly adjust, picking up the most dangerous player and leaving those farthest from the goal free. Whenever possible, defenders should stall and attempt to contain the attack allowing the rest of their team time to recover. However, once play has reached the circle edge, the defenders can no longer afford to stall for time. At this point they must immediately react to closely pressure the forwards into making a hasty (and, it is hoped, an inaccurate) pass or shot at goal.

Midfielders and backfield should be aware of where the opposition and their own teammates are *before* they tackle, intercept, or stop the ball. Once in possession, no time should be wasted in passing to the forwards. Any lack of organization on the part of the opposing defense should be exploited quickly by passing and mounting the attack before the defenders have time to reposition. Once a defender has fielded the ball and sent it upfield to her teammates, she must not feel that her job is finished. She should then immediately follow up behind her line in order to give depth on attack and possibly shoot through herself onto the forward line.

SKIING

Coaching Emphasis

1. Structure a preseason training program that includes endurance, strength and power, flexibility, coordination, and speed and quickness.
2. Practice skiing movements specific to downhill, slalom and giant slalom in gates and free skiing.
3. Emphasize technique that produces the least amount of skidding and braking of speed.
4. Emphasize use of knees and lower body while upper body remains balanced in a neutral position.

Mechanics

1. Carving a turn
   a) Carving a turn in the snow properly—with weight on the inside edge, downhill ski—reduces the amount of skidding and friction in a turn.
   b) The less skidding, the more efficient the turn.
   c) A racer should not have to rely on skidding to slow down; she should be able to turn across the hill, i.e., turn out of the fall line to control her speed.
   d) Many ski technicians divide a turn into three parts. The first part is the initiation of the turn. As the racer approaches the first phase, she put her outside ski on its inside edge and begins to transfer her weight to that ski.

The second part of the turn is the fall line phase in which the direction change occurs. The last third of a turn is the acceleration phase. If done properly, the speed gained from the fall line phase is used to accelerate the skier out of the turn with increased speed. If done improperly, the last phase is where skidding or loss of control occurs.

e) If the turn is longer, as in many GS turns, then the outside ski remains in a flat or outside edge position while the weight shift occurs. The ski is then rolled over to the inside edge as the first third of the turn is initiated. The goal is the same as in d), but in a longer turn, everything is delayed just a bit.

f) The crucial action for carving a turn is driving the knees, especially the downhill knee, into the hill. To do this, the knees must be in a flexed position.

g) Driving the knees laterally into the hill accomplishes important actions: (1) at the end of the second part of the turn or arc, it will achieve edge lock and prevent sideslipping, (2) It will to a great extent allow a natural and necessary angulation of the hips to maintain balance and proper weighting of the downhill ski.

h) The pressure exerted on the outside ski by the knee is intensified by increasing the lateral thrust of the knee into the hill. Greater pressure is necessary in the second and third parts of a turn to prevent skidding.

i) Leverage is also being applied to the skis by a skier's body weight through either a forward, neutral, or back pressure.

j) This can be effected by subtle movement of the hips and knees. It must not be caused by bending at the waist.

k) Forward pressure=weight just ahead of the boot by pressing on the ball of the foot. Neutral pressure=weight evenly distributed between ball and heel of foot. Back pressure=weight on heel of foot.

l) Usually, slight forward or neutral pressure is used to initiate the turn. Neutral pressure begins to take over at the second phase. Back pressure is essential at the third phase to prevent the tails from skidding and to aid in acceleration. It should be noted that back pressure does not literally mean that weight is over the tails of the skis. Nor does forward pressure mean that weight is over the tips of the skis.

m) At the end of the third phase, when a change in direction has been accomplished, the edge lock of the downhill ski is released. This is done most often by up-unweighting. The quickness of the turns and the terrain will warrant more or less pronounced up-unweighting (the quicker the turn, the less time there is to fully extend before going into the next turn).

n) Up-unweighting allows the skis to accelerate by abruptly releasing the edges from a back pressure position. It requires a subtle extension of the knees and hips.

Christine Gortschel of France during International Ladies Races at Grindelwald, Switzerland, in January, 1963. (Courtesy of Ski *Magazine.)*

o) The body must still maintain a balanced, agile position, so that the skis do not come off the snow or shoot away from the body out of control.

p) Do not allow the body to be fixed in any one position—a static low position is as inefficient as being too erect. The ankles, knees, and hips should be flexible and fluid, always ready to turn the skis in any kind of terrain or situation.

q) The thighs, in most instances, parallel to the ground is as low as you should ever be, i. e., the hips should not drop below the knees. A totally erect posture, with locked knees and hips is also not desirable.

r) Shoulders and hips should remain square, facing down the fall line, anticipating the next turn.

s) Arms should be in a balanced, comfortable, *natural* position, ready for the pole plant.

t) The pole plant is made before the first part of the turn. It is crucial for timing and should never be done once the weight has shifted and the turn has been started—at this point, it is too late.

COACHING HINTS

a) Practice making snowplow turns on a beginner slope, exaggerating weight transfer, weighting downhill ski, driving downhill knee into hill, and experimenting with forward, neutral, and back pressure.

b) Many racers have a tendency to rotate their shoulders around the turn. Observe if the racer's shoulders and hips follow around the turn. This will cause unnecessary skidding and may decrease the speed of the racer. Be sure she is using a type of counterrotation whereby the shoulders and hips are facing more toward the fall line.

c) Watch the knees closely. They should be flexed into a low body position during the middle and end of the turn, and should be simultaneously driving laterally into the hill. Knee movement is extremely important.

1. Lateral step or lateral projection

a) This is not a skating step. Rather it is a technique that increases the radius of the turn with the skis, while the upper body remains square and actually follows a straighter line down the hill than the feet do. Lateral stepping has become one of the most important tools used by racers to increase their speed in turns.

b) At the end of a turn, i.e., the end of the third accelerating part of the turn, the uphill ski is moved slightly ahead and laterally. The ski is placed subtly on its inside edge, and is weighted more and more as the racer initiates the turn.

c) The upper body stays square to the fall line and the necessary angulation by the hips happens almost automatically.

d) Lateral steps can be so subtle, as in slalom turns, that they are difficult to perceive, being only a weight shift from the inside edge of the downhill ski to the inside edge of the outside ski.

e) This type of turn might not be used in extremely tight or quick turns where there isn't enough time to make a proper lateral step.

2. Starts

a) Poles planted in front of starting gate.

b) Knees flexed, body leaning slightly forward.

c) On "Go," bring feet back and up in the air by kicking up with one foot first.

d) At this point, the upper body should also be leaning in an arc ahead of the feet, and out over the starting gate timing wand.

    e) Arms, shoulders, and hips explode forward from this position with a tremendous push with the poles. The feet are the last part of the body to pass through the starting gate, and the only part of the body to trip the starting wand (to touch the timing device).

3. Race day

    a) Memorize the proper line, especially know blind turns and technically challenging sections of the course, changes in terrain, etc.

    b) Racer should be able to visualize her run with eyes closed, from start to finish.

    c) Warm up with stretching exercises and a few free skiing runs before race. A racer may or may not want to run a few practice gates before the race; this should be left up to her.

    d) Never ski through any of the gates in the course—this will lead to disqualification (except in downhill, where practice on the course is necessary and mandatory).

4. Taking care of skis—sharpening edges

    a) New skis must be prepared just as used skis must be maintained.

    b) Flat file bottom of ski so that edges are perfectly flat. A 10-inch mill bastard file is usually adequate.

    c) Be careful to keep file *flat* while filing, putting pressure directly on the metal edges, and not bending the file.

    d) You want a *square*, not a rounded, edge.

    e) You should round the edges at the shovel of the tip to prevent catching in the snow.

    f) Check edges for burrs (rough spots), and lightly file or rub with emery cloth to smooth these out.

    g) Wax after filing.

5. Waxing

    a) Base of ski should be cleaned with carbon tetrachloride or commercial ski base cleaner.

    b) New skis should be sealed three times with base wax, which is a special sealer.

    c) Wax should be applied with heat, by brushing on melted wax or by ironing, or both.

    d) Skis should be at room temperature when waxing.

    e) There are many variables to consider in choosing what wax to use, and what mixture. For example, snow temperature, humidity, texture of snow, terrain, etc.

    f) Wax manufacturers provide instructions with their product regarding the use of proper wax for a particular air and/or snow temperature.

g) After applying wax, scrape down to bare base. Wax soaks into the base of modern skis, so you ski on a wax-impregnated base, not on the wax itself.

h) There is no need to polish except for very cold snow (below -10°C). If necessary, polish with colorless nylon cloth.

i) Rescrape skis at start when extremely cold.

j) Bury skis in snow before start of downhill.

6. Setting courses

a) By writing to the Unites States Ski Team Office, and for a small fee, you may receive the current international and national rules and guidelines for ski racing as established by the Federation of International Skiing (FIS).

b) For basic reference, it is helpful to know some of these rules: (1) in Women's Slalom, the minimum number of gates is 40. The maximum is 60. The distance between two gates should not be less than two feet from each other. The two poles of each gate should not be less than 12 feet apart. (2) in Women's Giant Slalom the minimum number of gates is 30. The nearest poles of two successive gates should not be less than 5 meters. The poles of each gate should not be less than 4m, nor more than 8m. (3) in downhill, the poles of a gate should not be less then 8m wide. It is a good idea, but not a regulation, to set a gate so that it is visible from the previous one.

c) In downhill, flags should be placed at right angles to the racing line. This is a good rule to follow for GS also, but is a little more difficult to do when using off-set and closed gates.

d) It is a good idea to set the first three or four gates open and to make the last three or four gates open, so that the turns are a bit easier.

e) See Fig. 9–18 for various gate combinations.

7. Racing

a) Picking the proper line through a course depends somewhat on the racer's ability.

b) A line fairly tight with the inside pole of the gate is desirable. However, the ultimate correct line depends upon where the next gate down the hill is located. Because of this, the straightest line from gate to gate is not necessarily the fastest line.

c) It is important to realize that because of hip angulation, allowing the upper body to take a straighter line (leaning to the inside of the turn), the skis must take a wider line from the pole. The radius made by the skis must be longer to allow the body enough room to pass by the inside pole. In many cases, the posterior side of the inside shoulder brushes the pole in slalom, and occasionally in giant slalom. If the tips of the skis are directed too closely to the inside pole, they must slide during the second

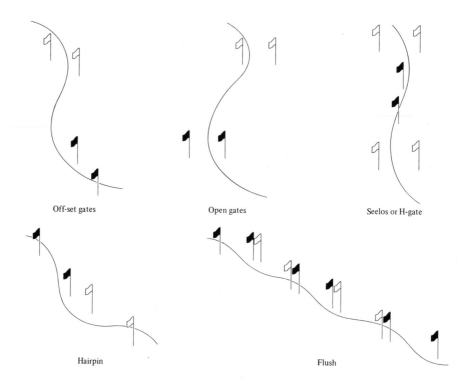

Off-set gates   Open gates   Seelos or H-gate

Hairpin   Flush

Fig. 9–18 Positioning of flags for racing variation.

phase of the turn to make room for the rest of the body. This sliding or skidding will continue through the entire turn and greatly decrease speed. It can also throw the racer's timing off and make her late for the following gate.

d) Turns must be initiated early, so that direction change is occurring by the time the racer reaches the inside pole. As soon as she passes the gate, the direction change should have been completed, and the racer should already be preparing for the next run. To do this, she must always be looking ahead, concentrating on the next two or three gates down the hill.

e) The finish is as important as the start. The racer should pick the straightest line possible from the last gate to the finish line. She should not attempt to turn or slow down until well past the finish gate.

One important note—free skiing is essential. Skiing in all kinds of weather, snow conditions, and terrain is probably the most important single facet of racing that a skier can do. It builds competence and confidence. It should be a learning experience as well as an enjoyable experience. A racer should get in many miles of skiing every year.

CROSS-COUNTRY SKIING

Cross-country skiing, or touring, has enjoyed increased popularity in our country the last few years. Many people have turned to cross-country skiing in order to get away from the crowds on the ski slopes, while some prefer it because of the natural surroundings and the freedom of exploration it allows. Others have found that it is much easier to learn than downhill skiing is. At any rate, young and old are spreading out to enjoy snow-covered lumber trails, rolling hills, frozen lakes, and out-of-the-way places.

The basic movement for cross-country skiing is a kickoff from one foot, and a gliding step with the other. Skilled individuals move in a relaxed, easy stride, alternating kickoffs and glides from one foot to the other. These rapid, pushing movements and long glides allow the skier to move smoothly and rhythmically, while having the weight balanced entirely on one ski or the other.

Many skiers find it easier to relax their head and shoulders if they focus their eyes about forty feet ahead of them. Relaxed movements and proper techniques allow one to conserve energy and to move swiftly through the snow.

The arms and poles help the skier maintain balance, while the main force comes from the kick. In executing the "diagonal stride," the opposite arm plants the pole while the leg on the other side of the body starts the kick. Then the diagonally opposite arm and leg move together. The kick involves moving the weighted ski backwards vigorously, while transfering the weight off the back ski to the other ski to allow it to move forward on the gliding stroke.

Many individuals prefer to practice without poles when first learning to ski cross country. This allows them to get the kick motion going properly, without depending on the poles for anything other than support and balance.

One variation of the diagonal stride involves planting both poles instead of one. This double-poling technique is useful in picking up speed on gentle down-hill areas.

SOFTBALL

Coaching Emphasis

1. Three most important skill factors in determining a team are throwing and hitting ability, and speed.
2. Should work on fundamentals of catching, throwing, batting, and pitching.
3. Special work on sidearm throw, bunting, pitching, placehitting, fielding, base-running, and sliding (bent leg, straight leg, and hook), and specific position play.

Mechanics

1. Sidearm throw
   a) The sidearm throw is used when the fielder does not have time to come up into an erect position for throw, or when the baseman catches a low

ball and must release it quickly for a double play, or whenever a quick release is needed on a charging play from the outfield.

b) Grip is same as for overarm throw.

c) While body is in low position, swing arm back below shoulder level and then forward almost parallel to ground; finally extend arm and snap wrist for force. When you release the ball, your thumb should be on top, your first and second fingers should grip the underside of the ball, and your third and fourth fingers rest on the side of the ball.

d) Body movement: (1) Lift up with throw while rotating forward; (2) shift weight from rear to forward foot; (3)extend arm about waist high and in the direction of the throw.

Problems with Sidearm Throw	*Corrections and Coaching Hints*
Throw goes to right of intended target. Cause: ball released too early in throw.	For accuracy, wrist snap and release must be consistent. Hold wrist flexion and release a second later. Hang a tire or a hula hoop up and practice throwing through it.
Ball goes to left of intended target. Cause: ball released too late in the throw.	Snap wrist and extend elbow a second or so sooner.
Ball goes too high or too low. Cause: arm swing and follow-through not parallel to ground. If hand drops down, arm swing is upward, causing ball to go too high. If hand comes back too high, swing is down, causing ball to go too low.	Bring hand back no lower than hip and no higher than shoulder.

2. Batting

a) Grip: (1)The hand about an inch from end of bat is the usual grip for power and control. (2) For accuracy in placement, and for times when pitcher is very fast, keep hands 3 or 4 inches above end of bat (choke grip). (3) When power is more important than control, use the long grip (hand at end of bat).

b) Relax hands while waiting for ball; just before hit, tighten grip.

c) Stance: (1) Face plate, a bat's length from outside edge. (2) Vary position according to pitcher, by moving back or forward in box. (3) For fast balls and curves, move back in box to allow break and time to react; or you may prefer to move forward to hit curve or drop ball before curve or drop develops. (4) For bunts or hit-away situations, stand forward in box so you are closer to first base. (5) Keep feet about shoulder width apart. (6) Point rear foot toward plate and turn forward foot at about a 45-degree angle to allow good weight shift.

d) To hit ball: (1) Bend knees and place weight evenly on both feet. (2) Bring bat back at about shoulder level, while rotating shoulders and hips away from pitcher. (3) Keep arms out and away from body. (4) Cock wrists and watch pitcher over left shoulder. (5) Watch ball all the way.

e) Just before release, shift weight to rear foot. Start swing by shifting weight to forward foot (or even step with forward foot). Rotate hips and shoulders toward ball, and swing bat forward and parallel to ground.

f) Arm action: (1) Let left arm pull bat forward while right arm pushes; (2) snap wrist on contact. (3) Follow-through: wrists about shoulder high, palm of left hand faces up, and palm of right hand faces down.

g) Push off with forward foot. For run to first base, take first step with rear foot. See Fig. 9–19.

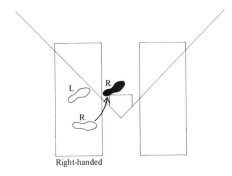

Right-handed

Fig. 9-19 Batting stance, with right foot taking first step toward first base.

3. Place hitting

a) Change direction of hit by swinging bat faster or slower, using extreme wrist action, or changing position of feet at plate.

b) To hit to left field, swing more quickly; to hit to right field, swing late.

c) Remember that change in wrist action is hard to control.

d) Since change in position of feet lacks deception, move forward foot at last possible second.

e) To hit to left field, use an open stance (pull forward foot back 2 or 3 inches). To hit to right field, use a closed stance (move forward foot farther toward the plate). See Fig. 9–20.

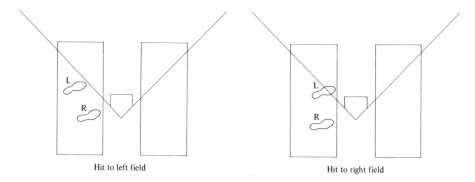

Fig. 9-20   Open stance to hit to left field; closed stance to hit to right field.

4. Bunting

   a) Bunting is used to advance runner on base, or to get fast runner to first.

   b) For deception, use regular batting stance.

   c) Hit ball down first- or third-base line, preferably halfway.

   d) To bunt: (1) Use regular stance; pivot and face pitcher at last moment. (2) On pivot, keep body low. (3) Slide right hand up bat to about trade mark. (4) Hold bat loosely by thumb and index finger of right hand. (5) Hold bat firmly with left hand at end of bat. (6) Let bat "give" when contact is made.

   e) Pivot on forward foot, stepping up with rear foot. Be careful not to step out of batter's box.

   f) Get bat over plate and parallel to ground before ball reaches plate.

   g) Slant bat in direction of desired hit.

   h) To drop ball close to the plate, hit it on top, "giving" on contact for slow roll. Hitting below center will result in "pop-up."

   i) Don't try to bunt high pitched ball.

   j) If runner is on second or third, don't bunt to third-base line.

Problems in Batting	*Corrections and Coaching Hints*
Lack of power. Causes: wrong grip; incorrect stance; failure to shift weight; lack of wrist action.	Use regular or long grip (long grip for most power); use open stance; shift weight from rear to forward foot; uncock wrists as contact is made.
Lack of control. Causes: wrong grip; failure to watch ball; lack of timing on swing.	Choke up on bat with hands three or four inches from end; keep eyes on ball until ball is actually hit. Concentrate on hitting to a particular area during practice.

Poor balance. Causes: poor stance; batter too far from plate; batter too close to plate; feet too close or too far apart.

Move closer to plate to prevent lunging at balls on outside corners; move back slightly to prevent falling back on inside balls. Place feet approximately shoulder width apart. Players who step toward the ball when they hit should not use as wide a stance (usually feet should be about 6 inches closer together).

Ball hit too far to right. Causes: stance closed; swing late; wrists not uncocked soon enough.

Keep stance square to plate; swing a fraction sooner; uncock wrists just before contact.

Ball hit too far to left. Causes: stance open; swing too early; wrists uncocked too soon.

Keep feet parallel, but forward foot turned at about a 45-degree angle; swing fraction later than usual; delay uncocking of wrists.

On bunt, ball rolls too fast. Causes: right hand does not "give" to allow bat to move backward as ball hits it; because of incorrect positioning, bat is moved toward ball before ball gets to plate.

Allow right hand to be relaxed and to recoil slightly as ball hits bat; get bat into position over plate before ball gets there.

On bunt, ball goes into the air. Cause: ball hit below center.

Keep eye on ball; try to hit on top of ball; don't bunt high inside balls.

On bunt, ball rolls toward pitcher rather than down base line. Cause: bat not angled toward base line as it is held in position over plate.

To get the correct angle for hit toward third base line, push tip of bat forward; for bunt down first-base line, push handle out slightly and pull end of bat back.

5. Pitching
    a) Two common wind-ups are the figure-eight and the windmill.
    b) For figure-eight wind-up, ball is brought to chest with pitching hand holding ball and with other hand covering back of pitching hand. All motion must stop for at least one second. For deception, let the ball follow a figure-eight path as the swing goes sideward, then let it move back and behind the body, upward slightly, then continue downward and forward to complete the delivery. During the movement of the swing behind the back, the hips should rotate away from the batter, then toward the batter on the forward and downward motion of the arm [50]. The left foot steps toward the plate, and the ball is released with a snap of the wrist. Both backswing and forward swing should be on line with the pitch. Follow-through consists of bringing right foot up parallel with left foot, with fingers pointing at the plate.

Pitcher versus batter—a challenge. (Courtesy of UTA News Service, James Russell.)

c) In the windmill wind-up, the arm makes almost a complete circle before release of the ball. Bring ball to chest in both hands; let pitching arm go forward and then upward, with weight shifting to right foot. Let arm continue up and back as left foot steps toward plate. On downward swing, wrist is cocked back. This arm rotation builds up momentum, which adds to the speed of the ball. During circling motion, keep the arm almost straight, and snap the wrist at the last moment to release the ball. After the release, take a step forward with right foot to put yourself in position to field any balls hit your way.

d) Another method used by some skilled pitchers is to lean backward by arching the back before the wind-up; this means that the stomach muscles help snap the body forward, which adds power to the ball. This method is very hard on the back, and in most cases is too difficult for the pitcher to maintain throughout the game.

Problems in Pitching	Corrections and Coaching Hints
Ball too high. Causes: release too late; step forward shorter than usual.	Snap wrist and release ball sooner; take same-length step each time. Mark spot on ground for first step if necessary.
Ball too low. Causes: too-early release; first step too long.	Delay release fraction of second longer; be consistent in first step.
Illegal delivery. Causes: throw side-armed; pitcher takes too many steps before release; incorrect position of pitcher before wind-up; pitcher not at full stop before wind-up.	Hand must be below hip and wrist not out beyond elbow. Take only one step during delivery. Face batter and keep shoulders square with plate. Stop and hold position from 1 to 20 seconds before wind-up.
Poor control or loss of balance. Causes: first step taken with wrong foot; weight shifted incorrectly; body not rotated back to face batter on the release; arc not flattened; release too early or too late.	Take first step and shift weight to left foot as arm swings downward. To start forward swing, rotate trunk toward batter. After release, bring right foot up parallel with left foot, and let fingers follow through toward batter. Determine best point of release by practice.

6. Types of pitches
    a) Pitch is determined by grip, spin on ball, and delivery.
    b) Types of pitches are: curve, drop, rise, fast ball, change of pace, and slant. (For grips, see Fig. 9–21.)
    c) Fast ball: (1) grip ball between thumb and first and second finger, (2) let ball leave from tips of fingers, and (3) turn palm slightly to left.
    d) Change of pace: (1) hold ball in palm of hand, (2) keep thumb and all four fingers on ball (knuckles may be bent under), (3) release ball from hand rather than fingertips (this prevents spin).
    e) Drop ball: (1) place thumb on right of ball, (2) place first three fingers close together, (3) bend little finger, (4) bring hand forward so that palm faces batter, and (5) let ball roll off fingers with top spin.
    f) Out-curve: (1) position thumb and first and second fingers in triangle on ball, (2) turn palm slightly to left, (3) pull second finger away from ball and snap wrist to left to create right-to-left spin. (Ball leaves little-finger side of hand.)
    g) In-curve: (1) use same grip as that for fast ball, (2) snap wrist to right to create left-to-right spin, (3) let ball leave from between thumb and first finger, creating a clockwise spin which makes ball curve toward the batter.

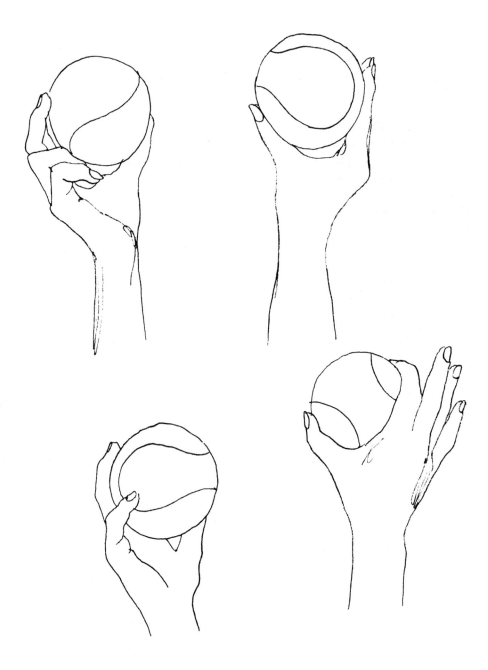

Fig. 9-21 Grips for pitching softball. Top left: In-curve and fast ball. Top right: Rise ball. Lower left: Drop ball. Lower right: Out-curve ball.

h) Rise ball: (1) hold ball with thumb pointing down, (2) place first and second fingers on top of ball, (3) place third and fourth fingers slightly to right, (4) let knuckles face batter as hand comes forward, (5) snap wrist upward to create back spin (push with thumb and pull upward with fingers).

i) Slant: (1) stand on extreme corner of rubber (to hit outside corner of plate, stand to extreme right of rubber—to hit inside corner, stand to extreme left), and (2) pitch ball diagonally to opposite corner of home plate. Vary by releasing ball from a low position (without spin), so that ball goes upward to cross plate at about level of batter's shoulder.

7. Fielding the ball

a) Wait in a crouched position for batter to hit ball.

b) Move quickly to get in line with ball.

c) Keep eyes on ball all the way as it comes toward you.

d) On balls that are hit high, allow ball to drop slightly in front of head; for grounders, move toward ball and stop it immediately after bounce if possible.

e) In catching ball, turn palm of glove hand toward ball. Cover ball with other hand, keeping both palms facing each other. Field off inside of left foot if right-handed. When ball is hit to side, turn and run at a slight angle to intercept the ball. Try to move to ball with glove low to ground since it is easier to raise glove up than to drop it down if the ball takes an unexpected hop.

f) Learn to get rid of ball as soon as possible after you make catch. This can be done by: (1) catching ball with arms flexed, (2) taking ball out of glove as hand begins to move back into throwing position, (3) taking step in direction of throw as you cock your arm and wrist, and (4) snapping arm and wrist forward quickly.

g) Save time by looking the situation over before the ball is hit to determine which base the ball should be thrown to.

h) If ball is hit over your head, turn and run as fast as possible to point you think ball will come down; then look over shoulder to locate ball before making turn for catch.

i) If in doubt, let ball bounce in front of you rather than taking chance of overrunning ball or letting it go over your head.

j) When fielding fast low balls and grounders in outfield, go down on one knee with body low and in position to block ball if you miss catch with glove. On slow and medium balls, bend body forward, letting legs and feet remain positioned for a quick throw after the catch.

k) In fielding fly balls, if ball is hit over right shoulder, pivot on left foot, drop step with the right, crossover with the left foot, and run to intercept ball while looking back over shoulder. Extend and rotate glove hand to face ball, extend body fully if leap at ball is necessary.

l) On short fly balls, anticipation is important. Player must have body in motion as ball is hit. Good balance, speed, and the ability to extend arm out and down while running full speed is necessary on short fly balls.

m) Line drives are very difficult to judge because of the rising and dropping factor. Keep eye on ball. Generally, a line drive to left or right field will be curving toward the line.

8. Base-running

a) If you are a right-handed batter, when you start run to first base, take first step with right foot.

b) Keep motion low at start of run, using short strides to build up speed.

c) When going to first base, run out every hit at full speed.

d) To determine whether to continue run to second, watch base coach. If hit is only a single, go across first without changing stride and slow down only after you have passed the base. If you are going on to second, swing out to the right when you are about 10 to 12 feet from first base, touching inside of bag with the foot as you turn back toward the next base. (Left foot is usually used to make turn easier.)

e) Once you are on base, threaten to steal or go for the next base on a hit. You can't leave the base until the pitcher releases the ball, but you can get set for a fast start by waiting with your left foot on the corner of the base and your right foot about a foot behind your left. This enables you to start your body in motion by pushing with your right foot as the pitcher's arm starts the downswing, and yet keeps your left foot on the base for the legal lead at the release of the ball. Bend your body forward and keep low while waiting.

f) Unless it is a hit-and-run situation, change your movements to a side slide about 10 feet down the base line, with your body facing the batter to see whether you can proceed to the next base or must move back quickly to the base you have just left.

g) If the catcher fumbles the ball or can't get to a wild pitch, go immediately to the next base; if it is a high fly, go back and tag up and be ready to grab any chance to go to the next base. On a ground ball, if a runner is behind you, don't hesitate to break for the next base immediately.

h) If the baseman is playing tight, don't lead off farther than your ability to beat the throw back in a pick-off situation.

i) Some things to remember about sliding are: (1) when approaching a base for a force play, particularly second base where a double play might originate, you should always slide unless the throw is clearly way ahead of the runner, (2) by using a bent-leg slide, you are able to quickly advance to the next base on an overthrow, (3) the hook slide is used mainly

Calling the close one. (Courtesy of Tommy Geddie.)

to avoid the tag if it is an extremely tight play, and (4) sliding creates additional pressure on the defense; therefore, opening up offensive opportunities.

9. Base coaching

   a) Two coaches—one on first and one on third—should be used to help the runners. The most experienced person should be stationed at third base because of the chances to score from this position.

   b) The first-base coach controls the movements of the runner approaching and leaving first base; the third-base coach controls the runner approaching or leaving second or third base. The third-base coach also gives signals to the batter.

   c) The purpose of batting signals is to help the batter and runner know when to take the pitch, steal, bunt, or hit and run. To throw off the opponents, batting signals can be very complex and contain useless devices. The coach gives many signals that the batter and runner ignore; then the coach gives the cut-off signal (a signal predetermined by the team, such as coach touching ear). The next signal after the cut-off sign is the one the players follow. The cut-off signal may be changed each game, to prevent the opponents from reading the signals.

   d) Running signals are sometimes given with the hands, sometimes verbally. Some common coaches' signals are: (1) circling arm high over head (keep running), (2) both arms held high over the head with palms facing runner (stop), (3) quick downward movement with hands (slide), and (4) circling left arm over head with right arm held high, palm facing runner (continue to next base, make turn, and stop to locate ball and determine whether to continue).

10. Reading batters and signals

a) The catcher signals for the type of pitch; however, the pitcher must also be aware of the batter's weaknesses. The pitcher has the final say on the type of ball to be thrown.

b) The catcher signals by showing the pitcher a prearranged number of fingers on her bare hand. (For instance, one finger means a fast ball, two an in-curve, etc.) While the catcher is in the crouched position, she hides this hand from the opponents with her legs and her glove.

c) Once the pitcher has agreed to type of ball to be thrown, the catcher goes into a semicrouched position, with feet about shoulder width apart (left foot usually slightly forward). The catcher holds up her glove to give the pitcher something to aim at, and maintains balance by keeping her weight on the balls of her feet. This enables her to push off quickly to stop any stray balls, or to make the throw to a base.

d) Pitcher and catcher can pick out a batter's weaknesses by looking at: (1) her grip, (2) her stance, (3) her position in the box in relation to the plate, (4) her preliminary swings, and (5) her attitude.

e) Generally, a batter likes to swing her bat back and forth in her strongest hitting area as she waits for the pitch.

f) If the batter is choking up on the bat, curves to the outside corner are effective because of her limited reach. A good change of pace is a high inside ball.

g) If the batter is using the power grip at the end of the handle, balls thrown to the inside corner usually cause her to hit with the weak part of the bat.

h) If the batter takes a long step forward as she swings at the ball or tends to swing upward, high balls usually result in pop-ups.

i) If the batter steps toward the plate on her swing rather than toward the pitcher, inside balls are effective.

j) If the batter's position is away from the plate, or if she tends to steps away from the ball on her swing, place the balls to the outside corner.

k) If the batter seems to be nervous or crowds the plate, inside balls usually increase her nervousness or cause her to hit balls off the weaker part of the bat.

l) If a batter seems to be impatient or eager to hit the ball, pitcher and catcher should take their time between deliveries. A bad pitch usually draws the batter into a swing, while a slow ball may catch her off balance and throw her timing off.

m) When you're pitching to a power hitter, keep the ball away from the center of the plate, and vary the pitches. Don't use the fast ball, since this speed plus her own power usually results in a long hit ball when the batter does make contact.

n) When the situation calls for a bunt, place the ball high and inside. The fast ball is usually best because it's hard for the batter to eliminate the speed for an effective bunt.

o) If the count is two strikes and no balls, throw a ball slightly outside the hitting area. The batter will probably swing at anything that's close.

p) Pitchers and catchers should file away all the information they can get about batters. In a crucial situation, a good memory can win the ball game.

Strategy

The best way to win a softball game is to keep the opponents from getting hits, because hits are what give them the chance to score. Preventing hits is mainly the pitcher's job. Here are some general things to remember about pitching: (1) Against the player who chokes up on the bat, use outside curve or high, inside ball. (2) Against the power hitter, or the hitter using the long grip, use inside curves or inside slants. (3) In bunting situations, use high, inside, fast balls. (4) Against the hitter who crowds the plate, use inside pitches. (5) Against players who stand back from the plate, use outside balls. (6) Against hitters who swing hard, use change of pace. (7) When you are pitching to a good hitter and want to determine her weakness, aim for corners and use several different types of ball.

When the count is at two strikes and no balls, or two strikes and one ball, throw close to the corners of the plate, to tempt the batter to swing at a bad pitch. When there are runners on base, keep balls low to increase the likelihood of a ground ball and a chance at a double play.

Thinking Ahead and Making Calls

Every player on the team should at all times know: (1) the exact score and the number of outs, strikes, etc., (2) positions of the base-runners, and (3) the best place to play the ball when a player catches it. If there are two outs, try for the easiest out. When the ball is hit to the outfield, the person who catches it should throw it immediately to the infield, aiming it one base ahead of the runner. When the ball is hit between an outfielder and an infielder, the outfielder should be the one to call for the ball, since she is in a better position to move into it and make the throw after the catch. A call for the ball should be made any time it is hit between two positions, with the player going from right to left making the catch when possible; this allows an easier throw-in.

On infield flies, the pitcher and the catcher should let another player take the catch whenever possible. If a runner or runners are on base, a player who does not have to cover a base should catch the ball; otherwise the infielder might be pulled too much out of position to make a play if she needs to. When a catch is being made by a baseman, however, other players should always be prepared to cover her base. On ground balls, the player closest to the ball should try to field it in order to save time in making the throw. If there is doubt as to who should take the ball, the person in the best position to throw to a base after the catch should call for the ball. If the sun makes it hard for players to see, a player who can turn partly or completely away from the glare should play the ball. High flies over first and third bases should be taken by the second baseman and the shortstop, respectively, since they have a better view of the ball than other players.

On a force-out play, the ball should be thrown about chest high. On a tag-out, it should be aimed about a foot above the ground. On tags, the person on base should touch the runner with the back of her glove to prevent losing the ball on the tag.

Positioning of Players

A team plays deep (infielders move almost back to grass of outfield) when a strong hitter is at bat or when there are no outs. A team plays tight, or "in" (in-fielders come in several feet from base paths), when a weak batter is up, or when a runner threatens to score. A ground ball is more likely to get by the infield that has pulled in, so this formation is not used when a strong hitter is up at bat, unless there is a runner in position to score.

Pitcher's Responsibilities

Ordinarily, the pitcher fields all balls hit toward her and any bunts along the base lines. If she can't stop a ball going to her left, she should move over quickly to cover first base, since the first baseman will be drawn off the base to field the ball. On outfield hits with runners on base, the pitcher covers behind the third base-man or the catcher to cut off any overthrow. She also backs up the third baseman when a runner is on first, and the catcher when a runner is on second. If the catcher loses a pitched ball, and there is a runner on base, the pitcher moves in quickly to cover home plate.

Catcher's Responsibilities

The catcher's responsibilities include: (1) fielding hits and bunts close to the plate, (2) getting rid of her mask quickly to catch pop-ups at the plate, (3) calling for curves, fast balls, etc., (4) throwing to side of base away from runner, (5) picking off players attempting to steal, (6) backing up first baseman if there are no runners on base, (7) blocking home plate on scoring plays, and (8) helping run down player caught between third and home.

First Baseman

The first baseman's position is about 10 feet toward second base and about 8–10 feet behind the base path if there are no runners on base. If a ball is hit to her, she must make the stop and then throw to the pitcher covering the base. With a run-ner on first, the first baseman plays tighter for a possible pick-off. If pulled off base to stop the ball on a possible double-play situation, she throws to second and moves back to first for the return throw. If the pitcher has come in to cover her base, she moves out of the path of the ball from second to first. On a throw-in from right field, the first baseman moves into position to intercept the throw, if necessary, and relay it on to home. If the runner has already crossed the plate, she may be able to make a play at one of the other bases. When receiving a throw, tag base with foot opposite glove hand (tag inside corner of bag on throw from third, middle, or side of bag on throws from shortstop, and outside corner on throws from second baseman). First baseman should develop ability to stretch for balls low, high, or to the side of the base.

Second Baseman

The second baseman usually plays about 15 feet to the left of second base (second baseman's left) and about 8 feet behind the base path. Balls to the right of second base are fielded by the second baseman and thrown to the shortstop, who should be covering the base. Balls to the left of the base are fielded by the shortstop, while the second baseman covers the base. With a runner on first, the second baseman watches for a possible steal. Second baseman tags base with left foot as she receives ball for double play and immediately pushes off to right foot and then throws to first. If throw is late, she tags with left foot behind base, and steps toward first with throw.

Shortstop

The shortstop plays about 18 feet to the right of second base and about 15 feet behind the base path. She covers the left side of the infield, backs up the second baseman, relays balls thrown in from left field, covers third base when the third baseman is pulled off, and helps with run-down plays. Shortstop tags base with right foot and throws to first as she pushes off the bag and out of the base path. Tagging the outside corner is more common on a throw from the second baseman.

Third Baseman

Third baseman must field all balls hit down her baseline, takes pop-ups in area between third base and home and those near the pitcher, and helps with run-downs between third and home. Her position is usually about 8 feet to her left of third base and about 5 feet behind it.

Fielders

The left fielder backs up the center-fielder, shortstop, and third baseman. The center-fielder backs up the right and left fielders, the shortstop, and second baseman. She also backs up second base on an attempted steal, pick-off, run-down play, or force-out. The right fielder backs up the center-fielder and the second and first baseman. Fielders should return the ball to the cut-off or infield as quickly as possible.

Waiting for the good one. (Courtesy of UTA News Service,
James Russell.)

Batting Order

The first batter in the batting order should be the one most likely to get on base.
The second batter is usually chosen on her ability to bunt or to hit behind the runner, while the third, fourth, and fifth batters should be consistent or power hitters. The fourth player should be the strongest hitter on the team. The other batters are usually the weaker hitters, with the pitcher batting last.

Hit-and-Run

The hit-and-run is initiated by the third-base coach, who signals the play to the
batter and the runner. As the ball is pitched, the runner breaks for second to draw
the second baseman in, and the batter tries to hit the ball through the hole between second and first. When there is a runner on first, or runners on first and
third, the hit-and-run can be used. The signal for the hit-and-run should be given
only on a count that forces the pitcher to give the batter a fairly good ball. This
play is hard to execute, and often ends up with the batter hitting into a double
play.

Squeeze Play

In a squeeze play, the objective is to get a runner home from third by a sacrifice
bunt. It can be executed two ways: (1) The player on third starts for home as soon
as the pitch is released. (2) The player on third waits until the ball has actually
been bunted.

   If there is a runner on first base, the batter usually lets the first ball go by, to
give the runner a chance to steal second. The batter should try to hit behind the
runner to right field, or attempt a bunt down the third-base line to force a long
throw to first.

SLOW-PITCH SOFTBALL

Slow-pitch softball has grown rapidly in popularity. Although fundamentals are basically the same in fast pitch and slow pitch (except for pitching), rules, and consequently strategy, differ between the two games. Some of these differences are:

a) Slow pitch has 10 players.

b) Can use extra fielder in the infield behind second base or in the outfield as a short fielder (between the infield and outfield in left field for right-handed batters, or in right field for left-handed batters). Most teams utilize the extra fielder as another regular outfielder so that they have a left centerfielder and a right centerfielder.

c) Runners may not steal. A runner may not leave the bag until the ball is hit or crosses the plate. However, unless the ball is hit, the runner may not advance.

d) Bunting is illegal and so is a chopped swing. A full swing or cut at the ball must be taken.

e) Slow pitch obviously gets its name from the type of ball thrown by the pitcher. In pitching, the ball must have an arc of at least three feet from the point of release and must never travel higher than ten feet from the ground. The strike zone is from the knees to the shoulders rather than from the knees to the armpits as in fast pitch. Since the batter has time to alter her stance and grip after the ball is released, hitting the ball is much easier in slow pitch, making it necessary for the fielders to catch more balls, and to make more tags and plays at the bases during a game.

SWIMMING AND DIVING

Coaching Emphasis for Swimming

1. Practicing strokes for speed events, with special work on butterfly stroke.
2. Developing efficient starts and turns.
3. Working on endurance.

Mechanics

1. Start for front crawl, breast stroke, and butterfly:

   a) Two variations are given here. Select the variation that seems to be the most effective, and then work hard to perfect it. (One well-known coach [49] believes that the circular arm swing is more effective. This variation is discussed in subsection (g).)

   b) Racing start [2]: (1) Place feet three to six inches apart, or in comfortable position. (2) Curl toes over edge of pool or starting block. (3) On "take your mark," bend forward from trunk, with weight concentrated on balls of feet, knees flexed, and arms back. (4) Keep head up, with eyes on far end of pool. (Some people prefer to focus on a point about halfway down the pool.) (5) Take 2 or 3 deep breaths and hold until the gun. (6) On starting signal, throw your weight forward by moving your arms back even more, then reversing their swing forcefully to throw them straight out ahead of body, and by flexing and extending knees and ankles with a final push by the toes. (7) Go as far out as possible, and as parallel to water. (8) To increase buoyancy, take deep breath before hitting water. (See Fig. 9–22.)

c) As your body is in the air, place head between arms and keep body extended in as straight a line as possible. Your hands should touch the water first, then the rest of your body.

d) Let your body go under water slightly, to cut down water resistance on top where it is choppy.

e) Stay in glide until speed has slowed to maximum swimming speed, then start stroke. Don't turn head for 2 or 3 strokes, until rhythm has been established.

Problems with Start	Corrections and Coaching Hints
Start too slow. Causes: Incorrect position before starting signal; lack of concentration on starting signal; slow reflexes.	On "take-your-mark" signal, bend knees, curl toes over side, and put arms back. Take two deep breaths and hold until starting signal, listening only for the gun. Practice starts while someone uses signals that are differently spaced, to learn to react automatically to signal rather than to movement of others around you. Experiment with the circular arm motion to see whether this gives you a faster start.
Dive too shallow. Causes: keeping head up; turning hands up at an angle toward the surface. Result: less speed, because of resistance of water on surface.	Put head between arms on dive; keep fingers and hands in straight line with arms and body.
Dive too deep. Causes: putting head down too much; bending from waist. Result: glide slowed, since swimmer must come back up to surface.	Don't duck head; try to keep body horizontal, with legs, trunk, head, arms, hands, and fingers in a straight line. After body is under water, lift head slightly and use hands as rudder to keep body from going too deep into the water.

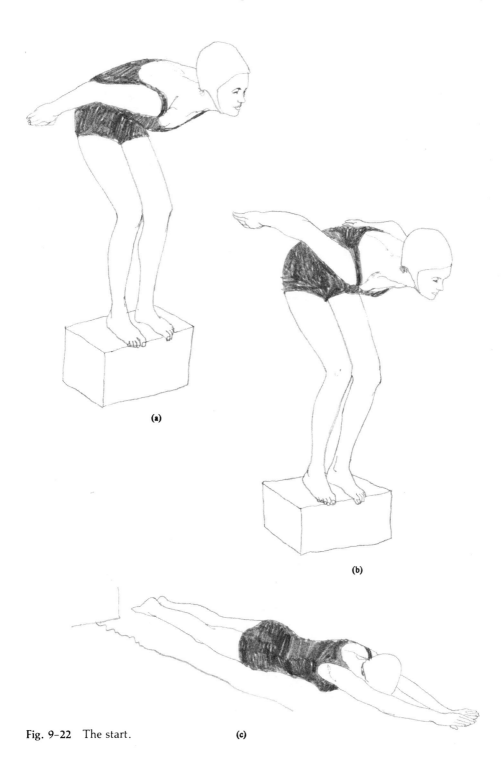

(a)

(b)

(c)

Fig. 9-22   The start.

f) On the breaststroke, let the angle for entry be a little deeper than the angle for the crawl, in order to take your first stroke under water, to increase your speed before surfacing. In the butterfly stroke, as the glide slows down to swimming speed, your legs should begin to recover (let knees bend, bringing heels toward the surface). Your feet are then in position to make the kick downward as your arms begin to pull.

g) Variation of start. Circular arm action is used as follows: (1) Let arms hang down, with arms almost straight, and with palms facing away from pool. (2) Bend body forward at waist, but with less hip and knee flexion than in start previously described. (3) On starting signal, let arms go upward and back in circular motion, and then down and out to help take the body forward. As arms reach their peak and start downward, the heels lift from the starting block, and the bending motion at the hips and the flexion of the knees is increased. (4) When the arms reach the knees, let the legs and ankles push off.

h) A third technique is to use the standard starting position without any knee flexion. At starting signal, flex knees quickly and bring arms downward and out as your legs and ankles push forcefully.

2. Start for backstroke

a) Racing Start: (1) In water, face starting block. (2) Grip starting board or side of pool (hands about 1 to 1½ feet apart). (3) Brace feet against side of pool (anywhere from surface to 3–5 inches under water) with legs about hip width apart. (4) On "take your mark," bring body up and out of water with head forward ("coiled" or tucked as close to wall as possible) and with knees against the chest. (5) At gun, throw arms and head backward. (6) Push legs forcefully against side trying to send body out over the water rather than pushing through it. (7) Arch back slightly so arms and head enter water first. (8) As head and shoulders hit the water, raise head to keep glide near surface (about 15–18 inches from surface).

b) When speed of glide slows to maximum swimming speed, start flutter kick, then first arm stroke. (Although any type of backstroke is permissible under the rules, all good swimmers use the back crawl for competitive swimming.)

c) Take breath during push-away and hold through most of glide (some swimmers prefer to exhale through the nose slowly on glide to keep water out of nose).

Problems with Backstroke Start	*Corrections and Coaching Hints*
Hips and legs hit water first. Result: poor glide. Causes: lack of arch in back; throwing arms and head back weakly.	Fling head and arms back forcefully; arch back slightly. Throw body up and out, rather than just out.

Glide too deep. Result: slowing-down of movement. Causes: wrist hyperextension; keeping head back too long.

Glide on surface. Results: friction and slow glide. Causes: lifting head too soon; not throwing head and arms back enough.

Keep wrists and hands in line with forearm; when head and shoulders enter water, bring head up.

See to it that head and shoulders are under water before head is lifted; throw head and arms back forcefully at start of race.

3. Turn for front crawl

   a) Learn to make turn with either arm; look at wall when about 10 feet out to judge which hand will be leading at turn. (A more advanced turn does not use the hand reach to the wall, but consists of throwing the head downward, bending at the waist, kicking downward with the feet in a "fishtail" action, and pushing downward with the hands as in a surface dive.)

   b) To execute somersault or flip turn:* (1) As you reach out with your hand, duck your head with chin against chest (turn head toward armpit opposite that of reaching arm). Hand must touch wall near the surface. (2) Tuck knees close to body. (Many feel that making the turnover in a pike position is faster.) (3) During somersault, body does a quarter twist (results from turning of head). (4) Extend knees to about 90-degree angle, then straighten forcefully as feet touch side of pool. (5) As feet push off against wall, let body take another quarter turn; end up in glide on face. (See Fig. 9-23.)

   c) To get an effective somersault, duck head quickly when hand touches wall; make the somersault, turn and push off all in one motion.

Problems with Flip Turn

Getting too close to wall before making somersault. Result: shoulders and back hit wall and push-off is poor. Causes: Delay in ducking head; poor timing.

Corrections and Coaching Hints

When you use hand reach, duck head just before or just as you touch wall. Extend arm when touch is made; for maximum strength, let hips be about two feet from wall on push-off. Touch with hand just below the surface. If hand reach is not used, begin flip turn a second or two sooner than usual. (Last arm pull is usually made when swimmer's head is about 4-7 feet from the end of the pool.)

Lack of sense of direction on turn. Causes: closing eyes; taking reaching

Keep eyes open; keep hand in contact with wall until turn is almost com-

---

*Developed by Dave Armbruster in 1936.

(a)

(b)

(c)

(d)

Fig. 9-23 Flip turn from front crawl.

hand off wall too soon; lack of practice.

Lack of power on push-off. Causes: too far from or too close to wall; too little extension of ankles following extension of knees.

pleted; practice turns until movement is done naturally.

Make turn close to wall to allow knee flexion before the push, but not so close that heels remain tight against hips (knee flexion should be about a right angle); straighten legs and then extend ankles forcefully.

4. Turn for backstroke

a) For tumble turn: (1) Reach for wall. (2) Take breath. (3) Let the other hand continue its pull as hand touches wall. (Fingers are pointing inward.) (4) Bend arm to allow head to come close to wall. (5) Tuck legs tightly and turn over shoulder of arm reaching for wall (on turn, let legs, from knees down, come out of water and swing to side). (6) Push feet against wall. (Usually place feet about 14–18 inches below the surface of the water.) (7) As you push, extend arms over head for glide. (8) When glide slows to maximum swimming speed, start stroke. (See Fig. 9–24.)

b) To help with turn, use free hand, with palm inverted, to scull, and use hand touching wall to help exert leverage. Remember: This turn is a spinning or pivoting action on the back rather than a somersault.

Problems with Tumble Turn

Body stays on surface during turn. Result: turn slows down. Cause: failure to lift knees and lower part of legs out of the water on the swing to the side; hand placed too high on the wall.

Making complete somersault. Result: person ends up on face or side rather than back. Cause: legs turned over head rather than swung to side and around shoulder of touching hand.

Lack of force on push-off. Cause: too much flexion in arm, causing hips to be too close to wall; pushing off with hand before turn, forcing hips too far from wall.

Corrections and Coaching Hints

Lift legs from knees down out of water to make the pivoting action; touch wall with hand in a line directly over head (some prefer to touch from 6–10 inches beneath the surface).

Swing legs to side, up and over water as they turn over the shoulder of the arm touching the wall. Remember: The motion is a spinning action on the back.

Extend arm as hand reaches out, but, for maximum push-off power, allow hips to come in close for about a 90-degree knee flexion. Maintain contact with wall with reaching hand during spinning action, but as you throw your legs sideward let your touching arm begin to straighten to push the upper part of your body away from the wall. Use free hand to scull.

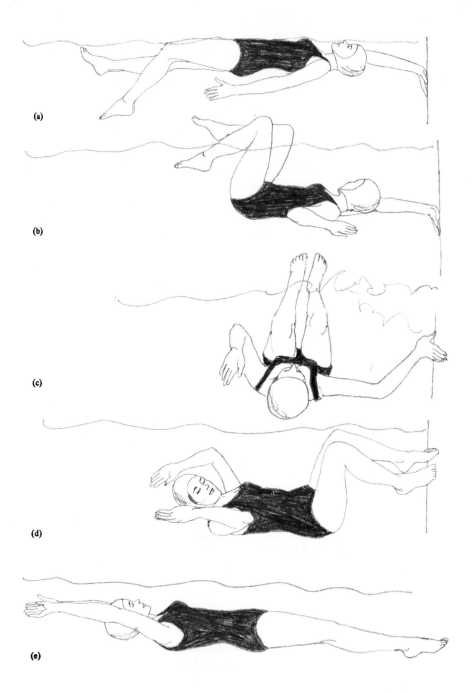

(a)

(b)

(c)

(d)

(e)

Fig. 9–24 Tumble turn from backstroke.

5. Turn for breaststroke and butterfly

    a) To execute: (1) Make contact with wall during arm recovery. (2) Touch wall with both hands (hands 4–8 inches apart, fingers slightly above surface of water). Grasp gutter, or place both hands against wall about water level. (3) Bend arms to allow head to come in close to wall, and bring legs into tight tuck. (4) Push hands against wall to help turn hips to side. (5) Let hand on side of turn come away from wall and pull water across chest to help with turning action (turn head in direction of spin and keep legs tightly tucked until turn is made). (6) For glide on stomach, place feet against wall and push. (Feet usually placed against wall about 2 feet below the surface.) Before feet begin push, take breath and submerge for the glide beneath surface of water. Since the breaststroker is allowed one stroke under water, angle the push-off on the breaststroke turn downward slightly to keep yourself deep enough to take advantage of this stroke under water. See Fig. 9–25.

Problems with Breaststroke and Butterfly Turn	*Corrections and Coaching Hints*
Glide to side rather than straight ahead. Cause: pushing off before complete turn has been made.	Be sure head is completely turned around and both feet are against side of pool before pushing.
Lack of power. Causes: too far from wall on turn, resulting in legs being extended too much when feet touch wall; failure to extend ankles on push-off.	Bend elbows; let head almost touch wall before turn; after extending knees, extend ankles and push with balls of feet and toes.
Glide too deep. Causes: hands placed too low; head lowered too much or too soon; feet too far below surface of water.	Let tips of fingers be just above surface; lower head just before touch, but either lift head for air on the turn, or let it remain under water. Place feet about 2 feet below surface; submerge head to allow glide about 2 feet beneath surface.
Glide too much on surface. Causes: hands placed too high; head not lowered before contact with hands on wall; head and shoulders lifted high out of water on the turn; head lifted too quickly on push-off; feet placed too high on wall.	Place hands properly, fingertips barely at surface; lower head just before touch with hands; keep shoulders in water, and don't let mouth get more than a few inches above the surface of the water; don't lift head on push-off, but submerge it after taking breath of air. Be sure feet make contact with wall about 24 inches below surface.

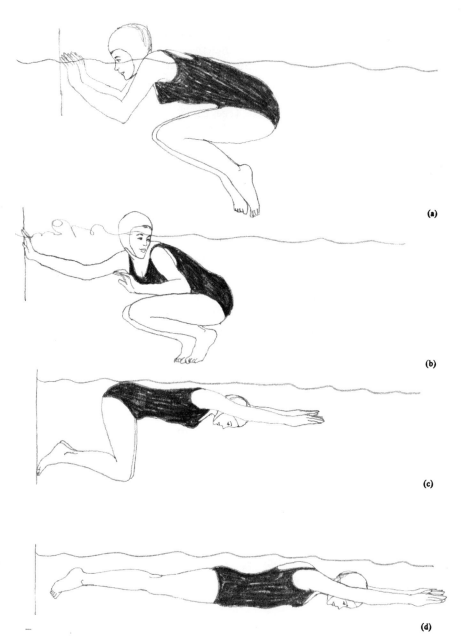

Fig. 9-25   Turn for breaststroke or butterfly stroke.

6. The butterfly stroke (see Fig. 9–26)

a) This stroke demands strong abdominal and shoulder muscles, as well as good ankle flexibility.

b) You must synchronize leg action (dolphin kick) with arm stroke to conserve energy and get the most power possible.

c) Dolphin kick: (1) To start upward beat, lift hips; as legs pass line of body, begin to bend knees. (2) As feet near surface of water, start downstroke, with knees flexed about 90 degrees at last part of downbeat, then straighten out knees forcefully. (3) On upbeat, point toes back. (4) On downbeat, hyperextend feet, with toes turned slightly in. Keep knees and ankles flexible for the up-and-down motion while the whole body weaves in an undulating motion.

d) Raise your hips upward on the downward kick and drop them slightly on the upbeat as your legs propel your body by a fishlike or whipping action.

e) Let your legs go up and down twice during one complete arm motion. Do first kick (legs going down) just after hands have entered the water. Do second kick when arms start their recovery. The first kick is usually the most forceful of the two.

f) Arm motion: (1) Start with arms over head, with palms turned downward and slightly outward (keep arms and fingers relaxed). Hands should enter water before arms. (2) As arms hit water, start stroke immediately. (3) Pull arms obliquely downward and outward. After the press outward, let hands begin to come closer together, but then move apart again as stroke continues outward and backward. (Arm pull pattern has been described as an hourglass or double-S pull [49].) (4) Lift arms out of water and shoot forward (keep few inches above surface to decrease water resistance). Use straight-arm recovery (start with elbows bent slightly). (5) Let arms go back into water in front of shoulders. (6) Repeat stroke.

g) Lift head for breath of air either at end of arm pull backward or during the recovery. You should complete your breath before your arms move by your shoulders on the recovery. Most swimmers breathe only every other stroke, although timing of breathing depends on the distance of the race. In short races, take a breath after every three strokes. When you are swimming long distances, you may have to take a breath with every stroke. Don't lift your head any higher than you have to to get your mouth clear of the water.

h) Timing of arms and legs is big factor in speed.

i) To start butterfly stroke after glide: (1) Bend legs at knees to start upbeat. (2) Let arms start pull backward and legs go into downbeat. (3) As arms continue pull to hips, let legs start back up on second upbeat. (4) As arms

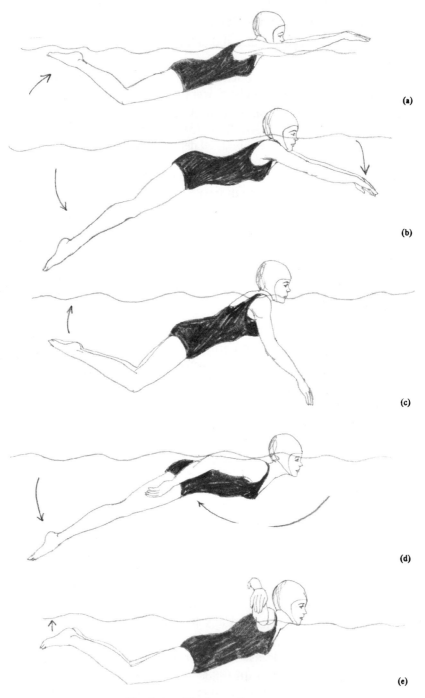

Fig. 9-26 The butterfly stroke.

come out of water for recovery, let legs start second downbeat. (5) When arms are about halfway through recovery, legs are moving up for second upbeat of the cycle.

Problems with Butterfly	*Corrections and Coaching Hints*
Lack of timing. Causes: arms too slow on pull or recovery; leg motion has too great a range.	Increase speed of arm pull and recovery; decrease distance covered by legs by stopping upbeat sooner. Body and leg movements should be relaxed.
Lack of power. Causes: poor timing; failure to get full thrust with legs because of incorrect kick or lack of stomach and leg strength; weak pull with arms.	Work on timing to get arms and legs synchronized; start upbeat with legs straight, bending them after legs have passed line of body, point toes, then on downbeat turn toes inward slightly, straighten knees forcefully. Use hourglass pattern on pull, with fingers relaxed but together. Build up strength by sit-ups, leg lifts, etc.
Inability to breathe. Cause: lifting head at wrong time in stroke.	Your head will automatically be lifted partially by the pull back and the downbeat of arms and legs during recovery; lift head slightly at completion of arm pull and as arms fly through the air during recovery.

Strategy

Speed swimming or competitive swimming is a matter of speed in the short events and speed and endurance in the longer events. Therefore you should plan your strategy accordingly. In short races, strategy involves getting a good start and swimming at top speed for the entire race. In the longer events, strategy involves a good start, quick turns, and the ability to conserve energy if you cannot cover the entire distance at maximum speed.

Work on establishing the best rhythm, the rhythm that will enable you to swim at top speed without wasting effort and energy. Sticking with an established rhythm during a race enables you to turn in your best possible time. Don't look around during the race because that throws your rhythm off and cuts down your speed. If it's a close race and you need to know how close the competition is, glance to the side during the normal breathing action.

In many cases, poor performance is a result of improper breathing. During competition, many people tighten up too much and begin to breathe differently from the way they ordinarily would during practice; this causes them to tire more quickly. Take 2 or 3 deep breaths before you start, and then try to breathe normally.

If you are entering endurance events, there is no substitute for conditioning. In order to perform at top efficiency, you have to build up to the event by practicing your start and turns until they are as perfect as you can make them. Only then will you achieve the best strategy: performance at maximum speed.

In some competitions, you may have a choice of lanes. If so, choose one of the two middle lanes, since the water is not as choppy and it gives you a better view of your opponents during the race. Before the race, check to see whether your lane has a warning mark 4 feet from the turning wall, and whether the lane markers are on the bottom of the pool or on the surface of the water.

When swimming middle and long distances, learn to pace yourself in order to save enough energy to finish strong. Decide whether you want to expend extra energy to take the lead at the start, or to swim at a consistent pace in hopes that your opponent will not be able to match the pace. Avoid building up a high oxygen debt at the beginning of the race.

In swimming against others of similar skill, never let an opponent get more than a length or a length and a half ahead of you; preferably less than that. If you're behind in the last part of the race, you may decide to pass the opponent and then try to hold this lead for the rest of the race. You can take the lead by trying faster turns, by increasing the speed of your strokes, or by holding to a pace that will tire the opponent.

Decide on your strategy before the race, but be able to adjust this plan according to the way the race is going. Sometimes a race is won by strategy; oftentimes, it is won by pure heart and determination.

In the 400-meter medley, one has to swim the backstroke the first 100 meters, the breaststroke the second 100, the butterfly the third 100, and freestyle the last 100 meters. Anyone training for the individual medley should be proficient in at least three strokes and have exceptional endurance. In the medley relay, the same order is used. Team members should be selected according to their strengths in the specific areas.

Coaching Emphasis in Diving

1. Practicing of approach, take-off, execution of movement in air, and entry into the water, with special emphasis on the three basic positions in the air: the layout, the pike, and the tuck.

2. Work on the five basic dives (forward dive, backward dive, reverse dive, inward dive, and forward dive with one-half twist).

3. Developing skill in doing a somersault in a tuck or pike position (forward, backward, inward, and reverse), in combining a twist for various combinations, and in executing a "save" when body is at wrong angle for the entry.

Mechanics

1. Somersaults

   a) Keep in mind that the body rotates faster in tuck position than in pike or lay-out position, and that the head largely controls the movement of the body.

b) To come out of somersault correctly when timing is off: (1) if turn is too slow, tuck body even more, and (2) if turn is too fast, straighten out body to slow turn down.

c) When you are combining multiple twists with multiple somersaults, use the pike position rather than the tuck position, to enable yourself to go from one move to another.

d) The forward somersault and the inward somersault are executed in the same way, except the the take-off for the inward one is backward (facing board). To execute forward somersault or inward one: (1) Start movement after feet have left board. (2) Bend knees and bring heels in close to hips, meanwhile throwing arms, head, and upper body downward. (3) Grip legs about halfway between knees and ankles to help tighten tuck. (4) Hold position until desired rotation has been accomplished. (5) For entry into water, come out of tuck position (straighten legs and lift chest and head up to come out of tuck).

e) If you are entering water feet first, straighten arms, place hands against thighs, and point toes; if entering head first, extend hands over head (toes pointed).

f) To avoid hitting diving board on the inward somersault, use same take-off as for the inward header, completing the press (spring) before starting the spin. (See Fig. 9-27.)

g) To do a backward somersault: (1) Start movement during thrust from board. (2) Lift arms, chest, and head upward. (As you move your arms above your head, tilt your head backward.) (3) Bring legs up close into tuck position. (4) Grasp legs with hands. (5) Hold tuck until you reach desired position. To help keep entry straight, keep your eyes on the end of the board.

h) To gain more rotation for a move such as the one-and-a-half, use more force in throwing upper body backward, or use a tighter tuck. (See Fig. 9-28.)

Problems with Somersaults

Corrections and Coaching Hints

Going too far over. Cause: waiting too long to open tuck, which results in poor entry.

Extend legs sooner; lift head. Open tuck usually when you have completed three-quarters of a turn.

Not going over far enough. Causes: lack of spinning action; opening tuck too soon. Results in poor entry.

On forward somersault, bring arms, head, and upper body forward forcefully. On backward somersault, throw arms, head, and chest back more. Pull legs in with hands for tighter tuck; hold tuck longer before opening up.

Fig. 9–27   Inward somersault.

Fig. 9-28 Backward one-and-a-half.

On one-and-a-half, going too far over. Causes: tuck opened too late; arms extended over head at same time legs are straightened out.

On one-and-a-half, not going far enough over. Causes: coming out of tuck too soon, poor spinning action. May also happen if tuck is too loose.

Straighten legs by kicking out, pull head back before bringing arms over head (backward one-and-a-half). If entry is still long, open tuck sooner.

Hold tuck longer; on backward somersault, swing arms over head at same time you extend legs and throw head backward. On forward somersault, bring tuck in tighter, throwing arms, head, and upper body down forcefully to start spin; hold tuck longer. Tighten arms around legs to make tuck more compact.

i) Reverse somersault: (1) Execute in same way you execute back somersault, except that direction of take-off is forward rather than backward. (2) To avoid hitting board, complete press *before* executing spin. (3) Open tuck when body is about three-fourths of the way around. (See Fig. 9–29.)

Problems with Reverse Somersault

Inability to get over quickly enough. Causes: too little arm, head, and chest movement; too loose a tuck; leaning too far forward when leaving the board.

Going over too fast. Causes: throwing arms, head and chest backward too forcefully; staying in tuck too long.

Coming down too close to board. Cause: starting movements for spin before full press is completed.

Corrections and Coaching Hints

After complete press, and after the arms have reached upward, tilt your head and chest backward; tuck legs close to body. Don't lean too far forward out of fear of hitting board.

Don't use as much force in throwing upper body backward; come out of tuck sooner; delay arm reach over head until after you extend legs.

Wait until you have completed press and body is well into the air before executing backward spin.

2. Pike dives
   a) Remember that abdominal strength and hip flexibility are very important.
   b) Develop flexibility in ankles especially, for graceful line when pointing toes.
   c) To execute pike dives: (1) Use more force than in tuck position. (2) Keep legs straight. (3) Place hands behind the knees. (4) For deeper pike, relax hips. (5) Point toes and extend ankles. (See Fig. 9–30.)

Fig. 9-29   Reverse one-and-a-half.

Fig. 9-30   Somersault in pike position.

Fig. 9–31 Forward dive layout with one-half twist.

3. Twists

    a) For more difficult dive, combine twist with somersault, pike, or lay-out.

    b) Control speed of twist by: (1) extending arms (for slower turn), (2) bringing arms in closer to body (for faster turn).

    c) To execute twist: (1) Move both arms at same time in direction of turn. (2) Bring one arm up and behind head (for twist to left, use left arm). (3) Let other arm "reach" across chest (for twist to left, right arm does this). (4) Keep the arm that goes up over head close to the head. (You may bend elbow.)

    d) To execute forward dive lay-out with one-half twist to the left: (1) Use same take-off as for swan dive. (2) On the lift, let arms begin the turn. (3) As body leaves board, swing arms up over head. (4) Move right arm into position as for a swan dive. (5) Move left arm into same position, but pulled backward. (6) To continue twisting movement, keep left arm back. (7) Just before entry, let right hand join left hand. (See Fig. 9–31.)

Problems with Twist	*Corrections and Coaching Hints*
Body hits water sideways rather than vertically. Cause: pressing laterally from the board.	As you leave board, twist slightly but smoothly.
Inability to make complete half-twist. Result: body ends up turned to the side rather than with back to board on entry. Cause: too little motion to start twist as arms swing overhead on leaving board.	Pull left arm backward from swan position as body leaves board, resulting in first quarter of twist. Hold arm behind head to continue twisting movement before entry.

4. Saves [24]

    a) Use a save to correct the angle of entry, to eliminate excessive splashing.

    b) To execute reverse save: (1) Use reverse save when timing is off on backward-spinning dive. (2) Keep same arch until body is in water to waist. (3) Then increase arch of back (by raising head and using arms to make entry shallow). (4) Bend knees to allow lower legs to enter on a vertical plane. (See Fig. 9–32(a).)

    c) To execute forward save: (1) Use forward·save when spinning action is forward and timing is off for entry. (2) Start correction movements when lower legs are still above water. (3) Go into forward pike position by bringing head and arms forward. (4) Use arms to pull on water to deepen pike and to turn upper body toward the surface. (See Fig. 9–32(b).)

Fig. 9-32 (a)   Reverse save.

Fig. 9–32 (b) Forward save.

Strategy

Strategy in diving involves both physical and mental readiness. Try to increase the flexibility in your hips and ankles by a sound training program. Strength in the abdominal region is especially needed for dives involving the pike position. You should be able to control all the muscles of your body, and they should all be *firm* muscles. This gives you poise and grace in the air and strength and control upon entry into the water.

Practice under competitive situations. Before you use a particular dive in competition, work on it until you feel you have it really under control; confidence plays a big role in competitive diving. To help your timing, use a trampoline, or a diving board with an air mattress underneath, during off-seasons. It may help you, while you are practicing feet-first entries into the water, to use a nose clip; this may prevent nasal and sinus congestion. Avoid excessive bouncing on the board, since this may lead to shin splints. Try to develop courage, since advanced dives require daring and the ability to take occasional hard smacks on the water.

While in the starting position, concentrate on the dive you're about to execute; visualize it in your mind and picture yourself doing it perfectly. To relax, take two or three deep breaths before the approach.

Before a meet, practice as much as possible on the board you're going to use, so that you can make any needed adjustments in spring, space perception, etc.

Strive to analyze your mistakes so that you won't repeat them the next time you attempt the same dive, or a similar one. In diving, performance depends on the individual alone. Therefore strategy in diving means being at your best, both physically and mentally.

TENNIS

Coaching Emphasis

1. Controlling forehand and backhand.
2. Placement and variety of serve.
3. Developing strong overhead and volley, and "touch" on the drop shot.
4. Practicing the lob as a defensive stroke.
5. Strategy.

Mechanics

1. Twist serve
   a) The twist serve requires much back and abdominal strength; for some girls, it may create too much strain on the back.
   b) To execute American twist: (1) Use backhand grip. (2) Use stance slightly more parallel to base line than stance in slice serve. (3) Toss ball behind head and a little more to left than for slice or flat serve. (4) Bend body

backward, with knees bent. (5) Keep weight on balls of feet (concentrate weight on rear foot during toss-up; shift it to forward foot during hit). (6) Snap body, arm, wrist, and racket up and out, in that order. (7) Let racket face go up and slightly over top of ball to create top spin. (8) Let follow-through go to right side of body. (See Fig. 9-33.)

Problems with American Twist	Corrections and Coaching Hints
Poor toss. Cause: ball does not go high enough or far enough behind head.	Let arm action be slightly backward; make toss slightly higher than one can reach with racket.
Poor balance. Causes: weight on heels; lack of knee flexion; improper spacing of feet.	Keep weight on balls of feet; on toss-up, shift weight to rear foot; on hit, shift it to forward foot. Bend knees on toss-up, straighten them on hit; space feet comfortably.
Lack of top spin. Cause: incorrect wrist action. Result: inadequate bounce or "kick" when ball hits ground.	Immediately on contact with ball, roll face of racket over ball, snapping wrist and whipping racket out to right.
Lack of power. Cause: incorrect body and wrist action.	Cock wrist and then snap it forcefully. You get more power if you snap body and arm forward before contact.
Lack of accuracy. Cause: inconsistency in stance, toss-up, or shoulder rotation.	Take same stance each time; practice toss-up to get it in same place each time; keep left shoulder toward net as long as possible.

2. Volley

   a) Use modified Eastern or Continental grip, because fast play at net does not allow time for change in grips. (In this grip, the hand is placed in a way that is halfway between a forehand and a backhand grip, with fingers slightly closer together than in the regular grip.)

   b) To execute volley: (1) Keep weight low and knees bent. (2) Keep racket head above wrist. (3) Rotate upper body to get shoulder toward net if possible. (4) Watch ball. (5) Keep wrist firm. (6) Block ball and use short follow-through.

   c) Keep body weight in motion by bouncing slightly on balls of feet as you wait for ball at net.

   d) Make contact with ball slightly in front of the body.

   e) If ball drops below net before hit, angle racket face up slightly to clear net on volley.

   f) Work on deep placements and angled shots on the volley.

(a)

(b)

Fig. 9-33 American twist serve.

Problems with Volley

Corrections and Coaching Hints

Lack of confidence. Cause: inadequate practice. Results: unsure and weak hits.

Get someone to hit soft volleys to you until you feel confident in your ability to volley. Practice volleying against a wall which has a line drawn on it at net height.

Too much swing. Results: lack of control and inability to get ready for next ball.

Just block ball and then "push" it back; if you have a firm wrist, this will give the ball enough power so that the rebound will go back over the net.

Too much wrist action. Results: inaccuracy, caused by cocking and uncocking of wrist.

Don't allow wrist to break back; keep wrist locked and firm; let wrist act as an extension of the arm.

Too much spin on ball. Results: ball goes into net; ball bounces too high. Cause: racket head dropped on contact.

Keep ball on strings as long as possible; lock wrist and make contact with ball slightly in front of body, pushing forward about a foot on the follow-through. Keep racket head above wrist. Don't cut under ball be angling racket face back unless ball has dropped below the net and the angled face is necessary for clearing the net.

Lack of power and accuracy. Causes: no follow-through at all; wrist "gives" with ball; ball hit behind body; lack of strength.

Take short follow-through; keep wrist firm; contact ball in front of body. Build up arm and wrist strength by practicing backhand and forehand strokes, swinging *slowly* with the press on the racket.

Ball hits wood. Causes: lack of concentration; moving in too close to ball.

Watch ball all the way; position body to allow room for volley without too much crowding of arm.

Poor positioning at the net. Results: balls hit at feet of player; player can't reach balls.

Practice stroking ball from base line, then move in to net on strong returns for the volley; go beyond service line; set up position on side of center line, as previous placement, to cut off the shortest return.*

---

*For example of cutting off the shortest return, see Fig. 9–8.

Poor reactions. Causes: inertia of the body; lack of knee flexion; inability to anticipate.

Bounce lightly on toes; keep body moving while waiting; keep weight low with knees bent; try to anticipate opponent's best possible return.

3. Smash or overhead stroke
   a) Use motion similar to that used in slice or flat serve.
   b) To execute smash or overhead stroke: (1) Get in position under ball (let ball drop slightly in front of right shoulder). (2) Bring racket back behind head, cocking wrist. (3) Shift weight to rear foot as you bring racket back. (4) Time swing to hit ball at height of reach. (5) Extend arm and snap wrist through ball while shifting weight forward. (6) Let follow-through be to left side of body. (See Fig. 9-34.)
   c) Turn left side slightly toward net while waiting for ball.
   d) If you're having trouble with timing, try two things: (1) Wait for ball with racket on shoulder rather than taking full swing. (2) If lob is high, let it bounce before smashing it.
   e) Practice positioning by tossing balls high into the air, then moving under ball for hit.

Problems with Smash

Corrections and Coaching Hints

Poor timing. Result: ball not hit solidly. Cause: ball too high or too low on hit.

Move into position quickly; let ball bounce if lob is high; reach up to hit ball so that arm is extended as you make contact with ball.

Poor Positioning. Result: ball hit into net or out of court. Causes: player not getting in line with ball; player hitting in an off-balance position.

Hustle into position; get in direct line with ball and allow it to drop in front of right shoulder. If ball goes into net, you may have let it drop too low or may need to get more directly under it before contact. If ball goes out of court, body is too far under ball or wrist snap is too late.

Lack of power. Result: weak hit. Cause: incorrect wrist and body action.

Cock wrist and snap it through ball; shift weight from rear to forward foot before hit, and follow through across left side of body.

4. Drop shot
   a) This shot requires soft touch and "feel."
   b) You can execute a drop shot by allowing racket face to give slightly on contact with ball; this is even more effective when you apply spin.

(a)

(b)

(c)

Fig. 9–34   Overhead.

c) Try to place ball just over net.

d) Use the drop shot when: (1) opponent plays deep at baseline, (2) opponent's movement has previously been away from net, and (3) you want to pull opponent up to net for a passing shot.

e) To execute the drop shot, use the same movement you use for any other stroke, except at the last moment, stop forward stroke and let racket "give" or recoil slightly as you hit the ball. For spin, angle racket face and move down or across ball gently.

5. Spins

a) Top spin: (1) You are using top spin when your racket face moves up and over the ball, with the movement starting behind the ball. (2) To keep ball in court more easily, use top spin on forehand and backhand drives. (3) The top spin gives a lower line of flight. (4) The top spin causes faster and lower bounce.

b) Side spin: (1) Use side spin for change of pace, or on service, to achieve a slice. (2) To make ball have a side spin, let racket face move down and to the side of ball. (3) Note that bounce is sideways and higher than usual. (4) To execute a side spin, you must snap wrist toward ground.

c) Back spin: (1) Use back spin to create a chop; this is very effective on drop shots. (2) To execute a back spin, let racket face move downward and slightly under ball from the back. (3) Note that bounce is higher than usual, and almost vertical.

Strategy

Work continually on perfecting your strokes and on obtaining endurance. Set up your practice sessions with the aim of achieving accuracy on specific strokes. For example, if you're weak in hitting the backhand cross-court shot, practice this two ways: (1) Stand in the left-hand corner of the court and stroke balls across the net into the right-hand corner (preferably by hitting with another player, but you could use a bucket of balls). (2) Run across the court to take the backhand and stroke it to the opposite corner; then move back to the center of the court to repeat the movement. Or take a bucket of balls and practice your slice service by aiming at specific areas marked out in the service box.

Practice against another good player is a must. Hitting a thrown ball is not the same as stroking a ball hit at you by a racket. In tennis as in everything else, there's no substitute for real live people and gamelike situations.

Playing the Opponent

Everybody plays a different game of tennis. Within certain limits, you must adjust your game to cope with a specific type of game.

To beat the steady player, either play more steadily than she does or play very aggressively to get the sure put-away shots. When you're playing against a

Keeping the ball in play with a back-hand. (Courtesy of Tom Smart.)

girl who likes to rush the net, keep her off-balance by keeping the drives deep. If the net player does come up to the net, use lobs to force her away from it, or try to pass her down the sideline. If the opponent hits the ball hard, use soft returns to prevent her from increasing her power by combining her force with a hard-hit return; drop shots, chops, and soft angled shots are good against this type of player. You may even lob the ball back continually, provided you keep it deep to prevent a smash. This again prevents her from combining her power with your power on regular strokes.

Surface

The type of surface you compete on can make quite a difference in the type of game you play. On hard surfaces, the player who has a strong game with a fast serve and a good volley has the advantage, because of the fast bounce on the court. On clay and other soft-surface courts, the ball bounces more slowly. Drop shots, chops, and slice or twist serves are effective on this type of court because the spin takes hold better. Slow-moving players have an advantage on clay and soft-surface courts (the bounce gives more time to get to the ball) such courts are a disadvantage to the power hitter.

Grass courts give the edge to the aggressive player because of the low bounce and skid. It is almost impossible to get to a hard-hit ball on grass courts because of the speed of the ball as it rebounds off the court. Here the advantage definitely belongs to the player with a hard serve, strong strokes, and an accurate volley. Drop shots can be effective at times, since a person has trouble starting or stopping quickly because of the footing on the grass.

Wind

Wind can also affect a person's game. If the wind is blowing toward you, you should: (1) Keep lobs to a minimum. (2) Hit ground strokes harder than usual. (3) Use drop shots if opponent is playing deep. (4) On passing shots at the net, keep ball low and to opponent's weak side.

If wind is coming from behind you, you should: (1) Keep lobs to a minimum. (2) Use top spin to keep balls in court. (3) Keep drop shots to a minimum. (4) Let high lobs bounce before smashing them. (5) Move in closer to receive service. (6) Keep ball in play until opponent hits weak shot into the wind; then be aggressive for put-away.

When hitting into a cross wind: (1) Allow a margin for error. (2) Get in position quickly, allowing for movement of ball toward or away from you, according to direction of wind. (3) Keep ball in play. (4) Try to let wind carry ball away from opponent rather than toward her. (5) Don't rush net indiscriminately.

Sun

When you're facing the sun and serving, throw balls up more to the side, so that you won't have to look directly up into the sun on the service. On overheads, position yourself with the same idea in mind. If you're serving and the sun is to your right, the toss for the twist serve may be easier to see. If the sun is directly over your head, the toss for the slice or the flat serve is better. If you do have to look into the sun when you're serving, don't follow your serve up to the net. If your opponent is having a sun problem when she is serving, hit the serve to a corner and follow it to the net. A lob over the net player's head when she is facing the sun is also an effective shot.

General Strategy

The subject of strategy in tennis can be divided into factors applicable to singles and factors applicable to doubles; but individual readiness is basic to both. Learn not to choke up under pressure (this usually comes only with experience and confidence). Learn to concentrate, and watch the ball until you have actually hit it. (Some coaches tell their players to try to read the name printed on the ball as it comes to the racket.) Another thing you must be able to do if you are to play well is to relax. If you're too tense, and your play is tight as a result, you have what is commonly called "the elbow." Remind yourself constantly to go ahead and stroke the ball rather than playing too cautiously.

If you're winning, stay with the strategy that has put you ahead. If you're losing, change your strategy, in hopes that your opponent will not be able to cope with your new tactics.

The skilled player should be able to hold her serve, since a well-placed serve gives anyone a definite advantage. Therefore she should concentrate on breaking the opponent's serve. If you return the service down the sidelines and deep in the court, this keeps the opponent from taking advantage of a rush to the net behind her serve, and may help in breaking the serve.

When the score is 4–3, this is probably the most crucial point in a set. At this point, a service break or a service win can throw the game either way. Another critical time in a game occurs when the score is 30–5. Winning the point can give the receiver a fighting chance. Losing the point can put the score at 40–5, which is quite an advantage for the server. However, don't forget that *every* point is important. It gives you a psychological advantage if you can win the first two points of a game; you should therefore work especially hard at the beginning.

Try to hit the ball to the opponent's weaknesses, and play the percentage shots. If you know that one type of play is giving you more points and fewer losses than another, stick to this type of play. Don't get upset when you miss a shot; learn to take each point as it comes.

Strategy for Singles

1. When serving
   a) Vary your serves. The slice and twist give greater control and are effective as second serves.
   b) If your serve is hard and effective, follow it to the net.
   c) Place serves deep and to the corners.
   d) If receiver is overplaying, hit serves away from her.

2. When receiving
   a) Position yourself according to the power and spin on the serve. Move in closer for: (1) weak serves, and (2) serves with spin.
   b) If server rushes net, hit return low and deep, preferably down the sideline. Use lobs to force her away from the net.
   c) Hit weak serves deep to backhand corner and go to the net.
   d) Keep weight on balls of feet; for most effective return of serve, keep weight in motion.
   e) When serve is angled toward sideline, best return is high lob or shot back down sideline.
   f) On a fast, hard serve, if you cannot stroke ball, keep wrist firm and attempt to just "block" shot.

3. Ground strokes
   a) Place ball deep and to opponent's weak side.

Hitting a high forehand. (Courtesy of BYU Sports Information.)

b) For better control of forehand, use top spin on ball.

c) Run opponent as much as possible; when she is running fast to get back into position, hit ball behind her.

d) Use drop shots, chops, and angled volleys to make drives more effective.

e) If opponent is slow, hit one drive deep and then on the next one drop the ball right over the net.

f) Always get racket back *before* the ball gets into hitting position.

4. Net play

   a) When opponent hits the ball short, hit return deep and go to net.

   b) Stop forward body motion before volleying.

   c) To prevent balls hitting at feet, go beyond service line.

   d) Be aggressive; keep opponent on defense.

   e) When ball drops below level of net, angle racket face up slightly.

   f) When hitting toward sideline or baseline, allow 2–3 inches for error.

   g) To come to net on a ground stroke, hit ball deep to middle of court or to deep backhand corner; then move up.

   h) When the opponent angles balls to one side, move slightly in that direction to cut off the shortest return back down the sideline, but be ready for crosscourt shots.

   i) Keep weight low, racket head above wrist, and be firm.

Stretching for a volley. (Courtesy of Madison Sports Information.)

5. Overheads
   a) When you hit an overhead from a position close to the net, angle it as much as possible; when you hit ball from area close to baseline, smash ball deep and go up to net.
   b) If ball is too far over head for safe smash, put racket up and hit ball as deep as possible, with a soft but firm blocking action.
   c) If opponent hits a high lob to your backhand side, if possible run around the ball for the smash after it bounces.
   d) When you can, let lobs bounce before you smash them; this helps your timing (provided lob will take high-enough bounce).
   e) Allow for wind; keep eye on ball; get into position quickly.

6. Lobs
   a) Lob over opponent's head when she is at net, to force her back.
   b) Use lob when you are out of position, or when you need extra time before next stroke.
   c) Place lobs as deep as possible and to the backhand corner.
   d) Don't lob often when you are up against a player with a good overhead.
   e) As a defensive stroke, lob high. As an offensive stroke, send lob barely over opponent's reach.
   f) When opponent is off-balance and must hurry back to return a lob, go to net.
   g) When wind is blowing, keep lobs at a minimum.

7. Other strategy

   a) Return to middle of court (behind baseline) after each stroke.

   b) Don't get caught between baseline and service line ("no man's land").

   c) Play balls that hit close to a line.

   d) Don't give up on a point; don't relax until ball has been put away.

   e) When you are distracted while your opponent is serving because of a ball rolling across court, or other uncontrollable factors, call for a "let" immediately.

   f) When you return a serve, or go in to the net to volley, follow angle of ball to cut off shortest return.

Strategy for Doubles

1. When serving

   a) The best server of the team should serve first game of each set.

   b) Follow first serve in, but stay back on second, unless it is also a strong serve.

   c) Move to net immediately; try not to get caught between baseline and service line.

   d) If you serve with a lot of spin rather than power only (flat serve), this gives you more time to go to the net.

   e) Server coming in to net must be ready to reverse direction and take a lob placed over partner's head.

   f) Try to get to net at first possible chance, since in doubles there is a definite advantage in net play.

2. When receiving

   a) If both players are right-handed, the best backhand player should take the left court.

   b) If possible, return ball deep or at an angle and go to net.

   c) Best shots are: (1) lob over head of net player, (2) ball hit at feet of server coming in to net, or (3) sharply angled shot away from net player.

   d) To allow faster move to net, play as close to service line as possible.

3. General strategy

   a) Work as a unit; when one player moves to the side, other one should too. This prevents opening up a large hole between the two players.

   b) Be aggressive at the net; keep balls low and angle off when possible.

   c) Poach on signals or when there is a sure put-away shot.

   d) Player with best forehand should take all shots in middle of court.

   e) Hit between players; when players pull into middle, hit to alley.

f) When out of position, lob ball to allow time for yourself and your partner to get set up.

g) When ball is lobbed over you at net, change sides with partner.

TRACK AND FIELD
Coaching Emphasis

1. General conditioning.
2. Specializing in skills and conditioning for specific events.
3. Working on starts, running, hurdling, jumping, and throwing.

Mechanics

1. Starts
   a) The object is to start body from "set" position in fastest possible time.
   b) To start effectively, body must be in an unstable position (obtained by
   moving center of gravity forward so that body must move quickly to regain balance).
   c) To execute start from blocks: (1) On "get set," move hips upward and
   forward, forcing most of body weight to fingertips. (Shoulders usually
   move 2–3 inches beyond hands.) (2) Head position should be a relaxed
   one, with eyes focused about 3 feet ahead of the starting line. (3) On "go"
   signal, push hard against blocks with both feet to start motion forward
   (forward foot gives most power). (4) Keep body low when coming out of
   blocks. Arms move in opposition to legs. (See Fig. 9–35.)
   d) Spacing of blocks varies. Stance usually used is the medium-elongated,
   with first block about 6–12 inches (about two hand spans) from starting
   line, and rear block about 12–16 inches from front block. (Knee of rear
   leg is usually opposite arch of front foot.) In bunch start, feet are close together; in elongated stance, feet are spaced wider than in medium-elongated stance. Although the medium start is thought to allow the runner to
   go into her running stride more quickly, the bunch start gets her out of
   the starting position the fastest. However, this fast start out of the blocks
   by use of the bunch start forces the runner to lose valuable time in regain-
   ing balance before hitting her running stride.
   e) Forward leg should be strongest leg.

Problems with Starts

*Lack of balance when going into the
"set" position.*   Causes: center of
gravity moved too far forward for
hands to support weight; placing
blocks too close to starting line.

Corrections and Coaching Hints

Experiment with spacing of blocks;
find best position for concentrating
weight over hands and forward foot
without losing balance.

(a)

(b)

Fig. 9–35 The start.

Difficulty in holding "set" position comfortably until "go" signal.
Causes: incorrect arm and hand positioning; lack of strength in arms and hands.

Place hands slightly farther apart than shoulders; let fingers support most of weight, as thumb and fingers form an inverted V; lock wrists; keep arms straight (elbows locked). Build up strength in hands and arms with fingertip pushups and isometric exercises.

Too little power or push coming out of blocks.   Causes: blocks spaced too close or too far apart for maximum push; weaker leg placed in front position; push made with only one leg.

Experiment with spacing of blocks to get maximum push. Exchange lead legs to see if this increases speed coming out of blocks. Push against blocks with both feet.

f) After push out of blocks: (1) Keep leaning forward and keep body low, gradually coming up to normal running position (body lean should still be about 20–25 degrees). (2) Make first steps out of block as long as possible, while maintaining good balance. (3) Increase stride as you pick up speed (length of stride should become progressively greater until full speed has been reached). (4) Swing arms alternately (elbows bent at about a 90-degree angle, and hands relaxed). (5) Point feet straight ahead.

g) Speed depends on: (1) distance between feet on stride, and (2) number of strides per second.

h) Standing start is usually used for distance running.

Problems after Leaving Blocks

Swaying of body during run.
Results: loss of speed; body does not move on straight line. Causes: incorrect steps; failure to swing arms properly.

Corrections and Coaching Hints

Point feet straight ahead. If body sways, concentrate on swinging arms in straight line. Arms may swing toward the middle of the body but should not cross the midline of the body. Hands should not go above the shoulder or beyond the back of the hip on the swing.

Coming up into an erect position too soon after start.   Results: runner loses power in leg drive forward. Causes: taking too-long steps; not having head in correct position; body lean inadequate.

Shorten first 2 or 3 steps when coming out of blocks; don't life head when coming out, but keep head in line with body; body lean should be as great as balance will allow, with approximately 20-degree lean when top speed is reached.

Lack of speed and smoothness during stride. Causes: too little knee lift by front leg; head sways from side to side; exaggerated arm swing; not enough push on ground; too-short strides.	Lift knee of forward leg high; keep head steady, with eyes focused straight ahead; arm swing should be synchronized with leg movement; push should be result of leg and ankle extension, with greatest push against ground coming during first 7–8 strides. Increase length of strides.

2. Hurdling (see Fig. 9-36)

  a) Adjust running stride just enough to allow hips and legs to clear hurdle without spending an unnecessarily long time in air.

  b) To execute a hurdle: (1) Leave ground far enough from hurdle to allow good stretch between legs. (2) Increase body lean as lead leg starts over. (3) Let lead leg skim hurdle (lead leg should lift toward chest until heel is slightly above level of top of hurdle). (4) Snap lead foot down. (5) Let trailing leg come over hurdle in sideward motion (inside of leg is next to hurdle). (6) Turn foot outward to avoid hitting hurdle. (7) When lead leg hits ground (about 2 feet from hurdle), bring trailing leg forward quickly with knee high (reach forward and out to gain full stride). (8) Take three strides. (9) Repeat movement.

  c) Let opposite arm reach out at same time as lead leg, while other arm goes back about hip level. Arm action between hurdles is same as for other running action, following opposition pattern.

Problems in Hurdling	*Corrections and Coaching Hints*
Too much clearance between runner and hurdle. Causes: take-off too close to hurdle; too much push-off from take-off foot; lack of body lean. Result: loss of speed.	Distance between take-off and hurdle depends on individual, but usually about 5-6 feet; push-off is *forward* and across hurdle rather than up; lean forward with body. "Skim" hurdle with legs.
Runner hits hurdle with lead leg. Causes: take-off too far from hurdle; too little lift on lead leg.	Be consistent in steps taken between hurdles; let take off be closer to hurdle; lift forward leg to clear hurdle.
Runner hits hurdle with trailing leg. Causes: failure to swing leg to side; failure to rotate ankle.	Flex knee, swing leg to side, rotate ankle to allow foot to turn outward.
Inadequate stride when landing. Results: loss of speed; poor timing for next hurdle. Cause: failure	As leading leg hits, let trailing leg complete its swing over hurdle and lift toward chest, and then out, to

Fig. 9-36 Going over a hurdle. (a) Body leans forward as lead leg goes over. (b) Lead leg snaps down. (c) Lead leg has hit ground and trailing leg has been brought high to give long stride.

to lift knee toward chest after clearing hurdle.

give long stride for maximum speed.

3. Jumping

a) Jump depends on a build-up of momentum and the ability to direct this momentum in an outward or upward motion.

b) Increase height or length of jump by: (1) swinging arms upward or forward, (2) practicing leg action on the ground and in the air, and (3) increasing speed of approach. (In high jump, increase speed on approach is valuable only if this speed can be converted into an upward motion at take-off.)

c) For greatest distance in broad-jumping, the take-off should be at approximately a 45-degree angle. The arms and legs should be used for balance, and to gain a reaction from other parts of the body. For greatest height in high-jumping, the speed of the approach must be converted upward; leg and arm action makes this possible.

d) *Standing Broad Jump:*(1) Space feet about width of shoulders. (2) Rock back and forth, with weight going from toes to heels and back, etc. (3) Swing arms in time with rocking movement. (4) Push with legs forcefully, swing arms forward at same time, and lean in direction of jump. (5) Give final thrust, extending ankles and toes. (6) As body is in air, pull legs up and extend them forward as arms reach out. (7) Flex knees on landing. (8) Keep body lean forward. (9) Swing arms forward and down.

Problems in Standing Broad Jump	*Corrections and Coaching Hints*
Illegal jump. Causes: both feet not kept in contact with board; feet not behind scratch line.	If raised beat board is used, toes may be curled over edge but must not touch floor or ground; otherwise, keep feet behind line. Keep part of both feet in contact with board at all times.
Lack of timing. Cause: incorrect arm movement.	As arms swing forward, shift weight to toes; as arms swing backward, shift weight to heels.
Landing off-balance. Causes: inadequate body lean; failure to use arms.	While body is in air, and upon landing, the body leans forward. Arms are extended forward until landing and then are brought forcefully downward to keep body from falling backward.

e) *Long Jump:*(1) Approach take-off board at about 90 percent of top speed. (2) Shorten last stride about 6 inches. (Runner should relax during last 3-4 strides. This "coasting" action is not a reduction in speed, but a controlling action as runner gets ready for the take-off.) (3) Hit take-off board with knee bent. (4) Straighten leg and push hard with leg, ankle, and toes (body weight rotates from heel to ball of foot). (5) Throw arms, head, chest, and shoulders upward and outward, and lift lead leg. (6) As body goes into air, swing both legs forward. (7) Use hitch-kick for balance and to keep feet in the air as long as possible. (8) As feet hit ground (heels first), bend knees to absorb force of jump. (9) To help body continue forward motion, extend legs forward, pull head and trunk forward, and swing arms forward and then backward.

f)   Speed of approach is very important for the long jump. Most girls use an approach of about 90-120 feet, although a longer distance may be used by a person who is in good condition. Check marks should be used.

g)   The three main factors in a successful long jump are the sprint down the runway, the foot plant and push-off, and the leg lift.

h)   To execute hitch-kick: (1) After take-off, straighten lead leg. (2) Bring lead leg back as take-off leg moves forward and upward (in flexed position). Take-off leg then straightens as it reaches out. (3) Move lead leg forward again. (4) For the landing, let the take-off leg and the lead leg meet in extended position. This leg action for the hitch-kick is like taking a step in the air.

Problems in Long Jump	Corrections and Coaching Hints
Poor take-off. Causes: failure to use check marks; incorrect foot plant; not enough leg lift.	Check marks vary according to individual's stride, but are usually approximately 60 and 30 feet from take-off board. Plant foot heel first; then let weight roll from heel to toes, extending leg and pushing from the toes; lift leg up forcefully as head and shoulders also lift.
Jump too short. Causes: inability to gain enough momentum and then relax during last few strides; inability to shorten last stride; lack of flexion in take-off knee; insufficient leg lift and upward movement of head, shoulders, and arms.	Increase length of approach; relax during last few strides, but don't slow approach; shorten last step about 6 inches; plant foot and lower body by flexing knee; lift lead leg, arms, head, and shoulders as leg pushes off.
Falling backward on landing. Causes: too little body lean; failure to pull arms down; insufficient knee flexion.	Body should lean forward; arms should pull forcefully down; knees should "give" as heels hit. (If arms are carried high, they are moved forward; if carried low, they are pulled forward and then backward.)

Sore, bruised heels.   Cause: tremendous force of foot plant.

Insert piece of sponge in the shoe to absorb shock of foot plant.

i) *High Jump:*(1) Start approximately 7-8 strides back. (2) Build up speed gradually on approach, from a relaxed trot to a relatively slow run. (Approach should be at about a 45-degree angle to the crossbar; some prefer an approach of 30-40 degrees for a straddle roll.) (3) Quicken and lengthen last three strides. (4) Let take-off point be about an arm's length away from bar. (5) Plant heel of take-off foot and lean backward (for push-off force, bend knee). (6) Keep other leg straight as it swings upward. (7) As leg swings upward, lift arm on that side up forcefully and transfer weight from the heel to the toes of the take-off foot as it straightens for the push-off.

j) The techniques most used for the high jump are the Western and the straddle roll. The approach and the take-off are the same for both techniques (the inside foot is used as the take-off foot), but they vary in the lay-out as you go over the bar. For the Western, you go over on your side; for the straddle roll, you go over on your stomach. Many people think that the straddle roll is the more efficient of the two.

k) To execute straddle roll (after take-off): (1) Swing lead leg up and over bar. (2) Start to turn body toward bar (body facing bar). (3) Tuck arm next to bar in close to side, with elbow bent. (4) Straighten push-off leg and rotate it outward to clear the bar. (5) Let right arm and right leg touch pit first. (6) Roll to back to absorb force of landing. (See Fig. 9-37).

Problems with Straddle Roll

Corrections and Coaching Hints

Take-off forward rather than vertical.   Causes: taking off too far from bar; failure to lengthen last three strides to help backward lean. Result: jumper goes into bar rather than over it.

Move take-off point closer to bar; make last three strides the longest and fastest of the approach; lean backward after planting take-off foot.

Insufficient upward motion.   Cause: poor take-off. Result: inability to clear bar.

Flex knee of take-off foot and plant heel, and then rock weight to toes; straighten other leg and lift up while arms go up to aid in lift; extend take-off leg and push hard with ankle and toes.

Improper action going over bar. Results: failure to get hips over; trailing leg hits bar.

As you straddle bar, duck head and right shoulder slightly to help lift hips; as body passes bar, straighten trailing leg; this helps trailing leg to clear.

(a)

(b)

(c)

Fig. 9-37   Straddle roll on high jump.

Leading leg hits bar on way up.
Causes: take off point too close to
bar; swing is toward bar rather
than parallel to it.

Move take-off point back; place take-
off foot in line with approach; make
initial swing-up almost parallel to
bar.

4. Throwing

a) The objective in a throwing event is to transfer body momentum to the object being thrown.

b) For best results in throwing events: (1) Throw object at 45-degree angle. (2) Use body rotation and/or rotation of throwing arm. (3) Shift body weight. (4) Direct force in one direction by proper sequence of weight shift, truck rotation, elbow extension, wrist snap, etc.

c) In the shot put, strength is the biggest factor, though glide helps the shot-putter to achieve distance. In the discus throw, strength and speed of movements in the circle are important. In the javelin throw, speed on the approach, ability to stop suddenly, and strength affect distance.

d) To execute the *shot put*: (1) Start in rear of circle, facing away from direction of throw. (2) Hold shot in fingers of right hand, with hand behind and underneath shot. (3) Tuck shot under jaw and against neck just back of the ear. (4) Keep elbow close to body and pointed toward ground. (5) Bend forward and put weight on right foot. (6) Flex left leg and kick back while straightening right leg (this starts glide). (7) Keep body low and upper trunk almost parallel to ground during glide. (8) Place left foot down near toe board. (9) Begin to rotate trunk, with power coming from push by right leg, trunk rotation, arm extension, and wrist flexion. (Release shot at end of sequence of power resulting from rear leg thrust, hip rotation, shoulder, arm, hand, and finger push.) (10) Follow through by extending arm in direction of throw. (11) Reverse step (bend right knee to absorb force of body weight shift). (See Fig. 9-38.)

e) To help your balance, extend your left arm during glide.

f) In reverse step, your right foot simply trades places with your left.

g) To execute the *discus throw* with one and three-quarters turn: (1) Stand in rear of circle, facing away from direction of throw. (2) Press discus against palm with tips of fingers around edge. (3) Spread feet comfortably, flex knees, and keep head up. (4) Swing discus back parallel to ground while rotating upper trunk. (5) Repeat swinging motion once or twice to build up momentum. (6) On final backswing, shift weight to right foot.(7) Transfer weight back to left foot, which has dropped back 16-18 inches from right foot, and begin pivot (from heel to ball of foot). (8) When left toe faces front of circle, push with left leg. (9) Jump to right foot (which is placed in center of circle). (10) Continue pivot on right foot while swinging left leg around and letting it come down at front edge of circle and about 6 inches to left of center line. (11) Throwing arm is still

Fig. 9-38 Shot put. (a) Beginning of knee bend for kick back. (b) Glide as result of kick back and extension of right leg. (c) Body almost parallel to ground. (d) Left foot set down near toe board. (e) Follow-through after release.

(a)

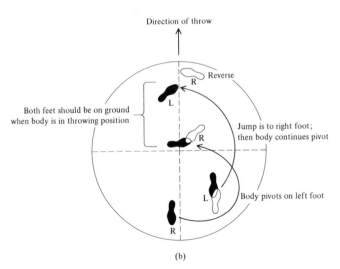

Direction of throw

Reverse

Both feet should be on ground
when body is in throwing position

Jump is to right foot;
then body continues pivot

Body pivots on left foot

(b)

Fig. 9–39   Discus throw. (a) Hand position, with fingers spread and tips of fingers over edge. (b) Footwork for discus throw.

trailing body at this point. (12) When left foot is planted at front of circle, begin body rotation from hips (keep right knee slightly bent). (13) "Explode" by forceful extension from hips of right leg as discus reaches hip. (14) Continue swing forward at 45-degree angle while you pull your left arm back and down to help body to rotate. (15) Release discus on thumb side. (16) Follow through. (17) Reverse step. (See Fig. 9-39.)

h) To execute *javelin throw* with front cross-over: (1) Approach should be approximately 90–100 feet (about 15–17 running strides). (2) Grip javelin in palm of hand with middle finger and thumb at back edge of cord (tip of thumb on top of binding and middle finger curled around shaft), fore-finger hooked slightly around grip, and other two fingers curled naturally around the binding (Finnish grip). (3) Carry javelin above shoulder (near top of head) with elbow bent and tip slightly down. (4) Build speed up during approach. (5) Use last five steps for cross-over. (6) First step of cross-over: point right foot slightly out (about 45-degree angle to direction of throw). (7) Second step: bring left foot almost parallel to right foot (about 60 degrees to right of approach direction). (8) Take javelin back with arm extended (keep point close to face and tail just off ground). (9) Third step: cross right foot over left and place it at a right angle to the line of approach (flexing knee to allow backward lean). (10) Keep javelin as far back as possible. (11) Lift left leg and lean backward for the throw. (12) Fourth step: force left leg down to ground and push hard with right leg. (13) Bring javelin forward powerfully as right leg pushes and pull left arm downward and backward to aid the release at approximately a 45-degree angle. (14) Follow through. (15) Reverse step to stop forward momentum. (See Fig. 9–40.)

Strategy

For sprints.   The strategy for sprints involves coming out of the blocks correctly and immediately when the gun sounds, building up maximum speed as quickly as possible, and then maintaining this speed until the end of the race. The sprinter should not slow down until she is well past the finish line. In the 220, try to reach full speed for the first 60 yards, conserve energy by maintaining a fast pace or a "floating" pace for the next 100 yards, and then go all out for the last 60 yards. The better sprinters are able to maintain their top speed for a greater distance.

For hurdles.   The start for the hurdles is just as important as the start for the sprints. The runner should continue to build up speed as she clears the first two or three hurdles, and then maintain her speed throughout the race. She must learn to skim over the hurdles as if they weren't there, maintaining three strides between each hurdle and sprinting all the way. When she has taken the last hurdle, she should concentrate on maintaining her rhythm until she is well past the finish line.

Reverse
after throw

R

L

R

L Crossover

R

L

Direction of
run and throw

(a)

(b)

(c)

(d)

(e)

Fig. 9-40 (a) Last five steps of javeline throw involving crossover. (b) Feet cross over. (c) Right leg begins push for throw, (d) the throw, and (e) reverse after javelin has been released.

Relays.   For relay races, the second-fastest runner is usually selected as the lead-off runner, unless another team member has more experience or can be depended on more not to make a false start. The third-fastest runner usually runs the second leg, while the slowest member of the team runs the third leg. For psychological reasons, the coach sometimes runs the slowest girl on the second leg and the third-fastest girl on the third leg. The fastest runner runs the last leg. This decision is usually based on the lineup of the chief opponent in the race. However, other factors should be considered in placing runners, such as ability to run straightaways and curves, psychological advantage of having fastest girl give team a good start, ability of a girl to come from behind, and efficiency in the baton exchanges.

Middle-distance running.   Strategy in middle-distance running is a little more involved, since the runner must maneuver for the lead, prevent opponents from boxing her in, and pace the run so that she can challenge for the lead or maintain the lead at the end of the race. The runner's main objective should be to enter the first and last turns in a good position, either as the leader or within easy reach of the leader and to pace herself correctly. In the 440, the girl should learn to run the second half of the race at the same pace as the first half. The time between the first and second half of the race should not vary more than a couple of seconds. In the 880-yard run, a shorter stride is more economical from the standpoint of energy, but overstriding or understriding can put one at a disadvantage. In an ideal run, each 220 would be run at the same pace. In middle distances, if the girl can take the lead on the first turn and still have enough energy to run strong for the rest of the race, she definitely has the advantage.

Reaching the last turn in a good position is important because if the leader has too much of a lead, the other runners won't be able to close the gap, or if the leader has not overextended herself, she can hold off any challenge by other runners. If you're trailing the leader on this last turn, in order to have a chance to overcome her lead during the remaining distance of the race, you must stay within at least 9 or 10 feet of her.

When you're going into the turns, decide whether to follow the curve in the pole position, in order to travel less distance, or to expend extra energy and try to move up in the order of runners by passing on the outside. If you decide to move up, don't hesitate. Ordinarily, do your passing on the straightaway, so that you cover the shortest possible distance on the pass. When running a curve, stay on the inside of your lane, lean into the curve, and increase your speed as you go around the curve.

If you're leading and want to maintain your lead, you must anticipate the challenge from your opponent and accelerate your pace accordingly, to keep your lead and the inside position. Going into the final stretch, you must start your sprint in time to hold off any challenge while choosing a spot to open up that will allow you to finish the race. Usually if you are leading and have not been challenged before, begin your "kick" 40 to 50 yards from the finish line. If you are challenged earlier in the straightaway or on the turn, accelerate at that point to maintain the inside position and the lead, and try to continue at the necessary pace until the end of the race.

If you're trailing the leader, don't make your move too soon in coming off the last turn, or the leader may force you to run extra distance around the curve by speeding up and keeping you on her outside shoulder. Instead, choose a pace on the straightaway where you can sprint the rest of the way to the line. When you come around any of the turns, hold the inside (or pole) lane and don't swing too wide; otherwise another girl will pass you on the inside.

Throwing and jumping events.   Mental readiness is especially important in the throwing and jumping events. Strategy for shot putting demands synchronization of all your body movements in order to have a total "explosion" action on the release. This involves practice, timing, balance, and strength. The shot-putter should follow a program of exercises designed to increase strength in her legs, hips, upper body, shoulder, arm, and wrist. It is also important for her to practice an efficient glide across the circle.

The javelin throw is based on the principle of coordinating your body movements to end up with a total effort to give the object thrown the most distance. This is accomplished by building up speed on the approach and stopping your body forcefully as you release the javelin. An adequate warm-up period is necessary. You must condition your muscles for the strain of the throw by weightlifting and isometric exercises; don't overthrow during practice sessions, because this could lead to shoulder and elbow injuries.

The discus-thrower needs a continuous movement across the circle, with the upper body and the discus trailing the hips and legs until the actual delivery. Force comes from the speed of the glide and the sequence of power derived from the toes, ankles, knees, hips, upper trunk, shoulder, arm, and hand, as the body uncoils and transfers momentum to the discus.

Strategy, in high jumping, must include an approach that gives optimum force that can be converted into a vertical direction, sufficient push-off and lift, and correct turn in clearing the bar. A mental picture of the body clearing the bar seems to aid the body in accomplishing this feat.

Strategy for the running broad jump includes: building up speed on the approach, shortening the final stride, push-off and leg lift, balance in the air, and a forward motion on landing. If you miss a check mark or feel that your approach is off, abort the try and save your energy for a better run.

General strategy.   In most track and field events, strategy is mostly a matter of preparation and practice before the event. The good athlete learns to relax during her performance, although her muscles are working at maximum efficiency. Self-confidence, attained by means of practice and experience, contributes to this ability to relax.

Mental readiness before an event is of prime importance. The athlete must concentrate and shut out all noise and other distractions. She must know what she wants to accomplish and believe that she can do it.

In events in which three tries are allowed, an athlete who knows what she has done wrong and knows how to make the necessary corrections before the next attempt has an advantage.

The good athlete does not let the performance of another athlete "psyche"· her out, but plans for her event by setting goals that are within the possibility of achievement, continually raising her goals as she improves her performance.

VOLLEYBALL

Coaching Emphasis

1. Practicing basic fundamentals, such as overhead pass, net recovery, serve, etc.
2. Giving special instruction in: two-arm forearm pass ("bump" or dig), one-hand dig, effective serving (floater, overhead top-spin serve, etc.), setting for the spiker (forward, backward, and short-set), spiking, recovery techniques, individual and team blocking.
3. Offensive and defensive strategy.

Mechanics

1. Forearm bounce pass
   a) Use the forearm pass for hard-hit balls below the waist, to recover the ball out of the net, or to hit ball when back is to net.
   b) Two hand positions are commonly used: (1) Hands together with one fist in the other fist, and with thumbs together and parallel on top. (2) Hands open (palms up) with back of one hand in palm of the other, and with thumb of bottom hand folded over palm of top hand.
   c) Execution: (1) Move in line with ball. (2) Bend knees and lean forward slightly (use forward stride). (3) Keep elbows straight and close together. (4) As ball hits forearms, straighten legs, lift body, and keep arms firm. (5) Use little arm motion for hard-hit balls, but lift upward more on slow balls. (6) Keep feet on floor.

Problems with Forearm Pass	*Corrections and Coaching Hints*
Inaccurate passing. Causes: body out of line with ball; having one forearm higher than the other; failure to pass ball from a low position.	Before hit, get directly in line with ball; let arms form an even hitting surface. Practice by getting someone to throw balls at your arms, first gently and then harder, to simulate a spike or hard-hit serve. Practice against a wall.

Forearm bounce pass. (Courtesy of Tommy Geddie.)

Ball hit too high. Causes: too much arm action; in some cases, too-forceful leg extension.

Let arms remain relatively still and firm and keep elbow and wrist action to a minimum. Let leg extension be firm but not forceful.

Ball hit too low. Causes: incorrect alignment with the ball; lack of leg power; in the case of slow balls, lack of slight upward movement with the arms, and bending over at waist with legs extended.

Line up with ball to prevent over-reaching. Flex knees and then extend them as you hit ball; in recovering ball from the net, use a solid upward movement with the arms, as well as push with the legs.

2. One-arm dig
   a) Use a one-arm dig to play the ball when good positioning for a two-arm dig is impossible; this is frequently used in returning a spike or playing a blocked ball.
   b) Objective is to get ball back up into the air to allow teammate a good hit, or to play ball back over net on last legal hit.
   c) To execute: (1) React quickly, since positioning depends on reaction time. (2) Try to have left leg extended to side and right knee bent under body when hitting with the right hand, and the opposite position for

hitting with the left hand. (3) Bend knees and get body low. (4) Keep weight on balls of feet, with most of weight usually concentrated on forward foot. (5) Use fist or slightly cupped hand for hit. (6) Hold wrist and forearm firm so that ball gets a good bounce just from its own force. (7) Use nondigging arm for balance by extending to side.

Problems with One-Handed Dig	*Corrections and Coaching Hints*
Ball rebounds from arm with too much force. Cause: swinging arm into ball.	Keep arm firm and let ball rebound off from its own force.
Hit inaccurate, out of bounds, etc. Causes: Failure to hit ball squarely; not enough concentration on flight of ball; not getting down low enough.	Keep eye on ball until you hit it; get hand and body down close to floor and try to get under center of ball.
Ball goes into net or forward rather than up. Causes: hand or forearm not under ball; on a slow ball, not giving enough upward motion with arm to give ball momentum.	Reach out and get under ball even if it means going to the floor; hit *under* and behind the ball; on net recoveries and other slow "saves," hit upward with arm on follow-through.

3. Floater serve
   a) A floater serve has an erratic flight because of the placement of the valve on the ball before the hit.
   b) Valve usually faces forward, but you can turn it to one side or down to get a different flight.
   c) For best effect, toss-up must be done without spin.
   d) To execute: (1) Have feet behind line in a comfortable front-stride position. (2) To ensure best transfer of weight, put left foot ahead of right. (3) Face net, with right shoulder turned away slightly. (4) Hold ball about chest high with left hand, steadying it with right hand. (5) Toss ball high enough to hit with extended arm (usually 2–3 feet) and about 1 to 1½ feet in front of right shoulder. (6) On toss-up, shift weight to rear foot and bring right arm up and overhead with elbow slightly bent (hand may be brought behind head with greater elbow flexion). (7) Shift weight to forward foot, reach for ball with elbow leading out. (8) Hit with heel of the hand, keeping wrist firm (make contact in center of ball). (9) Let the follow-through be short and in line of flight (sometimes arm is pulled back quickly after contact of hand with ball) and in line with right shoulder.

Problems with Floater Serve	*Corrections and Coaching Hints*
Ball goes high. Causes: hitting ball overhead rather than in front of	Throw ball up 1 to 1½ feet in front of shoulder. (Keep wrist firm throughout

body; lack of wrist firmness; hitting too much under ball.

the hit, without a wrist snap.) Watch ball, and try to make contact in the center.

Ball doesn't float, but spins. Causes: ball hit off-center; follow-through is incorrect; wrist snaps.

Pick out a spot in center of ball and hit it squarely; follow-through should be toward line of desired flight.

Ball goes into net. Causes: ball toss too far in front of body; incorrect weight transfer; not enough arm extension on hit.

Toss ball closer to body; transfer weight from rear to forward foot before contact; throw ball higher or don't let it drop so low before hitting it; reach up for ball.

Serve has no speed. Causes: not enough speed on arm swing forward; failure to shift body weight.

Bring hand back behind head; shift weight forward and then bring hand forcefully "through" ball on contact. (Some skilled players prefer to use a wrist snap.)

4. Overhead top-spin serve
   a) Spin makes this kind of serve difficult to return.
   b) To execute: (1) Use same position at line as you use for floater serve. (2) Hit ball with heel of hand, making contact in center of lower rear part (ball should be hit at a full arm's reach). (3) Snap wrist quickly to cup hand over ball (force is from heel of hand upward and forward to create over-spin). (4) On follow-through, extend arm fully in direction of serve, with wrist flexed and slightly pronated.

Problems with Overhead Top-Spin Serve

Corrections and Coaching Hints

Ball hard to control. Causes: inconsistent hand and wrist action; poor toss-up.

Heel of hand should hit center of rear lower part of ball; snap through with wrist, cupping hand over ball. Toss-up should be slightly higher than reach, and in the same spot each time.

Not enough power behind ball. Causes: Failure to transfer weight; failure to use abdominal muscles, elbow, and wrist snap.

Shift weight from rear to forward foot before hit; contract muscles in abdomen, pulling upper body forward; then snap or extend elbow, and finally snap wrist.

Ball hit too far. Cause: hitting too high on ball; not enough wrist snap.

Contact ball lower (on lower portion of rear). Snap wrist just as heel of hand contacts ball.

Ball goes into net. Causes: throwing ball too far in front of body; letting ball drop too low before hitting it; failure to reach up for the ball.

Toss ball slightly higher than reach; extend arm to hit it, reaching up with arm and body to contact ball.

Ball goes to right or left of target. Causes: ball tossed too far to right or left of right shoulder; using stance with side to net rather than front of body facing net; hitting ball with sidearm pattern.

Toss ball in front of right shoulder; extend arm straight upward from bent elbow, hitting up and over ball.

5. Forward set

a) Use forward set in controlled play when you have time to get into position under the ball; also use it to set up ball for the attack.

b) To execute: (1) Get body under ball and in line with intended pass. (2) Place side toward net. (3) Adopt a position that would cause the ball to hit your nose if you allowed it to drop. (4) Spread feet comfortably, knees bent, weight on balls of feet. (5) Hold hands up and in position (elbows shoulder high, wrists back, index fingers and thumbs forming a triangle, with thumbs about 5 inches apart). (6) Watch ball. (7) Extend arms and legs at same time, making contact with ball about 6 inches over head. (8) Hit with fingers only (last 2 segments of each finger). (9) On follow-through, turn palms in direction of ball's flight.

c) Place ball approximately 8–10 feet above net and about 12–15 inches back from it.

6. Backward set

a) Use the backward set for purposes of deception.

b) To execute: (1) Use same body and hand position as for forward set, except that you keep your back to the intended set, your wrists are flexed back more on contact, and the motions of your hands and arms are upward and backward (back may be arched). (2) Position of body with respect to ball determines degree of wrist tilt and angle of arm follow-through needed.

c) To avoid "throwing" calls, arch back and use a straight follow-through, or get directly under ball, tilt hands backward, raise head upward, and follow through in upward direction.

Problems with Setting Ball

Corrections and Coaching Hints

Inaccuracy because of poor positioning. Causes: player fails to face intended direction of set, sets on the run, or doesn't shift weight into set.

Face direction of set (in backward set, back is to intended flight); get under ball; stop body movement before hit; "step" into set by extending knees and arms.

Setting ball too high. Cause: too much knee and arm extension.	Learn, through practice, to gauge height; aim ball so that it arches and then drops in desired spot; don't push as hard with arms and legs.
Setting ball too low. Cause: not enough extension of arms and legs; contacting ball below face.	Bend knees before contact; then, as you make contact with ball, straighten out knees and extend arms.
Ball goes forward instead of up. Causes: failure to get into position; failure to hyperextend wrist or to hit under ball.	Move quickly to get under ball; lay wrist back, watch ball, and try to contact bottom of it.
On backward set, ball goes straight up instead of backward. Causes: not enough backward motion with arms and body; not enough back arch; not enough wrist tilt.	Let hands and arms follow through over and beyond back of head, with body weight shifting to rear foot. If back is arched, use a straight follow-through; if body is right under ball and wrists tilted back, use an upward follow-through.

7. Short set

   a) Use short set as change of pace and to add deception to attack.

   b) The short set is very difficult because of timing and need for signal between setter and spiker.

   c) To execute: (1) Receiver of ball sends it to setter. (2) Spiker approaches net. (3) Setter places ball a few inches above net as spiker jumps. (4) Set should be timed so that ball goes into spiker's hitting hand just as she is at the peak of her jump. (5) For variety, use semishort set, 2–3 feet above net.

8. Shoot set

   a) Use shoot set as change of pace, to add deception to attack, and to cause the middle blocker to be late on the block.

   b) To execute: (1) receiver of ball sends it to setter, (2) spiker times approach so that she starts her jump as ball leaves setter's hands, (3) setter sends ball approximately one foot from the sideline and 1–2 feet above the net, and (4) spiker hits ball from inside the sideline before set starts to drop.

9. Spiking

   a) Spiking involves hitting from 2 basic positions: (1) the off-hand spike, when set must cross your body to reach spiking hand, and (2) the on-hand spike, when set reaches your hitting hand without crossing body.

   b) If spiker is right-handed and is to left of setter, it is an on-hand spike; if spiker is to right of setter, it is an off-hand spike.

   c) To execute on-hand spike: (1) Start about 8–12 feet from net (far enough

(a)   (b)

Spiking action. (a) Elbow bent and wrist cocked for hit. (b) Player hits ball with an extension of the elbow and snap of the wrist while rotating shoulder toward net. (Courtesy of Madison Sports Information.)

back for 3-step approach). (2) Approach net at an angle from left sideline (with left shoulder slightly turned toward net). (3) Lengthen last stride, lower weight, and bring rear foot forward for two-foot pushoff. (4) Swing arms upward to help take-off and gain height on the jump. (5) Bring arm into hitting position (elbow bent and up, hand open or cupped, but firm). (6) To achieve maximum power, rotate right shoulder toward net, contract abdominal muscles, extend arm, and snap wrist, in that order. (7) After you hit the ball, the hitting arm moves downward and across the body. (8) Land with knees flexed, ready for next move.

d) When ball has been set close to net, use follow-through that is parallel to net; give ball a glancing blow to prevent hitting net with hand.

e) If your spike is blocked by opponents, move back from net for another approach as your team sets ball; if spike gets by block, stay at net, ready to block opponent's return shot.

Problems with On-Hand Spike	*Corrections and Coaching Hints*
Not enough power. Causes: facing net too squarely on approach; not enough contraction of muscles of abdomen; failure to snap elbow and wrist.	Keep left shoulder slightly toward net; then, as you make hit, rotate right shoulder into ball; move into ball with stomach, elbow, and wrist snap.
Hitting ball too long. Causes: hitting too much under ball rather than on top; approaching too soon.	Let ball fall in front of your right shoulder and contact top of ball; don't make approach until ball leaves setter's hands.
Hitting ball into net. Causes: hitting ball after it has dropped too low; jumping off floor too far from net.	When you make the hit, reach up with full extended arm. Practice jumping up with tennis ball in hand and throwing it over as close to top of net as possible. Jump off floor as close to net as you can without going into net after hit.

f) To execute off-hand spike : (1) Before hit, allow ball to cross over body to point in front of right shoulder. (2) Use same method of execution and hit as for on-hand spike.

Problems with Off-Hand Spike	*Corrections and Coaching Hints*
Not enough power. Causes: not enough elbow extension and wrist snap.	Allow ball to cross body to the hitting-arm side. Rotate right shoulder toward ball and extend elbow forcefully. Snap wrist when you hit ball.
Jump too low. Causes: push-off from only one foot; arms not used in lift; strides too short.	Let last stride be a long one; bring rear foot up and push off with both feet. Lift arms vigorously to add height.

10. Angles on spike
    a) Angle is obtained by hitting ball on side rather than in center.
    b) To angle the ball to the right, hit the ball off-center on the left side; to angle the ball to the left, hit it off-center on the right side.
    c) If you are the spiker, to get the most effective angle, you must be able to see the blocker's hands in relation to the ball.
11. "Dink"
    a) Use "dink" as a deceptive move to get ball by block when defense is expecting a spike.

    b) To execute: Hit ball gently with fingertips, keeping wrist firm.

    c) Use same movements as for power hit, but slow swing down and place ball to the side of, or just over, the block.

    d) To recover ball below net height, place hand under ball and return it with fist, knuckles, or heel of hand.

12. Rolls and dives

    a) Used to play difficult balls (such as hard serve or spike).

    b) Rolls may be partial or complete, and allow a player to save balls that force her backward.

    c) Dives are usually last ditch efforts to save ball by lunging forward or reaching out. After contact is made with ball, palms of outstretched hands contact floor, easing body down to the chest, abdomen, and thighs while head is held back.

13. Blocking

    a) Blocking may be executed by one, two, or three players.

    b) To execute: (1) When opponents pass ball to their setter, move in 12-15 inches from the net. (2) Determine direction of set to spiker. (3) Slide along parallel to net, following flight of ball. (4) After spiker has left floor, jump (usually when spiker has hand cocked to hit), (5) The deeper the set, the longer the blocker must delay her jump.(6) Place hands above net with thumbs close together, fingers spread and firm, extend arm downward from shoulders and tilt wrists forward. (7) Land with knees flexed.

    c) To execute two-player block: (1) Player closest to sideline "sets" block. (2) Second player moves to her side (to time jump so that you jump simultaneously, touch elbows). (3) Keep hands within 2–3 inches of hands of second player. (4) Execute as described in b).

    d) To prevent ball from being deflected out of bounds, girl on outside tries to turn block into the court (her outside hand should be turned to face the middle of the court).

Strategy

In volleyball, strategy includes knowing how to set the ball, and how to cover spikes, knowing the best hitting angles to evade blocks, establishing offensive patterns geared to personnel, knowing the best defense against serves, knowing the blocking options, and knowing how to cover behind the block.

Passing.   Ordinarily, the first pass should go to the center forward; she then makes the set to either side for the spike. As soon as the ball is on the way to the setter, the spikers should move back from the net for their approach. Whenever possible, the center forward should take the second hit, but if another player is in better position to play the ball, she should make the call for it.

Setting the block. (Courtesy of Donna Christiansen.)

When the pass goes to the right or left forward, a cross-court set can be used. If the ball must come from the back row on the second hit, a cross-court set should be used, since it allows the spiker more time to judge the ball's flight.

Spiking. Most tall players prefer to have the ball set close to the net, while a short player usually has more success in spiking from a position farther back from the net. If the set is too deep for a hard spike, the spiker should hit the ball with top-spin and aim deep in the court. When the opponents attempt a block, the spiker has several choices: (1) When blocker's hands are too far from the net, she may hit inside the block. (2) She may hit the ball at the blocker's sideline hand so that the ball will glance off the hand on the opponent's side of the net. (3) If the block is poorly set, she may hit around it. (4) She can use a change of pace, such as the "dink" to throw off the defensive team's timing.

Covering spike. The spiking team must be ready to cover their court and recover the ball for another offensive attempt in case the opponents block so that the ball comes back over the net. The player covering the spike should wait with her hands about waist level and her weight well balanced on the balls of her feet. (See Fig. 9-41 for team position when covering the spike.) If the spike clears the

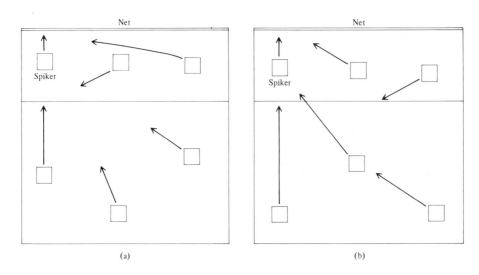

Fig. 9–41 Attack coverage. Two different methods of covering court in case spike is blocked. Positioning depends on direction of ball after block. (a) Player-back defense. (b) Player-up defense.

block but the opponents play it, players should quickly go back to their regular defensive positions. If the ball is blocked but recovered by a teammate, players should set up their offensive pattern.

Offensive patterns. Depending on the personnel the coach has available, she will set up a 3–3, a 4–2, a 5–1, or a 6–0 offensive pattern [27].

The 3-3 system is built on the pass-set-spike principle with the players working in two-player units for setting and spiking purposes. This system is used when there are only three girls on the team who can spike. The players are positioned so that the setter precedes the spiker in the serve rotation. The strongest spiker should always start in the left forward position, to enable her to stay on the front row longer. If a team has a left-handed spiker or someone who can spike with either hand, the coach should start her in the right forward position.

The 4-2 offensive pattern is usually used if your team has 4 spikers and 2 setters. As it is used for competition at the beginning of the game the two setters are in the center forward and center back positions. The server, left back, left forward, and right forward are the spikers. (See Fig. 9-42.) After rotation, if the team is receiving the serve and the best setter is in the left or right forward position, as soon as the serve is hit she switches into the center forward position to take the second ball. When the setter's team is receiving, she stands near the net and does not play the serve, but remains ready to move into the setting position. (See Fig. 9-43.)

The 5-1 offense is based on 5 spikers and a setter. Thus 3 spikers play at the net when the setter is in the back row, but they shift to a 4-2 when the setter is in

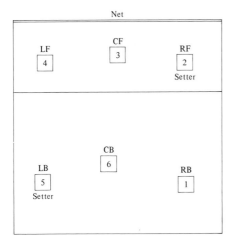

Fig. 9–42 The 4–2 offensive pattern: best spiker in position 4.

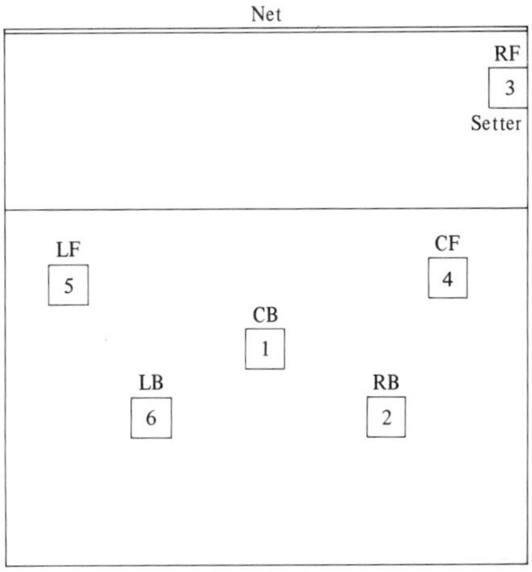

Fig. 9–43 In 4–2 offensive pattern, setter (number 3) does not receive serve.

the front row. If the setter is on the back row when she receives the serve: (1) She is shielded and does not play the serve. (2) She moves into the front court position as soon as the ball is served, so that she can set the ball. (3) The pass goes preferably to the right front side of the court for the set. (This allows her to set to the on-hand side of the spikers.)

The 6-6 offense is used when a team has 6 spikers who can also set the ball. Every center forward (regardless of number of rotations) is the setter and must be prepared to set from this position. On defense, the team tries to send the first pass to the center forward position for the set. When she is receiving the serve, the center forward plays near the net, while the rest of the team go into their receiving positions.

The 6-2 offense is a variation for advanced players. The 6-2 offense is used when a team has six spikers and two of these players have the ability to set. When a team is receiving a serve, the back line setter is left out of the service formation so that she can run up from the backcourt; when in RB, she positions herself in the right corner to set for the on-hand spikers and the one off-hand spiker. (See Fig. 9-44.) When a team is serving, all players take defensive positions against the spike, ready to go on offense if the spike is recovered; preferably with the right back moving up into position to set the ball.

Because of the fact that under current rules the setter in the 5-1 and 6-2 offenses may shift from the back of the court after the serve, the setter from back court should not take part in blocking, but should back up her spiker until the ball is sent into the opponent's court. She then runs to the right back position for defense, while the other two back court players position themselves in left back and center back.

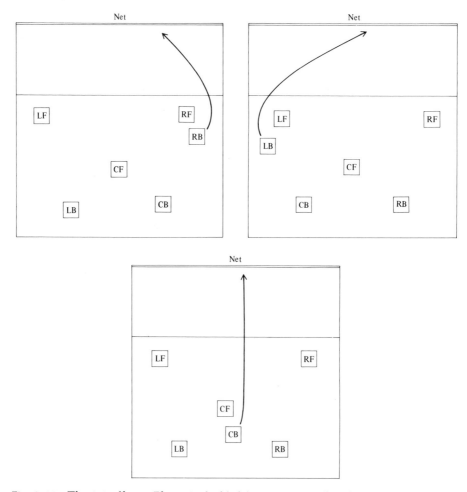

Fig. 9-44 The 6-2 offense. Player is shielded from serve to allow her to run up to net.

Serve defense.   Regardless of the offensive patterns a team uses, on defense the object is to cover the defensive court effectively and to be able to execute the overhead pass, the forearm pass, and the one-handed dig well enough to hit the serve into the air by one of these methods, so that a teammate can control the ball. The forearm pass should be used to play most serves, since it eliminates "throwing" and "lifting" calls.

      Under current rules, players must be in their position until the serve is contacted, and then may interchange positions. A team may use the half-moon formation or the "W" formation (front line back from net and center back playing up) depending on the type of serve being hit and the abilities of your personnel. (See Fig. 9-45.) When receiving the serve, players should wait with their body weight low and their hands in position for an underhand hit. Most players find

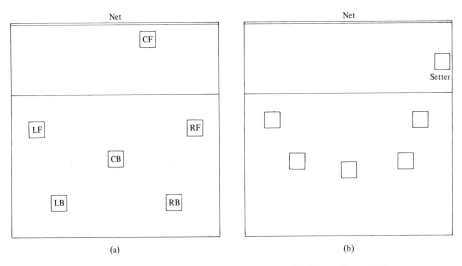

Fig. 9–45 Positioning for team receiving serve. (a) Method usually used for 4–2 offense. (b) The half-moon formation is another serve-receive variation (although there are several variations of this.)

that they can react more quickly if they keep their bodies in motion while waiting for the serve by bouncing lightly on their toes. As the serve comes over, the player should try to get her body in line with the ball, stop her body movement, and then play the ball as best she can.

Blocking. There are two reasons for blocking: (1) to intercept the ball before or as the ball crosses the net, (2) to block according to the spiker's weaknesses or the team's strengths in playing defense. Unless the opponents have executed a bad set, players should always be prepared to block. They can vary their blocks by: (1) blocking line hits, allowing only cross-court angles, (2) blocking cross-court angles, allowing only line hits, (3) blocking according to the spiker's ability to angle the ball, allowing line hits if the spiker is weak in this area, or only cross-court angles if the spiker has trouble with this type of hit, (4) trying to block the spike regardless of the angle attempted.

Any time a team uses the block, team members must be prepared to cover all possible areas for the spike, in case it gets by the block. When the opponents set for the spiker, the two closest defensive players set the block; the third front-row player drops back off the net. (See Fig. 9-46.) As the opponent gets set to spike the ball, the players move into their defensive positions, anticipating the direction of the spike. As shown in Fig. 9-47, players 2 and 5 cover spikes to their areas, as well as watch for the "dink" over the block. Player 6 covers the back-court area, and player 1 handles the cross-court spike, which is the most likely shot. When the spike is hit, the player in the area receiving the ball must move quickly and without hesitation. She has to try to hit the ball into the air to allow a teammate a controlled hit.

Attempted block. (Courtesy of Carol Olson.)

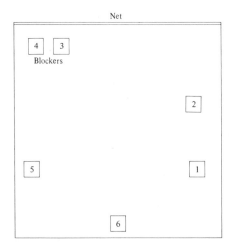

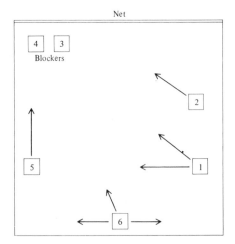

Fig. 9-46   Setting the block.

Fig. 9-47   Covering in case the block is successful.

CONCLUSION

I regret that, because of lack of space, this chapter has necessarily been limited. However, I hope that the techniques and strategy described here will be helpful to coaches and players; and that qualified people in the different sports will broaden the resources available by contributing to the body of published material written for the skilled woman athlete and for coaches of women's athletics.

I also regret that, because of a prior commitment to another publisher, I could not include basketball in this chapter. I realize that basketball is one of the more popular sports; and therefore this omission was not a matter of choice, but of decisions beyond my control.

Finally, let me stress once again that I sincerely believe that competition for women, when *properly* controlled and supervised, is of great value. However, a note of caution: There is evidence that some would like to carry programs too fast and too far, at the expense of the average girl. Conceivably, we could swing from one extreme to another, from providing for the average girl and ignoring the highly skilled, to providing for the highly skilled and ignoring the average. There are already instances in which this is taking place. Rules and programs geared only to the highly skilled athlete and to international competition could be just as much a mistake as programs geared only to the masses. Let us hope that these factors will be considered in the future, and that our athletic programs will be a challenge and a joy to every girl.

BIBLIOGRAPHY

1. Ainsworth, Dorothy S., *et al., Individual Sports for Women.* Philadelphia: W.B. Saunders, 1964.

2. Armbruster, David A., *et al., Swimming and Diving.* St. Louis: C.V. Mosby, 1958.

3. Barnes, Mildred, *et al., Sports Activities for Girls and Women.* New York: Appleton-Century-Crofts, 1966.

4. Bowers, Carolyn Osborn, *Gymnastic Workshop Report.* Salt Lake City, Utah: University of Utah, June 17–28, 1963.

5. Brown, Margaret, "Modern Gymnastics," *DGWS Gymnastic Guide* 1963–1965. Washington, D.C.: AAHPER, pages 14–16.

6. Bunn, John W., *Scientific Principles of Coaching.* Englewood Cliffs, N.J.: Prentice-Hall, 1960.

7. Burke, Jack, Jr., *et al., How to Solve Your Golf Problems.* New York: Cornerstone Library, 1963.

8. Dante, Jim, and Lee Diegel, *The Nine Bad Shots of Golf and What to Do about Them.* New York: Cornerstone Library, 1963.

9. Davidson, Kenneth R., and Lealand Gustavson, *Winning Badminton.* New York: A.S. Barnes, 1953.

10. Day, Frank, *If You Can Walk, You Can Ski.* New York: Crowell-Collier, 1962.

11. Edwards, C.B., and E.G. Heath, *In Pursuit of Archery.* London: Nicholas Kaye, 1962.

12. Forslund, Ellen, *Bowling for Women*. New York: Ronald Press, 1964.

13. *Golf Lessons from the Pros*, compiled by the editors of *Sports Illustrated*. Englewood Cliffs, N.J.: Prentice-Hall, 1961.

14. Hochman, Lou, *The Complete Archery Book*. New York: Arco Publishing Co., 1957.

15. Kentfield, John F., *Teaching and Coaching Tennis*. Dubuque, Iowa: Wm. C. Brown, 1964.

16. Kidwell, Kathro, and Paul Smith, *Bowling Analyzed*. Dubuque, Iowa: Wm. C. Brown, 1960.

17. Lees, Josephine T., and Betty Shellenberger, *Field Hockey for Players, Coaches, and Umpires*. New York: Ronald Press, 1957.

18. Mackey, Helen T., *Field Hockey, and International Team Sport*. Englewood Cliffs, N.J.: Prentice-Hall, 1963.

19. Martin, Dorothy, "Balance Beams," *DGWS Gymnastic Guide 1963–1965*. Washington, D.C.: AAHPER, pages 43–57.

20. Meyer, Margaret H., and Marguerite M. Schwarz, *Team Sports for Girls and Women*. Philadelphia, Pa.: W.B. Saunders, 1965.

21. Miller, Donna Mae, and Katherine Ley, *Individual and Team Sports for Women*. Englewood Cliffs, N.J.: Prentice-Hall, 1955.

22. Miller, Kenneth, *Track and Field for Girls*. New York: Ronald Press, 1964.

23. Mitchell, Viola, *Softball for Girls*. New York: Ronald Press, 1952.

24. Moriarty, Phil, *Springboard Diving*. New York: Ronald Press, 1959.

25. Neal, Patsy, *Basketball Techniques for Women*. New York: Ronald Press, 1966.

26. *Olympic Sports*, prepared by United States Olympic Committee. New York: Olympic House, 57 Park Ave., New York, N.Y.

27. Peterson, Sharon, *et al.*, *Volleyball*. Published Proceedings of Fourth National Institute on Girls' and Women's Sports, December 3–10, 1966, Indiana University.

28. Robertson, David H., and Bruce Harlan, *Competitive Swimming*. Chicago: Athletic Institute.

29. Sarver, Mary J., "Floor Exercise," *DGWS Gymnastic Guide 1963–1965*, pages 35–39.

30. Schaafsma, Frances, *Volleyball Workshop Report*. Salt Lake City: University of Utah, summer of 1966.

31. Scharff, Robert, *The Collier Quick and Easy Guide to Golf*. New York: Collier Books, 1963.

32. Scott, Phebe M., and Virginia R. Crafts, *Track and Field for Girls and Women*. New York: Appleton-Century-Crofts, 1964.

33. *Skiing International Yearbook, 1967*. New York: Ziff-Davis, 1966.

34. Tieber, Avis Andrea, "Preparatory Work on Uneven Parallel Bars," *DGWS Gymnastic Guide 1963–1965*. Washington, D.C.: AAHPER, pages 58–62.

35. Trotter, Betty Jane, *Volleyball for Girls and Women*. New York: Ronald Press, 1965.

36. Vannier, Maryhelen, and Hally Beth Poindexter, *Physical Activities for College Women*. Philadelphia: Wm. B. Saunders, 1964.

37. Wachtel, Erna, and Newt Loken, *How to Improve Your Gymnastics*. Chicago: Athletic Institute.

38. Wilman, Joe, *Better Bowling*. New York: Ronald Press, 1953.

39. Cooper, Phyllis, *Feminine Gymnastics*, Minneapolis: Burgess Publishing Company, 1968.

40. Cutler, Merritt, *The Tennis Book*. New York: McGraw-Hill, 1967.

41. Finsterwald, Dow, *Fundamentals of Golf*. New York: Ronald Press, 1961.

42. Gabrielsen, M. Alexander, Betty Spears, and B.W. Gabrielsen, *Aquatics Handbook*. Englewood Cliffs, N.J.: Prentice-Hall, 1960.

43. Hughes, Eric, *Gymnastics for Girls*. New York: Ronald Press, 1963.

44. Jackson, Nell C., *Track and Field for Girls and Women*. Minneapolis: Burgess Publishing Company, 1968.

45. Mortensen, Jesse P., and John M. Cooper, *Track and Field for Coach and Athlete*. Englewood Cliffs, N.J.: Prentice-Hall, 1959.

46. Smith, Hope M., *Introduction to Human Movement*. Reading, Mass.: Addison-Wesley, 1968.

47. *The Skier's Handbook*. Editors of *Ski Magazine*. New York: Harper & Row, 1958. 1958.

48. Thigpen, Janet, *Power Volleyball*. Dubuque, Iowa: Wm. C. Brown, 1967.

49. Counsilman, James E., *The Science of Swimming*. Englewood Cliffs, N.J.: Prentice-Hall, 1968.

50. Shaw, John, *et al.*, *Selected Team Sports for Men*. Philadelphia: W.B. Saunders, 1952.

51. *America's Ski Book*, Editors of Ski Magazine, New York: Charles Scribner's Sons, 1966.

52. Beattie, Bob, *My Ten Secrets of Skiing*, New York: Viking Press, 1968.

53. Jordan, Payton, and Bud Spencer, *Champions in the Making*, Englewood Cliffs, N.J.: Prentice-Hall, 1968.

54. *Hockey Coaching*, The Hockey Association, London: Hodder and Stoughton, 1966.

55. Klann, Margaret, *Target Archery*, Reading, Mass.: Addison-Wesley, 1970.

56. O'Brien, Ronald, *Springboard Diving*, Columbus, Ohio: Charles E. Merrill, 1968.

57. Poindexter, Hally B., and Carole Mushier, *Coaching Competitive Team Sports for Girls and Women*, Philadelphia: W.B. Saunders, 1973.

58. Read, Brenda, and Freda Walker, *Advanced Hockey for Women*. London: Faber and Faber, 1976.

59. Showers, Norman, *Bowling*, Pacific Palisades, California: Goodyear, 1973.

60. Talbot, Don, *Swimming to Win*, New York: Hawthorn Books, 1969.

61. *The Female Runner*, Runner's World Magazine, Mountain View, California: World, 1974.

62. Wein, Horst, *The Science of Hockey*, London: Pelham Books, Ltd., 1973.

63. Williamson, John "Gearing Up for the Bull's-eye," *Young Athlete*, May/June, 1976, pp. 44-45.